EDDIE FORDE has been writing for over 40 years. Attending courses at the Arvon Foundation in Devon and Yorkshire, where he was able to spend time with living authors, inspired him to become a writer himself.

He has had many different jobs, including working as a milkman, a postman, a meter reader, a barman, a shop assistant, and more. After spending six years at night school, he trained as a primary school teacher and spent eighteen years working in Lambeth schools.

He has published half-a-dozen slim volumes of poetry and written plays for the radio and for the fringe theatre in London.

Pier Head Gold is part of a trilogy with *A Dublin Childhood* and *Holloway Road* to follow later.

G000044696

By the Same Author

Poetry

Putney Poems
More Putney Poems
Pilgrim Poems
Feeling Funny
Seeking Sanctuary
Christmas Collection SW15
Christmas Collection SW15 (Second Delivery)
Christmas Poems Special Collection

Published by City Dragon Publishing
www.putneypoems.co.uk

Drama

Mild and Bitter
Fly the Flag
The Flea Man
A Dog's Life

PIER HEAD GOLD

Eddie Forde

SilverWood

Published in 2020 by SilverWood Books

SilverWood Books Ltd
14 Small Street, Bristol, BS1 1DE, United Kingdom
www.silverwoodbooks.co.uk

ISBN 978-1-78132-981-8 (paperback)
ISBN 978-1-78132-986-3 (ebook)

British Library Cataloguing in Publication Data
A CIP catalogue record for this book is available
from the British Library

Page design and typesetting by SilverWood Books

To my sister Mary and my brother Henry.
This is their story as well as mine.

In loving memory of my sister Joan,
my brother Pat and my Mother and Father.
May they rest in peace.

Acknowledgements

Thanks to Josie Forde for all the input, chat, listening, and cups of tea.

Thanks to Mandy Davies for her help in preparing the manuscript for publication.

With special thanks to Saints Anthony and Jude for continuing to answer our prayers with countless small miracles and some big ones too.

Chapter 1

"Get your *Echo*, read all about it," the news vendor was shouting, "Everton and Liverpool drawn to clash in next round." Dad said everybody was soccer mad in England but that didn't stop him doing his football pools coupon every week like clockwork.

As we went along the dockside there were many pitches and stalls set up offering a variety of advice to those landing on the English shores.

There was a man from the Catholic Truth Society on a soapbox encouraging the small group who surrounded him to remain practising Catholics.

"Once you set foot in this country, you risk losing your faith," the man warned.

"Will my religion get me a bed for the night?" Dad shouted.

A woman in the crowd shouted that the Pope was an idolater while another asked where in the Bible it stated that the Pope was an idolater while another asked where in the Bible it stated that priests must not marry?

I could hear music and as Dad had a keen ear for any kind of music we soon found ourselves looking at men and women in black uniforms, the men wearing peaked caps and the women wearing old-fashioned bonnets. They played a stirring version of 'Rock of Ages', which sent shivers down my spine and tears to my eyes because of the simplicity of their statement in these bleak surroundings. The Sally Army has always had the knack of turning up at the right time in the most unexpected places intent on relieving human distress even if only by offering some sweet tea and a bun. "Welcome to England," one of the Salvation Army men said to Dad, "have a cup of cheer."

"I'll accept anything free except a kick up the arse," said Dad.

This embarrassed me and showed me how ignorant Dad could be sometimes to people he thought of as his inferiors. Dad couldn't accept these people as God's representatives on earth. As far as he was concerned the only true Church was the Roman Catholic Church whose headquarters were in Rome but as far as my dad was concerned its real spiritual home was Ireland. His faith was a confused mixture of dogma and Irish Nationalism. He was having no truck with any types in uniform who were probably conspiring to destroy his Catholicism and therefore his Irish identity. Dad didn't appreciate that these people were doing the best they could for us. He didn't even have a good word to say about the free tea they gave us. He complained that he would have more milk in the cat's saucer on a Good Friday than they had put in our tea.

I looked at my dad. There he stood, an angry red-faced powerfully built man of about five foot eight who was much balder than I had noticed before. He was intent on having an all-out war with everyone and everything. The officer offered us a plate of bread and butter slices, saying that we should celebrate in the Lord. Dad bit into the bread and immediately spat it out, complaining that they were using margarine instead of butter. Anything these people tried to give us, Dad belittled. When they said that they had beds in their hostel in Scotland Road, Dad walked away in disgust, muttering under his breath that he had no intention of bedding down with these Protestant bastards.

In the early morning fog and cold we made our way to the Pier Head. The streets were very busy with ashen-faced Lowry matchstick men on their way to work. Black-coated, black-capped, they walked along the cobbles in hobnailed boots, roll-ups in mouths despite their coughing and wheezing. Dad remarked that you would never see so many people up at this early hour in Dublin.

I sat on a suitcase near the tea stall and looked across at the Royal Liver Building with what looked like an eagle perched on top as if it was about to take off. It couldn't because it was sealed down and trapped, as were most of the people arriving on the hundreds of buses dropping them off for work. Seagulls were competing noisily with pigeons for scraps of sodden food thrown by customers at the tea stall.

"Right, that should be better than the last lot," said Dad, handing me a cup of tea and a piece of pie.

"Thanks," I said.

"And you'd better have a couple of bob in your pocket, just in case."

11

Something really major must be afoot. The last thing Dad ever did was to put his hand in his pocket and part with money. Up to now he would only ever give me money to go and buy a specific item.

"In case of what?" I asked.

"In case we get separated," he replied. He said he would be able to get around faster on his own and, giving me two half crowns, said he wouldn't be long.

What could I do? I felt very much on my own, very aware that at twelve years old, there was not much I could do about it. I wondered how they were on the Quays in Dublin. They would be just getting up to have their breakfasts and not giving a damn about me.

As I looked at the ferries crossing the Mersey, I knew I was going to have to lead a solitary life. I felt angry as I watched the men going to and from the docks. No one cared or gave a fig about what was going through my mind. Eventually I saw Dad coming across the cobble-stones towards me. I could tell he was in a bad temper by the swagger in his walk. Despite myself, I was really delighted to be with him again. As Mam had said, blood is thicker than water. Dad said in his brisk voice we'd got a lot to do and asked for the two half crowns back.

"I spent one of them."

"You spent a half crown. Christ Almighty."

"I didn't know if you were coming back."

"That was no reason to throw caution to the wind."

I had no intention of throwing caution to any wind. I wanted to build up my financial assets and try to establish some form of independence. This was going to be a formidable thing to do given the domineering character of my unpredictable father.

Our plan was to leave the cases in the left-luggage office at the railway station. Left-luggage offices held a fascination for me as they seemed to be popular places to deposit bodies. Every so often there would be a story in the papers where a body or parts of a body had been discovered in a suitcase, often only after the ticket had run past its six-month date or when the stench was so great that even the porter was alerted to it.

As we waited for the ticket for our cases, I wondered how many bodies this gaunt little porter had come across in his time at the Lime Street left-luggage office. It seemed to me that he did look at us curiously as he took the cases from us but then he relaxed when he found the cases to be light.

Dad's idea was that we should have a look around Liverpool before we made any contact with anyone. Dad asked someone where the main street was and they just looked at him as if he was mad. We were looking for something like O'Connell Street, Dame Street or Grafton Street there. We were used to some of the finest streets in the world in Dublin. The British had built them. No point conquering a country if you didn't make it as good as what you had at home. Then Dad asked this sickly-looking man with his Adam's apple popping up and down his neck, making him look more like a turkey than a human being, where the main street was.

"There isn't really one la," he said in this peculiar accent. "You see it was all bombed, dockside targets if you know what I mean."

"Well, that's a great start," Dad said. "No streets, no shops, no houses, what a fecking place."

Dad went on alarmingly. I was getting tired listening to him and then in next to no time, we were back at the Pier Head again.

Dad didn't want to go and find Johnson too soon. He thought that would look as if we were desperate. Dad did all his thinking out loud except when he was in a church. Not that he stopped thinking then; he stored it all up to tell you when he came out. He thought about anything and everything except about the reason he was supposed to be in church, to pray to God. In church he was kneeling down. Perhaps that was what stimulated his thinking so much. Perhaps that would be a great new technique for psychiatrists. Instead of having their patients lying down, they should try the effect of kneeling. Most people who came out of church were at peace but he came out with a thousand and one ideas. The theme was always the dollar sign and new ways of making some money.

As we walked along he was thinking out loud about getting a place to stay. He thought it would be best to stay in a hotel, as this would give Johnson the right impression. He'd get the idea you had something behind you, not short of a bob or two. Didn't want him thinking we were a pair of spalpeens. We had our own business in Dublin, our own bank account and cheque book. Outside the Imperial, he thought aloud that this looked the place to give the right sort of impression to Johnson. It all depended on Johnson. Dad was really desperate for things to go well with Johnson. I knew this because he had mentioned lighting candles to St Jude, the patron of hopeless causes, one of the forgotten saints. Dad's logic was that this saint would not be as busy as the likes of St Peter and Paul. I don't think he realised that he was admitting how up against it he was in choosing this particular patron.

Inside the hotel at the reception desk, Dad said, "I want a room for myself, and I don't mind if you charge for the child."

There he goes again, I thought. I wish he wouldn't call me a child. I'll be thirteen in May.

"It's three pounds for yourself and it's thirty shillings for the boy," the receptionist said.

"You don't understand," Dad explained slowly. "We just want the room for one night."

"That is for one night," she replied.

Dad was flabbergasted. "Three pounds for one night in a bed and a little bit of breakfast."

"We don't supply breakfast without ration books."

"Come on Dad," I said, pulling at his coat as he stared at her, all the usual signs warning me that he was about to erupt.

Dad started thinking out loud again as we walked away from what he felt like doing to the hotelkeepers at the Imperial.

"I wonder did she realise who she was talking to, I think I'll go back and tell her."

"No Dad, don't bother with them. We don't want to waste time. We've got a lot to do. We've got to find some place to stay tonight and we've got to see Johnson."

This seemed to draw his mind away from the incident. We crossed over London Road beside the Murphy's Pub. For a moment I could see that Dad was struggling against the temptation to disappear inside for a gargle. Then suddenly he brightened up. He had remembered that someone had given him the name of a priest in Scotland Road who might know of places to stay.

"What's that over there Dad?" I asked, as we approached the top of Scotland Road.

"That's the entrance to the Mersey Tunnel. Irishmen built that," he said with pride. "It goes right under the River Mersey and comes out at Birkenhead. Many's the poor Paddy lost his life building that. You won't find many buildings, roads, tunnels or canals that a Paddy didn't have a hand in constructing. If I have my way, son, that's one thing you'll never have to do, no siree."

That was the fear. That was the stark reality if the cards were not played right, I would have to go on the building sites. That was our heritage in this country. Dad saw the pitfalls ahead for me but to give him his due, he tried to protect me and steer me away from the fast money waiting to be picked up working as a 'navvy'.

We were shown into the priest's house by a crotchety old woman.

"It won't be long before they're saying a few words over her," Dad whispered. "A strong wind would blow her over."

"Don't Dad, you'll only get me laughing." I knew that if I started laughing there was no stopping me.

The room was cold and damp like most of the rooms in Liverpool as I was to find out. The walls would run with water and the thing I couldn't understand was that no one took any notice. It smelt as if there hadn't been a fire lit in the room for years although a fire had been made up in the grate. It looked as if it had been made up since before the war. There were a couple of pictures of gloomy saints hanging on the wall, a couple of battered chairs and a sideboard with two headless statues on a tray like John the Baptist's. In the centre of the room was a round table.

We stood by the table waiting for the priest, afraid for our lives to sit on the chairs in case they collapsed. This was Catholicism trying to survive alongside Protestantism in Scotland Road. Not Protestantism trying to survive alongside Catholicism as in Dublin.

As we looked out the window we could see the smog lifting slowly like a curtain on a stage. Instead of revealing a set and actors, it was revealing a bombsite. In fact the Liverpool of the fifties was just one big fecking bombsite.

Dad was musing out loud that we might be offered a cup of tea here or maybe even a bit of breakfast. "That's the beauty of the Catholic Church. Wherever you go there are Catholics helping fellow Catholics. It's a marvellous religion to belong to."

Father Felix, a Franciscan, wore a Father Christmas beard. He pushed the door open with an air of authority. In a soiled brown soutane and formidable rosary beads twined round his waist he stood eyeing us in suspicious silence. He must have good reason for his suspicion. There must have been dozens of characters calling on him every day with hard luck stories of how they had been robbed, lost their job or other misfortunes. Later on, I came to believe that unlike the Salvation Army, the Catholic Church were never ones to dish out money or food freely. They were the experts at collecting it in, never ones for parting with it, except to bishops and to the Vatican in Rome. The silence felt very intimidating and clearly was embarrassing Dad, who coughed nervously. Father Felix switched on the solitary unshaded light bulb and went up to Dad so that their noses were practically touching. He examined Dad through his Churchillian spectacles. Then he turned his attention to me or rather to the top of my head as if he was looking for nits. Then he went back to the doorway and switched the light off. "We've come from Dublin," Dad announced with forced cheerfulness. "Father Anthony, of Merchant's Quay, I believe you know him, told us to come and call on you." I could see that Father Felix was not impressed. He probably thought we were a father and son team working our way round all the parishes seeing what we could get. Dad continued to show our credentials.

"We are Catholics you know, regular Mass goers. My son is an altar boy. I am trying to get him into a Catholic school."

"What kind of employment are you looking for?"

"Well I'm looking for something in the business world. Father Anthony said you might be able to put us in contact."

"The only vacancies I've heard of recently are in Kearley & Tongues, they employ a lot of people but you've got to be a Protestant."

"I am a Catholic," Dad protested. "Not a fecking Orangeman," he said under his breath.

I found out later that the Orange order was fairly strong but like most things in Liverpool, not taken all that seriously by the majority of people. On the twelfth of July when the lodges marched on Scotland Road, the Catholic kids marched with them. On the seventeenth of March, St Patrick's Day, the Orange kids marched with the Catholics. Everyone had a great time, as should be the case. Life was too hard for working-class people without further adding to their problems by getting all steamed up over King Billy and the Battle of the Boyne or St Paddy the snake charmer.

Dad repeated "I am a Catholic," looking at me wondering where in hell did this lunatic of a priest come from.

Father Felix was shaking his head in disappointment, "that doesn't help."

His advice to us was, if we had the fare, to take the next boat back to Dublin. Dad was thinking out loud again with a vengeance as we made our way once again over the bombsites. I noticed that there was a picture house on the next corner. As we got closer I could see that the film was *Henry VIII* starring Charles Laughton in the title role.

"That dirty bastard. They're all dirty bastards," Dad roared.

"But we've never been to the pictures in England Da."

"And we won't ever if that's all they're showing."

My heart sank and sank farther when he said that the most important thing for me was a good school.

I bled inside, not school again. I'm not a horse to be schooled. One of the reasons I had agreed to leave Ireland and come with him to England was that I hoped I would never have to go to school again. I could see that his mind was made up and that meant I would have to go along with him and bide my time.

We went to the advice centre in Dale Street near the cop shop. The woman was polite and well spoken but very discouraging. She told us that it was nigh impossible to get a furnished or an unfurnished room in Liverpool. She told Dad that if he was on his own he might have been able to get full board and lodging. She was fairly certain that no landlady or lodging house would take a man with a young boy.

"I suggest you go back to Dublin or at least take the child back there." She must have been listening to Father Felix.

"You won't be able to get him into school," this prophet of doom added.

Why not have done with it and throw me in the Mersey, I thought.

"You see he's at the wrong age," she went on, "you said he would be thirteen in May, well he's missed nearly two years' work. He would be mixing with English boys who have a different approach. He wouldn't fit in."

Fit in I thought, I've got my fists, I'd fit in with them.

By this time Dad had had enough. I have noticed that when he knows someone is talking down to him he has the knack of asking the right question, which is always short, sharp and to the point. Quietly, and with the coolness of a mountain stream, he asked, "Where do your sons go to school?"

More out of shock and surprise than out of politeness she answered, "St Patrick's College."

Dad smiled and I could see that this one was ruffled. The sickly smiling expression gave all her thoughts away as if she was shouting them at us.

"Don't think you can come over here with cow shite on your boots and claim what it has taken me and my family years to obtain."

So she tried to put Dad in his place.

"But it's very exclusive, lots of boys are turned down every year."

"Well I think that will be the place," Dad said.

"Well you must suit yourself," she said, "but I can assure you that you are wasting your time."

"You see," Dad said, rising from his chair, "I like nothing better than a challenge."

Her mouth hung open like a torn pocket as we left the centre. There was something about Dad that told her he would do it despite or maybe because of her advice.

Chapter 2

Not spitting distance from the entrance to Lime Street Station stood Johnson's single-storey white-painted cafe, The Cosy Cup of Tea.

We had been standing across the street casing the joint like a couple of Chicago private detectives. We watched a steady flow of people going in and out.

It looked like a gold mine. The people behind the counter had not stopped pouring teas and dishing up meals. I had thought we drank a lot of tea in Ireland but compared to this lot, we only sipped it. Dad thought the cups were too big. He wanted to make fifty or sixty cups out of a quarter of tea: smaller cups, more profit.

Dad started planning how he would give the outside a lick of paint, rearrange the counter area and knock an interior wall down to make it one large space.

"We can put a couple of mirrors on the wall to make it look bigger. You know there's nothing in the world people like better than looking at themselves in a mirror." Dad was getting into his stride. He had picked up a lot of nous during his time in America about how to design and market business premises to attract the maximum number of punters. He was ahead of his time in this and many other respects.

"Well son, all my prayers have been answered, good old Johnson. Let's go and see him."

"Two cups of tea," Dad said to the old one serving behind the counter. I turned down Dad's offer of a cake or sandwich as I knew the prices they charged in these places.

"That will be five pence please," the woman said, giving us the two cups of tea.

"I am a friend of Mr Johnson's," Dad announced proudly, making no attempt to part with any money.

"That will be five pence," she repeated, holding out her hand. She was not the least bit impressed by what Dad had said.

"Mr Johnson," Dad said, thinking she might not have heard him properly.

"Look friend or no friend," she said, "the notice there says all goods must be paid for on receipt. Look over there, large letters in black and white, that's if you can read."

Dad's mouth hung open in amazement.

"That's five pence."

"Oh yes," Dad said, taken aback, "certainly, five pence."

He gave her the five pence and asked if Mr Johnson was around.

"No, he's not," she said grimly, "the last time I heard of him he was somewhere in Blackpool, living rough and washing dishes."

"Blackpool," Dad repeated, "living rough, doing dishes," he said in amazement.

We had gambled everything on promises Johnson had made to Dad over pints of Guinness in Gilsen's pub in Dublin. Dad stood there shaking his head, his world shattered. I drank my tea and I vowed there and then that I would never believe in pub promises for the rest of my life. In the bonhomie of the pub, a person could promise anything. It made them feel good making out they could do something for you. Invariably they couldn't do up their own shoelaces. This was not so for Dad. He believed the promises made over drink. The promises had to be believed as they represented his only hope of escape out of whatever his current predicament was.

Still refusing to accept the harsh reality, Dad persisted in hoping the world would turn out to be the way he wanted it to be. He asked, "But doesn't he own this place?"

I felt really sorry for him as the woman laughed, not a happy belly laugh but a dried-up, humourless, angry one, developed over years to express disappointment and cynicism.

"I see he's been having you on as well. If you'll pardon my French, he hasn't got a pot to piss in."

We drank our tea quietly. I was nervous because I thought he was going to blow a fuse.

Dad was thinking out loud again as we left The Cosy Cup of Tea.

Somebody up there had let him down and he didn't think it could get any worse. He mulled over the encounters he had had with Johnson and marvelled that a man who had always looked him directly in the eye could have lied to him. There were some more thoughts about not counting your chickens and that he should have known better.

"Never mind Dad," I said, as I put my hand in his coat pocket and squeezed his hard hand, "you've still got me."

"Yes, we've got each other. All we've got in this world is each other. I only hope God spares me long enough for you to grow up so that you can stand on your own two feet. God knows it is a hard disappointing old world for the likes of us."

We walked along in silence for a few minutes.

"It can't get worse, it must get better."

I thought to myself that if nothing stays the same then it could get better or it might get worse but I didn't say anything to Dad as he went on, "As the song says, 'Pick yourself up, brush yourself off, and start all over again'. We'll survive son."

The November evening was drawing in on this strange disappointing city of Liverpool. After a nearly sleepless night and a long day trailing around the bombsites of the city, we were tired. The smog had hardly cleared all day. I was to find out later that this blanket of thick grey pollution formed from the outpourings of chemical plants on the other side of the Mersey and from the factories of inner Lancashire arrived in September and stayed with us all winter. No wonder the people coughed and looked ashen grey.

Dad was off again. "Coming all this way to this cursed place. Look at it. You'd be better off in a graveyard."

The disappointment of Johnson letting us down was biting again and driving Dad into mad rages. He heaped every curse he could think of on his lying head.

My biggest fear was that we might have to go back to dear old dirty Dublin. They wouldn't have called it dirty if they had seen Liverpool. I didn't want us giving up and going back so soon.

I thought of Mam, depressed after having my baby sister and not having enough money coming into the house. Now I realised that Dad was in an equally bad state. Life was not turning out any easier because we were in England. In fact, things were getting a lot tougher for us. I could see Dad asking himself if he had bitten off more than he could chew.

"Will we have to go back Da? Will we have to throw the towel in?"

I knew that this reference to the square ring would stimulate him into action and stop him feeling sorry for himself. "I've never thrown the towel in yet," he shouted, "and I never will. Oh that's what they'd love to see, me back to Ireland with my tail between my legs."

His face looked set, like a boxer stepping into the ring who was not going to go quietly. Then his face softened as he looked at my worried face.

"Do you remember what the little boy with the donkey said?"

"Never take no for an answer."

"Exactly, come on, this looks like a good place."

So we booked into the Salvation Army on Scotland Road. I was praying hard that we wouldn't come across the officer that Dad had told to feck off that morning on the dockside and that no one would throw me out as you had to be eighteen or over to get a bed there and I knew I was not very tall for my twelve years. Apart from all my fears and anxieties, there wasn't a happier boy than me. At least now we wouldn't be going back to Dublin. How could I face Marmo and the gang, Brother Kelly and his spelling tests and all the others, with one arm as long as the other.

"We'll find a room to stay in tomorrow," Dad said, as we tucked into our meal. It was a kind of a hotpot, a brown stew effort, sprinkled generously with bitter red cabbage. Dad was still moaning but more in fun, trying to find a bit of meat in his stew. This was my first introduction to 'scouse'. It was warm and nourishing. For a shilling a plate, with a large mug of tea and a thick slice of margarined bread, there wasn't much room for complaints. There was no pie in the sky about the Sally Army, a practical religious organisation. You didn't have to wait for the next life, they helped you in this one. They put their money where their mouth is.

Hunger being good sauce, we enjoyed the 'scouse' and repaired to our little cell cubicles for the night. Dad said to knock on the dividing partition if I got frightened. He told me not to read the Bibles that littered the room as they belonged to Henry VIII and King James. I was to keep well clear of these two buckos. Dad told me that the only true Bible was under the Pope's bed in Rome, next to his piss pot, and all the rest were written by a pile of deranged lunatics. So much for a liberal approach to other Christians, especially as they were putting us up for the night.

Henry VIII or Old Nick himself wouldn't have bothered me that night as I settled down under crisp white cold sheets and Salvation Army blankets emblazoned with their own logo, making it impossible for any of their guests of a thieving disposition to pawn them.

It had been a long twenty-four hours since we had left the North Wall the previous evening. Another boat would be on its way from Dublin tonight, carrying more people and cattle: an endless stream of hopefuls full of dreams like Dad and me.

In the morning, I had a better opportunity to examine the hostel and the clients. The Sally Army definitely believed that cleanliness was next to godliness. I had to be careful not to slip on the highly polished floors. Everything was clean. The toilets smelt strongly of disinfectant but I noticed on the corner of the door that

Kilroy had left his name in black ink. To think that I was following Kilroy himself, perhaps one day I would meet him in person. That would be some story.

At breakfast time we lined up with our trays and served ourselves to large mugs of strong tea and wedges of toast. We were under close supervision. A man in uniform gave you a big spoon of marmalade. Everyone thanked him respectfully by saying "Thank you, Major, God bless you Major." The tables and chairs were laid out in long rows similar to those I had seen in George Raft and James Cagney prison films. Bibles were scattered everywhere. It was clear to me that if you intended to stay a couple of nights and to keep in with the Major who dished out the marmalade with the big spoon, it would be prudent to browse through the Good Book as you drank your morning tea and ate your marmalade toast.

The Salvation Army people did not openly try to convert us. I don't think they would have stood much chance against our strong Catholic indoctrination. The chances that any one of us would change over was remote. Most of the Catholics who came over here lapsed but if roused they reverted to their childhood training.

There were notices all over the hostel walls, 'Jesus Saves', 'Believe in the Lord' and 'The End is Nigh'. Some other notices said things like, 'No Smoking', 'No Spitting', 'No Drink to be consumed on the Premises'. In one corridor there must have been a chapel as the notice read, 'Silence, Service in Progress'. It seemed to me that the Salvation Army heaven might turn out to be a very boring place with highly polished floors and smelling of disinfectant.

I felt most sorry for the old men who sat around the tables dunking pencils in their tea and then putting them in their mouths, pencils that were surrogate roll-ups because of the no smoking rule. They hoped that somehow the dunked pencils would land on a winner on the racing pages, which they had sandwiched between pages of the Bible. They were trying to escape the disapproval of the Major but if the truth were told, Major Marmalade turned a blind eye to many of the little peccadilloes practised by his socially disadvantaged flock.

Prayers were optional. We didn't go, instead we went to the Catholic Church right opposite the hostel. As we came out of Mass, Dad said, "Right son, the most important thing is to get you into a good school." My heart sank, not school again I thought. He was determined to show that bitch at the advice bureau that he was as good as his word and that I would be going to the best school alongside her sons. The fact that this woman saw dozens of people every week and probably treated them all in the same high-handed manner did not register with Dad. He had taken her remarks as a personal affront and he would go through hell or high water and use me or anyone else to get back at her. So we went to London Road to get the bus to St Patrick's College.

Chapter 3

The pressure was really on me now. If I didn't get into the school the whole adventure would collapse. It would be back on the next boat from the Pier Head for the both of us. I didn't enjoy the bus journey from Lime Street up London Road to Queens Drive. The only good things were the five or six cinemas sandwiched in between the big stores, all showing new films that had not yet arrived in Dublin. Past Penny Lane, we arrived at the Old Swan, a coaching inn, which in past times had been part of what was then the small village of Broad Green. Then onto Queens Drive where every one of the big detached houses had gardens the size of a park. Besides all the greenery the other thing that struck me was the quietness. You could see the sky through the November trees and I could hear birds singing. There was no smog here unlike the centre of Liverpool. When I saw the drive leading up to St Patrick's College, my heart leapt into my mouth.

"We can't go in there," I said, tugging at Dad's coat. "Come on," he said, pulling me by the back of my jacket. "It's best to hit them between nine and ten. They won't have their minds on us so much as on their morning coffee and biscuits." I don't remember going in the front door of St Patrick's College. It was one of those times like going for an operation or witnessing a horrendous event when you blank out and you just go through the motions. For the past twenty-four hours since I had left Dublin, I had been living in an adult world. In the reception room of St Patrick's College, I was forced back to being a child again.

The sun shone in through leaded light windows, which had been cleaned recently. No broken panes of glass boarded up with pieces of cardboard, as had been the case with my school in Dublin. No bird shit on the windows. Obviously a better class of bird lived in the suburbs. The red carpet was so thick that if you were to lie down on it, you'd have been asleep almost immediately. What a contrast to the polished floors of the Salvation Army. I marvelled at the oak panelling. This was the first time I had ever seen oak panelling live in the flesh. I had seen it in Hollywood films. With the press of a secret button, the panelling could be opened and the cornered murderer would make a quick escape. I was conscious as I stood there with Dad that a dozen eyes might be trained on us, watching our every movement from behind a concealed door. There were some large leather armchairs standing around a polished oak table.

"Well, this is more our style," Dad said. I whispered, fearing that they might be listening behind the wooden panels, "It looks very posh Da. It looks too posh for us." Immediately, Dad went into one of his rages. "Jaysus, you're just like your mother going cap in hand to everyone. Well there's nothing in the world that's too posh for us." I ignored him and I went on resolutely, "I don't think I'm clever enough to get in here." "You're my son, if I'm clever enough to be here, you're clever enough to be here." For a moment I thought that he was going to give me a swipe. I felt miserably unhappy. Why couldn't I just disappear of the face of the earth?

Then in came a very tall Christian Brother in a black suit, much cleaner than those worn by the Christian Brothers in Dublin. An officer type, straight as a petrol pump and as lean as a greyhound, he was a man full of confidence. "I am awfully sorry for detaining you but Thursday is such a busy day. I am Brother Cooper the Head," he said to Dad, extending his hand. Janey I thought he's an Englishman. What's an Englishman doing in charge of the Irish Christian Brothers?

The Head stared at me. It was obvious that he was used to assessing boys. His power and control over them lay in his steel cold eyes. I tried to smile. Dad broke the ice.

"I'm so pleased to meet you Brother Cooper," Dad said in a very posh accent. He sounded so posh in fact that I had to blink and look around twice as I had seen Stan do in the Laurel and Hardy films. Oliver got all posh when they were in the same kind of predicament as we were now.

"Your school had been recommended to me by the Christian Brothers in Dublin."

"Yes," the Headmaster replied.

Anyone could see that this would be a difficult fish to catch. But you can catch any fish if you have the right bait and you know when to use it. Dad looked at the shining head of this bald-headed man and then at his brown index finger. He had found the man's addiction. He was a smoker, as were most of the male and female population at this time.

"Would you care for a cigarette?" Dad said, offering the Head a box of fifty Players.

The Head's eyes opened wide with delight. Who could blame him? The people who smoked must have often had to do without because of rationing during and after the war.

"Keep the box," Dad said. "Oh I couldn't possibly," replied the Head. You could see that he only half meant what he was saying, like most well-bred English people who think it's the height of good manners to refuse. I could tell by Dad's swagger that he was on top. "Go on. Of course you can. There are plenty of cigarettes in Ireland. They are not rationed like they are here. In fact, my son's mother intends to send us a couple of hundred each week." Dad was freewheeling now in a fantasy prelude of how things could have been and not how they actually were.

"We have our own business in Dublin. My wife is looking after it while I establish another base over here. I believe in expansion" – Go on Dad, I thought. You've got him now. You tell him. You tell Brother Cooper that if he scratches your back you'll scratch his.

There was a knock on the door and a portly Brother entered. He must have got a whiff of the cigarettes from under the door.

"Brother Rowley," the Head said to his colleague, "would you take Mr Doyle's son and get him to sit the entrance test. It's only a formality," the Head said to Dad. "Right me little mister," Brother Rowley said, taking me by the hand.

At last, I thought, an Irish Christian Brother from somewhere down the country in Ireland.

So into the valley of death rode the six hundred. Cannon to the left of them. Cannon to the right of them. He took me down the corridor to a disused classroom where a solitary chair and table was laid out. He then gave me a question paper. It could have been in Double Dutch or Treble Dutch for all it meant to me. There were no sums on it, no adding ups or taking aways. It was all funny stuff with numbers missing. There were a^3 and b^3, x^5 and y^5, big As and little as and stuff with boxes, circles and squares. I never saw the likes of it in all my life. Why fill your head with stuff like this when there were so many more important things to know in the world.

Left alone after going through the paper, I knew that there wasn't a thing I could do.

I sat back and looked at the fat-arsed cherubs on the ceiling and wondered if they were any relations to the ones in Adam and Eve's church in Dublin where I used to serve Mass.

The Brother, smelling strongly of tobacco, returned. He looked at the paper. He smiled at me. He shook his head in sympathy. Then he took me by my sweaty little hand to go back to the reception room as the cherubs on the ceiling shamelessly and brutally laughed at me. Back along the corridors of power where photos of past students decorated the walls, this Irish Christian Brother tugged at my hand and the tears welled up inside of me. "Oh my little mister, you shouldn't take life so seriously." I said, "I've failed Sir. I've failed." "Sure what's life without half a dozen failures a day." He smiled lovingly at me, revealing his black teeth. His breath stank. I knew he meant to be kind. What a terrible thing it must be to grow old in the likes of Liverpool when your teeth and body become distorted and you are a source of fun and ridicule to almost everyone you encounter.

Suddenly Brother Rowley stopped in his tracks. "Just a minute," he said, "follow me. The pen is mightier than the sword. Sit down. Us Paddies have got to stick together little mister. Pick up the pen."

I filled in the answers, which made me feel great. What a world. It was right that you could never tell a book by the cover. Who, looking at this dishevelled old man, could know what was in his heart.

The papers were given to the Head by my ambassador, who whispered some words to him. Not bad, or something like that, I hoped was being said. I couldn't work out anything for certain. There was something going on but I was too far away to hear.

Another teacher took the papers out, I assumed to be marked. They were all Brother Rowley's answers and all of them must have been correct. Or was he playing some kind of trick on me. No. I put it out of my mind. He liked me, I thought, reassuring myself.

Dad and everyone else were laughing and enjoying themselves, which added more to my misery. After some time, the papers were brought back. They were given to the Head, who examined them. Then he spoke to my dad. "Very interesting, you see this one, a much more difficult proposition and concept. He's answered that. Didn't you understand all the questions?" the Head asked. "Not all of them Sir," I replied. "Oh that's quite possible," Dad said, "you see he's used to learning everything through Irish in Dublin. In fact he had to learn English through Irish there. So I wouldn't be surprised if he wasn't able to answer some of the questions."

Then the Head's face beamed and he held out his hand to Dad.

I was dropped as if by parachute into the junior playground during the morning's playtime break, surrounded by what seemed like hundreds of boys in uniform.

A group of them closed round me intent upon having a good laugh at my expense.

It was the third one that pulled my hood that got it from me. Eyes closed, chin in, I went after him. "Come on," I shouted,

34

"who wants one of these fists in your gob? Come on you lot of English bastards."

"Ah the fighting Irish," said one of the teachers who had hold of my arms as I was frogmarched off the playground and down another corridor, past sporting pictures of victorious cricket and rugby teams and famous old boys. They sat me outside the staff room and gave me a glass of water to cool me down. I thought they were going to throw me out the front door. If this type of thing had happened in Dublin, I would have got the walloping of my life and then been sent home to get another walloping there.

They couldn't phone Dad. We didn't have a phone. In fact no one knew where he was. What a cock-up. If only I could control my temper but I had to stand up for myself or my life would not be worth living. Instead of giving me a beating they put me in their uniform. First I had to take off my civvies, the uniform of a Dublin gurrier. So they took me to a room where the Brother with the bad breath was domiciled, to be kitted out.

"Try these on," he said, "and we'll have you looking like a proper little English scholar in next to no time."

With new blazer, trousers, cap, shirt and tie, I felt very strange. I looked at myself in the mirror and was a little frightened by the loss of my own identity. I was in their uniform. Would they accept me now?

A kid called Wezzo took me to the classroom where the boys waiting for the next teacher to arrive took the mickey out of me even more than they had in the playground.

At lunchtime, we were goose-stepped in single file to the refectory and sat at the tables nearest the servery. All the rest of the school took their turn before us. By the time we queued up with our huge trays, the size of riot shields, there was hardly any grub left. A minute portion of runny potato served from an ice cream scoop. Some kind of sausage and mashed carrot covered with a shit-brown gravy.

"Cheer up," Wezzo said, "you'll have to face worse before you get better. Fancy going to the pictures this afternoon?"

"We've got games."

"So."

Then Wezzo outlined the plan. "There's a non-kit group as well as the games group. No one knows where anyone is in the afternoon. All the registers are cocked up. Once the pips go we hide in the bog. Climb up on the seat. Don't lock the door. The prefects only look for locked doors. Once the second lot of pips go, the games lot go to change. The non-kitters are taken to the hall to be punished by having to read all afternoon."

On this Thursday afternoon, the various divides were already revealing themselves, games, reading or skiving by going off to the pictures.

"But the prefects have their eyes on us all the time," I said.

"If you serve the eye you can always get away with beating the system. So come on."

So I climbed onto the toilet and it seemed an eternity before I heard prefects checking cubicles and banging doors, shouting all clear. Then Wezzo came in giving me the nod that all was safe. I was glad to get out of the bog because there was a turd in the bowl about three by four that kept turning my stomach every time my eyes were irresistibly attracted to it.

We made our way down through the senior playground where we could hear the boys noisily, but happily, changing for games in the gym. They were so easily satisfied looking forward to passing a rugby ball around to each other on this cold afternoon. Ducking and diving, I felt like a commando or a cockleshell hero on one of those secret missions that I enjoyed so much in the war films. We headed towards the woods surrounding the ten full-sized rugby pitches. Under Wezzo's instructions, I jumped over a wall and it wasn't long before we were on our way to the Jolly Miller Pub, where we caught a bus into Liverpool.

I stood with Wezzo outside the Palais-De-Luxe Cinema looking at the graphic posters advertising in detail the horror, mayhem and despair suffered during the San Francisco earthquake. The film starred Clark Gable, who by the sardonic expression on his face seemed to be bemused by the whole shindig. The poster worked on me. The film was a must for me to see immediately. But besides having no money to get into the cinema, *San Francisco* was a certificate 'A'. If you were under sixteen, you had to have an adult to accompany you into the cinema, in case the shock of the stuff on the screen would cause you untold suffering.

So we stood there with our eyes well peeled, looking for someone to take us in. The plan was to make out to offer the bloke entrance money, which you didn't have. Most times they would not take the money from you. Wezzo warned me to ditch the bloke when I got inside, in case he was getting the wrong idea.

"Say if I don't get in? Say if no one comes along?" I asked.

"Say if the chippie burns down," Wezzo said disgusted. "If no one turns up, go down the side entrance where it says Exit. I'll open the fire door from the inside. Wait there. Watch an expert at work."

This bloke came along. Wezzo had a few words with him. He then offered him the pretence money, which the bloke refused. Then Wezzo followed him into the foyer and turned with thumbs up to me as the bloke bought the tickets.

I didn't have the bottle to approach a complete stranger and ask them to take me in, especially with my Irish accent. I had been in Liverpool for less than a week. Wezzo was a fairly presentable bloke. He was tall and dark while I felt disadvantaged because I was short, stocky, square-shouldered and had red hair. A ferocious scowl always appeared on my face whenever I felt threatened. I looked at a couple of likely candidates who came along but I didn't have it in me to go up to them. So I went down the side of the cinema where there were bins and rubbish stacked high, to the Emergency Exit sign. Looking up at the barbed wire on the opposite wall, I wished I had stayed in school. I could have been in a warm hall, pretending to be reading a book, instead of being in this alley where my undiscovered corpse could lie for weeks just like in one of those Hollywood films.

Suddenly the Exit door was opened and Wezzo popped his head out. He beckoned me into the dark cinema. The light flashing from the screen made it doubly difficult for me to see. I could hear Clark Gable's friendly Southern voice talking but I couldn't see a thing. My legs were giving way beneath me and big black humps kept going up and down in front of my eyes. Then as luck would have it, I fell over someone.

"Sorry," I said, as Wezzo started laughing.

"Sod you, you blind bastard. You've nearly broken my foot."

"You should be in the sodding earthquake," someone shouted.

"Just sit there," said Wezzo, pushing me into a seat. I sat down and my eyes adjusted to the darkness and I became part of the mesmerised audience.

My first half-day at the new school faded as I blotted out the thought that I would have to go back there tomorrow.

I met Dad outside of the Liverpool Exchange. I was in my new uniform with my Dublin gear wrapped up in brown paper under my arm. I could have just been conscripted and in a way I was. Dad shouted in celebration, "Sean, I hardly recognised you. If I didn't know you I'd have passed you by. Turn around. Let's see you. And straighten that cap. You're not in the bog of Allen now. Only tinkers wear caps on the back of their heads like that. Let's have a photo of you done and we'll send it back to Dublin to show them what we've achieved. We'll show them that we're not in the gutter but heading for the stars."

Personally, I thought I hadn't achieved anything. I was in a uniform, which they gave on tick to prevent me from being beaten up in the playground. Dad wanted to send home some photos of me to Dublin to show Mam and my sisters and brothers how well we were doing in Liverpool. This would put their backs up and give them the idea that I was getting preferential treatment at their expense. I was being used as 'piggy in the middle'.

God only knows why, Dad had chosen me to go with him when things had got tough at home. I was the second eldest and we had left my older and younger brothers and my two younger sisters to carry on with their life in Dublin. My youngest sister was still only a baby.

If Dad had been honest, he would have sent home photos of us living in the Salvation Army, eating scouse and praying to find a piece of meat in it. Dad's funds were quickly dwindling. He had done his rounds of the pubs that day. But all that was on offer were badly paid labouring jobs. Dad would only touch these as a last resort.

There were promises of work in Manchester, Birmingham, Coventry and London. But Dad wouldn't hear of any of these. I was in a good school. I couldn't be moved. If he had seen what I'd already seen in just one half-day, he wouldn't have said that.

Dad said it made blokes feel big as they downed their pints of Guinness to fantasise about all the big jobs with the great money. "The grass is always greener on the other side of the fence to those buckos," Dad said. As we made our way along a dismal alley towards the address of a room to let, I glanced around and thought that the grass must surely be greener anywhere else than here.

Dad was desperate to get work and somewhere to live. The mortgage on our shop in Dublin, where Mam and the family lived upstairs, was seven pounds fourteen shillings and eight pence, the equivalent of one week's wages, due in the middle of the month. Dad was ahead of his time in getting into the mortgage trap. A terrible load around your neck he called it. If only I didn't have that fecking mortgage. He had got wind of a proposed road-widening scheme. The Corporation would have to put a compulsory order on the place, ensuring that Dad got the top market price for the property. Dad wanted to hold onto the place and make a killing on it. What would happen to the family was in the lap of the gods. But meanwhile the mortgage still had to be found. That is if he could get a job. Two months were already owing. If another month remained unpaid, the building society would take the place over. They would make the killing with the Corporation.

Chapter 4

O n the recommendation of Johnny Mulligan, the French teacher, I was promoted to the top stream. It must have been because of my recitation of those few lines of Shakespeare. Goodbye to the Beta group, now I was in the Alpha stream where all the clever dickies hung out. No mickey taking here. No piss taking. No IRA. In the Alpha class no one made any disparaging remarks. They may have had disparaging thoughts about me. But they were all too cagey to say anything outright.

In this class, I was surrounded by boys who were old before their time. Everyone here took themselves very seriously. Boys of twelve acted and behaved as if they were well into their forties. Play and maladjusted behaviour would be put on the back burner and "high spirited" behaviour shelved until they were well established in their careers.

Surnames, not Christian names, were the rule of the form. It was considered girlish to use Christian names. They all had their hair cut short back and sides with a parting on the left-hand side as worn by many of the men in the services. No Burt Lancaster crew cuts, or D.A.s as worn by Tony Curtis, short for Duck's Arse. The hair on the back of the head is brushed in from the ears to meet at the back and form the eponymous D.A.

There were no loose-fitting school ties with Spiv knots or Windsor knots. Any other socks than grey ones were frowned upon. No suede or brown shoes were worn, only highly polished black shoes.

In this spawning ground of the elite, potential solicitors, lawyers, doctors, dentists, chiropodists and bank managers were being prepared to be the great men of the future work force. They would fight and even die in the world of commerce. They would spread capitalism in this post-war period.

Here the conversation verged on Virgil and Cicero; on geometry and trigonometry as well as on the serious issues of the day. Would the young Princess Elizabeth destined to be Queen be able to follow in her father's footsteps?

Suez; should Eden resign? How was the tour going? Would we retain the Ashes? Could we win the Triple Crown? And how would our 'Sevens' do against Birkenhead on Saturday?

I didn't understand any of their conversations. But I was pleased with the brief interlude I had of not having to fend off the good-natured hostility I had encountered in the Beta class from the scholarship boys. The Alpha stream was mostly fee-paying boys whose parents had the highest aspirations for them.

The pips went for the end of this silent lesson. It had been heads down, copying out of a textbook for the whole dreadfully long forty-five minutes. A lad with glasses who seemed a nice enough chap came up to me. He might have taken pity on me. So I let him help me put my books into my new desk, all of which were of better quality than I had been given in the Beta group. They were never used as missiles in this class. Peel stayed behind with me after the rest of the class had gone. "Are you Everton or Liverpool?" he asked. "I don't know," I said. I hadn't got a clue what he was talking about. "They're football teams silly," he said. "Everyone's got to have a football team." "What are you?" I asked. "I'm Everton," he said. "Then I'll be Everton too." I had a lot more things on my mind than football teams.

"I'm not really," he said, "I'm Liverpool." I didn't like the way he was playing about with me. So I said I would stay with Everton. "You can't be Everton. If you want an easy life here, you'd better be Liverpool." "It doesn't matter," I said, "I'll manage." "I'm sorry," he said. "Don't be offended." "I'm not offended," I said, shaking my head and pointing my jaw out. "If you want to play games that's up to you," I said. "I hear you're from Dublin." I nodded, as I kept packing my books into my desk. My business was my own business and it was going to stay my own business. So the less said, the better. I didn't want my affairs being gabbed about all over the school. "My Dad's in Walton," Peel said. "What does he do there?" I asked. "He's in the cemetery." Janey I wouldn't like to work in a cemetery. A bit too spooky for me, I thought. Peel read my thoughts. "He doesn't work there. He's buried there." "Oh I'm sorry." "It's life," he said. "How long has he been there?" "Three weeks. They gave me a week off."

"I've got to go now," I said. "Thanks for helping me."

"I'll walk with you to the bus." He was hanging onto me like a leech.

"Which way are you going?" he asked. "I've got to go to Liverpool."

"You're not going shopping now?"

"No, I mean yes."

I had told Peel my first lie. Our truthful friendship hadn't lasted very long. But then who could blame me? We were still at the Sally Army in Scotland Road. I was ashamed to tell Peel. He probably lived in a posh house on Queens Drive. His mother most likely had a car. The more I encountered in school, the more disgusted I felt about my own circumstances. I should have been annoyed by my poverty. I should have hated it and not held myself responsible for it. I felt guilty for the nothingness I had fallen into. If it got out that I was living in the Sally Army, that could stick to you the whole of your school life. In a matter of moments, some Liverpudlian wit would have coined a name for me: General Booth. Captain Marmalade. Salvation. Scottie Road. Or even War Cry, making me sound like an Apache chief. Although only a short time in the school, I had already heard some peculiar nicknames. Teachers were called, among other things, Biddy, Pip, Gus, Pop, Chops, Windy and Titch.

In the top of the bus, I thought about Peel who was trying to make friends with me. His da was dead. Mine was alive. What if the situations were reversed? Where would I go? What would I do? On the bus into Liverpool, I thought that I had to find a way to bring Dad back into the system. Put him on the stage, so that he could have some kind of life. In Liverpool, at the Salvation Army, he must have realised that this was some kind of turning point. I was always sensitive to when people were dislocated and suffering although they hadn't said it outright. I had been with him in Capel Street in Dublin during his happiest times when he was able to get lots of fun and enjoyment out of little things.

What he needed now was a routine and a simple structure and to forget about the overall Divine Plan. The past was the past. It could never come back. Dad never knew he was happy until he was really unhappy. Then he would look back and bemoan the fact that those happiest times had passed. He wished that he had not taken them for granted and had appreciated them more.

He hadn't been satisfied in Capel Street. He had wanted the family back from the country up with him in Dublin. But when he got them back, he soon changed his tune. I thought that by getting a bigger place on the Quays, things would work out. But that proved another cock-up. Someone had to look after him. I went with him. He wouldn't have gone on his own. If he didn't go, her relatives were advising Mam to have him committed to Grange Gorman Lunatic Asylum. She didn't want anything to do with that idea. I had been persuaded that I had to go with him to make sure he would go. I had been the one he always took with him when he had left home before. I felt responsible for his happiness. It pained me terribly to see him at war with himself.

The ticket inspector interrupted my thoughts by prodding me on the shoulder. I handed him my ticket, which I had totally shredded through. It was impossible for him to see the number or the boarding stage.

He was within his rights to charge me again for the journey. But something made him see the humorous side of the situation. "You've got bad nerves for a scholar."

I was feeling sorry for myself and loving towards Dad when I met him outside the Legs o Man public house opposite St George's Hall. But he soon knocked any pity and sentiment out of me by his unpredictable abrupt manner. "Where the hell have you been? I've been waiting for ages." "I had to wait for the bus," I said, seeing that he was very much alive. "We've got a place," he said. "Where?" I asked. "Don't ask so many fecking questions, come on."

So we gave a quick salute to Major Marmalade in the Salvation Army and moved out, hoping never to set foot in the place again.

We got full board and lodgings in a house on the Bootle end of Queens Drive in the north side of Liverpool. This elderly couple read the *Daily Mail*. Not that we were allowed to look at the paper. It was more than a hanging offence to turn the pages until the man of the house had been through it. "Mr Lloyd never likes his paper touched," I was told one morning by the landlady, as I left it scattered across the table like a pile of dirty washing. The food was almost non-existent. For breakfast there was a runny white substance, which they called porridge. It was packaged by a Quaker, a hardy lot of soul-searching creatures. Dad always made me drink a glass of water after I had this in case my mouth got stuck together. He feared that we might have been silenced by this substance, becoming as non-verbal as the real Quakers themselves.

For the evening meal, it was Marmite, scraped on a single piece of white toast, followed by an isolated biscuit with a weak cup of tea. The biscuits were locked away somewhere. So there was no fear that we could have got any more. Not that we didn't search. But as Dad said, you could pray to St Anthony till the cows come home, you still wouldn't find out where she put the packet of biscuits. All we could say was the prosperity of the British Empire wasn't in evidence around the table.

But to be fair to the couple, they had been through six years of wartime rationing. So the helpings on the plate weren't going to change for the likes of us.

We slept in a double bed in a room at the back of the house. It was colder than any fridge. When I put my foot on the lino in the morning, it stuck to the floor. A shudder went through the whole of my body. It was as if I was experiencing an electric shock. I would have worn socks in bed to counteract the shock treatment of the lino. But I could never sleep if I wore socks. I devised a method in the morning of sitting on the side of the bed and fishing for my socks, which were lying frozen on the lino, using a wire coat hanger, which I had dismantled from its rectangular shape into a fishing rod.

Dad dressed up to go to bed like the Victorians whom I'd seen in films. As he was bald, he always covered his head, with a towel or shirt, which acted like a bonnet. I never saw him wear his hat or cap in bed. But he always put on more shirts and pullovers than he'd normally wear during the day. He always had a ton of coats, which were the last thing to be put on the top of the bed. He looked like Old Mother Riley before he got into bed. But I never said anything because I knew I'd end up getting a wallop.

I would lie in bed with my teeth chattering in suspended animation under the covers. Then I would pull my legs up to my chest as if I were back in the womb. I then waited for Dad as he got ready to come to bed, putting on his Old Mother Riley gear, so that he could generate some heat.

The only good thing about living in this house was that the landlady, like myself, was picture mad. She used to take me out on a Wednesday night. Her husband had a bad chest so he wouldn't go to the cinema because the place was full of smokers. He'd have to be on his inhaler for the next week if he had spent a couple of hours in the smoky atmosphere of the cinema. I was useful to provide company for her to get out of the house as it wasn't done for a woman to go to the pictures on her own in those days.

It was funny sitting by someone in the pictures that I hardly knew. But once the lights went down, I would settle into my seat.

As the music blasted out and the credits went up, I hoped to myself that this would be a good one. All of our problems, sufferings and despairs would be taken away from us for an hour and a half as we entered worlds that had apparently insurmountable problems much worse than our own, which would be happily resolved by the time the two saddest words in the English language came up on the screen: The End.

Maybe these words "The End" on the screen, when the lights came up and we were brought back down to earth, put me in a bad mood. I don't think the National Anthem was played at this time, as was normal at the end of a performance, because the court was in official mourning for the death of George VI.

On this Wednesday night, on the way home, I remember having a fierce argument with the woman whose house we stayed in. We had been watching a John Wayne film. He was having a wonderful time on the screen. I said I'd love to be an actor like John Wayne because of all the different suits he wore in his films. She said that the actors in the films didn't wear their own clothes but that they were supplied by the costume department. I never heard so much bunk in all my life. And I told her so. Imagine being in a film and not wearing your own clothes. Surely you'd want to look your best in your own gear with all your friends, family and relations coming to see you. I certainly would. I was so annoyed that I walked all the way home behind her, not passing a word of hello or goodbye to the poor woman. Why was I so ignorant and rude to this kind woman? She always bought me a lolly ice out of her own money during the interval. And she always shared her sweets with me.

I think Dad got jealous of me going to the pictures, leaving him in the house to read the second-hand *Daily Mail* and having to listen to the man upstairs coughing his lungs up. He probably didn't like me manipulating this woman and becoming too cocky. I think he was afraid that I was finding my feet too quickly. He was not prepared to let me off the leash.

One Wednesday night, after I had announced to Dad that it was picture night, he asked me casually if I had done my homework. "Sure have, amigo," I said, brimming over with confidence and swagger. I saw Dad look at me. Immediately I realised my mistake. I should have said that we had been let off homework. "Then I'll have a look at it," he said. I was trapped. I had no alternative but to show him my crumpled-up Science book. You'd put more on a mousetrap than I had on most of the pages. "That doesn't look much," he said. "Don't worry, I'll finish it off later," still hoping to spring for the door. "Will you now?" he said. He looked at the sentence and a half I had put on the page. Then he looked at me. I knew in my water that things weren't going to plan. "Is that the way you spell Wednesday? Or do they spell Wednesday differently in this country than they do in Ireland?" "I must have got mixed up," I said. He closed the blue copybook. Looking at the cover, he said "is that the way you spell Science?" I couldn't spell for toffee. "I think, young man, you'd better do some homework." "But the pictures," I said, "Mrs Lloyd." "You tell Mrs Lloyd that you've got a lot of homework to do and that you can't go to the pictures tonight, or any other night." That was the hardest thing I had to do, to have to say to Mrs Lloyd that I couldn't go to the pictures. It was like cutting my own throat. It was so unfair just because I couldn't spell Wednesday or Science. I had to stay in and listen to Mr Lloyd coughing his arse off upstairs while Mrs Lloyd banged about in the kitchen, the way women do when they're in bad tempers. Dad sitting opposite me, twiddling his thumbs and whistling no particular air, which he always did when he was in a bad temper.

Dad didn't value education for its extrinsic or intrinsic self. But like many of those at school who tried to implement it, it could be used as an instrument to shatter one's already low self-esteem. I knew there was a reason why Dad was in a bad mood. He was taking it out on me because he couldn't get at the person he wanted to direct his real venom at. He must have had another bad day at work. When things were going bad for Dad, he took it out on the person nearest to him. As I was the only one around, it was my role and duty to take the flack.

It all stemmed from the fact that Corrigan, Dad's employer, wouldn't let Dad go travelling on the road in November trying to flog Corrigan's Cola. As it was coming up close to Christmas, he wanted all the staff he could muster to serve behind his counters. So Corrigan sent Dad to work in one of his shops, promising him that if he fared OK he would give him his own shop to manage within three months. So, clad in white shop coat and with what little hair he had left plastered down with Brylcreem and Brilliantine, Dad set about to serve behind the counter in a shop just off Hall Green. The manager was a Northern Irish man by the name of wee Billy McShane.

I told Dad to hang on till after Christmas, as things were bound to change in the New Year.

But domestically, they changed for us just before Christmas, when Mrs Lloyd, by a circuitous route gave us notice to quit her house. This couple were not going to put up with us over the Christmas period. We were Irish. They supposed that if Dad had drink on him he'd want to tell them a few home truths and have a fight or two and smash the place up. So they got rid of us by leaving our suitcases outside of the door and changing the locks. There was no sight or sound of them. Their neighbours didn't know anything about the couple. They kept themselves to

50

themselves. Not an unusual thing in England. They had spoken to the Lloyds once about forty years ago. I said to Dad that we were probably the first lodgers the Lloyds had ever had. "As long as we're creating firsts, what does it matter?" Dad said, as we waited at the bus stop with our cases for the bus to Brecknock Road.

Dad had met this Irish bloke at Mass. He was letting out condemned properties that stood empty for years as the council was short of the cash to implement their new housing programme. So for a fee, a certain councillor would let this Irishman know when and where the places were empty. For another lump of cash, the Irishman would let the likes of Dad know where to find such condemned properties. So we got a place off Brecknock Road. We were squatters before the word became fashionable. "Do you know son, you'll write a book about this one day, but they won't believe what we had to do to survive."

We didn't go in the front door. It was boarded up. But more frightening was the big white X on the door, beside the notice. Warning people to keep out as the place was in danger of collapsing. So we went in by the back window, loosening some pieces of timber that Dad easily pushed aside. This now became our main door. We did not remove the wood because we feared that the Council Inspectors of the Law would know that there were people illegally occupying the property.

Dad went through the house, sorting through the gibbles left by the different families who had previously inhabited the house. These people had been moved out to the suburbs to new houses. The Corporation were doing the same to the people in Dublin, clearing out the cosy inner cities for the freezing suburbs.

Dad found lots of stuff, which he put in one room where we made our headquarters. Surprisingly we had a gas cooker that mysteriously had not been cut off. I prayed and begged Dad not to light it in case the bloody thing blew up. "You've been to Mass and Confession this week, haven't you?" he shouted. "So what's there to worry about?" he said as he lit the gas. Mercifully, it didn't blow us to kingdom come but the flame on it wasn't very strong. It took a good hour to boil a kettle of water. "You're just like your mother," Dad said, as we waited for the kettle. You fill it right to the brim instead of half filling it, you daft eejit. And don't look at it. It'll never boil if you stare at it. You should know by now, a watched kettle never boils," Dad said, pouring half the water out. Still, we were used to mucking in for ourselves. In our position we learned to make the best of a bad lot, to thoroughly enjoy simple things and to get the maximum enjoyment out of them. It wasn't long until we had a home from home. Dining each night with our takeaway fish and chips from Bowler Street, eating by candle light, the rats envious of our culinary delights. Dad made me laugh by saying that he wouldn't call the Queen his aunt.

I was well aware that we had nothing. That probably all our lives we would have next to nothing. But we still had each other. Dad and me. Me and Dad. We got no quarter in the world and we gave none. It was only natural as I was growing older that we would have the odd flare-up. Sometimes we got under one another's feet. I had to be a dab hand at being able to recognise the pitfalls ahead. I had to be sensitive to his mood swings. Know when it was prudent to duck and dive in order to avoid one of his raging tirades. These could occur out of the blue over the simplest most innocuous matters. He harboured things, allowing them to fester until a time came when he vomited all of the poisons and hurts that had been inhabiting his mind. Naturally all of his problems were down to me as I was the only one around to take the brunt of his self-persecutory neurosis.

I had to be a good listener. You couldn't pretend to listen with Dad as a lot of people do. They have other things on their mind. They are only half listening. You couldn't do that with Dad. You had to give him your full attention or he'd pull you up. He'd ask you what you thought of the situation. And you'd have to come up with a sound appraisal. So at an early age, I developed the habit of listening, sharing and giving advice.

We had rats in this house. They were as big and healthy as some of the royal corgis. They usually hung around the broken lavatories, which stank. The toilets were out in the back yard. After seeing a couple of these corner boys playing hide and seek one day, I vowed never to use those toilets again. Now I had a whole new set of problems. I trained myself to go for days without having to go for a shite. I had read of a bloke somewhere claiming a world record for not having had a shit for over twenty-two years but it proved a very difficult record to establish as I suppose constant supervision of the candidate would be necessary to make the record legal for entry into the record books.

I was lucky because I could go to school. So I didn't have to wait over twenty-two years. It was impossible to use the cubicles during the break time at school. They were always packed with kids smoking. If you did get into one of the cubicles during the break, you could have a host of lads looking over the top of the cubicle, laughing their bollocks off as you tried to have a peaceful shite. So I had to ask permission from the teacher to go to the toilets during lesson time. My leaving the lesson so frequently and regularly caused ripples of laughter and comments from the odd boy. "Don't forget your matches." But unlike them, I never smoked. The myth being that smoking helped you think. God only knows where that came from. But as I didn't want to think, only survive, I had no need to smoke. I had not then heard of Maslow's triangle, although I was adhering to his principles. I was at the bottom of the triangle. Survival at all costs was the most important thing on my agenda.

Chapter 5

On Christmas Eve, Dad went to the pub. I went to the cinema, which was cold, lonely and empty. That Christmas Eve was the first time in my life when I couldn't escape into the film. I had seen hundreds of films. I always enjoyed going into another world. Any world was better than the one I inhabited. But that night, what was happening on the screen seemed wooden and empty compared to what was happening outside in the streets, houses and pubs. The excitement and build-up for the Christmas celebrations was passing me by. The birth of Baby Jesus was escaping me. I sat in this cinema watching some Hollywood nonsense. I felt that I was not a part of anything, neither the film nor the celebrations going on outside. I wasn't old enough to go into a pub and join in the drunken party celebrations, have a singsong around the piano.

When they advertised the forthcoming attractions on the screen, I hoped and prayed that I could be transported in time to the period after Christmas when things would get back to normal again.

In that partly empty cinema, I experienced loneliness, rejection and abandonment. By having to realise and accept that I had lost my family and friends, a big part of me was dug out, leaving a deep empty void.

In the morning things were to get worse. Dad said that he knew that I didn't believe in Father Christmas and that all that Christmas stuff was a lot of nonsense. So I didn't get a single thing for Christmas. I hadn't got him anything because I didn't have any money. Then I wondered what my brothers and sisters in Dublin got for their presents. I'm sure they all got something. Mam was a great believer in Christmas and the family. Not that we got a card from her. Which wasn't her fault. She didn't know where we were.

My face must have dropped a mile at the thought of getting nothing. Immediately Dad said that I wasn't to worry, when the January sales started, he would get me something. Everything would be half the price and I could choose whatever I wanted. Back in those days, there were real bargains to be had in the New Year sales. People would queue for days after Christmas, camping out on the pavements all night.

One such bargain occurred in Henry Street in Dublin. A fur coat valued at a thousand pounds was put in the window of Cohen's shop for a pound. When the fur coat was handed over to the lucky customer in the crowded store, a hole was found in the back of the coat, the size of an elephant's arse so that the coat was virtually worthless.

I was so disappointed. I realised that the magic of Christmas was gone for ever. What was I to tell the lads at school when they boasted about all the presents they had got for Christmas? I still didn't tell anyone where I lived, so why should I tell anyone about what I didn't get for Christmas, especially Peel. He had come top of the class in the Christmas exams. I had the distinction of being bottom of the class. But they couldn't post my report home. They didn't know where we lived, which all added to my anxiety and neurosis. I knew I was only warding off the day when the terrible truth would come out. I was no more than a dunce, a useless dunce. No better than some of the kids in Dublin who had to wear the dunce's pointed hat and were made to stand in the corner of the classroom.

Dad went to the pub on Christmas morning. I stood outside like a genuine Victorian orphan. I was too young and too small to be allowed into the pub. There were no shops or parks open. I had nowhere to go. So I had to stand outside of the pub for over two hours kicking my heels, listening to them singing their songs of loving each other to an out-of-tune piano that had the guts hammered out of it during the war when one's sanity often depended upon a sing-a-long together.

In Dublin, I was allowed to go into Gilsen's pub in Smithfield. But the rules regarding children going into parks and pubs were much stricter in Liverpool. I don't think those rules were there to protect children. In Liverpool, children had to be out of sight as well as out of mind.

Dad might have thought that he was doing a bit of missionary work in the foreign fields of Liverpool when he took these three men, blokes he had got drinking with in the pub, men he'd never pass the time of day with in Ireland, back to our condemned rooms for Christmas dinner. The three wise men followed the star from the Pier Head. We had got a leg of lamb that Dad had nicked with the help of Jim English from Corrigan's warehouse. Dad had been to see old Corrigan to wish him all the best for the festive season with his Christmas card. Not that Corrigan gave anything back in return except a wet handshake. Jim chucked Dad the leg of lamb on his way out of the warehouse, saying, "Bugger me Doyle, it'll be rotten after Christmas."

It was naive of us to think that the cooker would work in this condemned building. Nothing else did. Windows were broken. The roof let in. The place was rat-infested. The gas fire was broken. When you lit it, only half of it was alight while the other half gave out poisonous fumes. The 'wise men' sat around in their overcoats and caps looking like figures from a Jack B. Yeats painting. You can take the man out of the Bog but you can't take the Bog out of the man, Dad would often say. We had nothing. No power in the gas. No nothing. So Dad got out the uilleann pipes and played this mourning sorrowful instrument and played to these abandoned men. Men who probably didn't want to be reminded of anything, least of all nostalgic Ireland, which was responsible for them being in this country in the first place.

It was a long painful Christmas Day, not a bit like the cut and thrust ones we had in Ireland as a family. Thoughts of home came recurring throughout the long day. Here we were, with nothing to do but to pray that this supposedly happiest day of the year would pass as quickly as possible. Dad's 'three wise men' sat around the table drinking their carrying out, talking about all the great jobs that were coming up. Next year could be a great year for the work, the year they would make a killing. They fantasised over jobs and the great money they were going to make.

What optimists these men were. The three of them had been in the country over ten years, which seemed like an eternity to me, most of my lifetime, as I was twelve and a half years old. But they still talked of making it during the next year. They couldn't see how the odds were so stacked against them. But as Mam used to say, "If you knew what was waiting for you around the corner, you'd never get out of bed in the first place."

After Christmas I was reduced to the ranks. My dismal showing in the Christmas examinations got me sent back to the Beta form. I got nought for Maths. I must have spelt my name incorrectly. My English composition was nothing compared to the article I had submitted to the school's Christmas magazine, with the help of Dad. "As Dublin City Lights Went Out".

Dad had written down the words as I told the story of our overnight journey on the SS *Munster*. He was amazed at the detailed observations I had made of the journey. He had seen little or nothing of what had been going on, on board.

Even then, I was a suspicious little character, trying to see what was going on behind the surface of things.

I always wanted to know what was behind what they were trying to do to us at school. Dad often used to tell me that I was my own worst enemy. But somehow I instinctively knew that if I swallowed their educational crap, I'd end up being a regulator, just like them. Most of the other boys did not see things the way I did. They were empty vessels so they allowed the teachers to fill them up with material that would further them in their careers. But I wanted to examine all of the shit inside of myself before I could take on any more shit from them.

The fierceness and the evangelical belief of those who had control of the print culture and those aping their positions never ceased to amaze me. Trained in Latin and Greek, they considered themselves so superior to those who had a more practical intelligence who could build a ship, paint a door, fix a seat on a lavatory or lay out a garden. Not that I could do any of those things myself. All I could do was to observe and remember, and observing and remembering could be a painful and solitary occupation.

Now I was back with Wezzo and the gang in the Beta group. I had been in the Alpha group of high flyers for less than six weeks with boys who had been studying Latin, Algebra, Geometry, Trigonometry and French for years in preparation for exams. Some of them had had their names down for the prep school since before they were born while I had just come off the boat. Now I was having to suffer rejection, failure, and further loss of self-esteem because of the unrealistic expectations of an overambitious father.

Something would have to be done, but what? I would have to get help from somewhere, but where? Certainly not from the Christian Brothers. They were running an educational business. It didn't seem to have much in common with the ideals of their founder St Ignatius Rice. He had taken the roaming orphan kids of the streets of Waterford in Ireland, fed them, clothed them and tried to educate them. St Patrick's College in Liverpool was more interested in the affluent middle classes who sent their offspring to their preparatory school to drill them for entrance to the fee-paying school. The scholarship boys who passed the eleven-plus came mostly from the council estates. They often found themselves at loggerheads with the fee-paying middle classes. Within six weeks I had visited both zones. As in any war, there were good and bad on both sides.

All we were doing in the Beta class was marking time. As many working-class people did in their places of employment. The joy of work and achievement had been taken away allowing a cynicism to develop. The playing of cards to pass the time was tolerated in most workplaces, but forbidden in the classroom. So

60

ways and means had to be devised to counteract the boredom. After thumbing through the latest editions of *Tit Bits* and *Health and Efficiency*, one of the ways the lads occupied their time while waiting on the changeover of subject teachers, who arrived later and later, was to examine each other for blackheads. They would sit at their desks and search each other like you'd see chimps do in the zoo. You would only allow your special friend to do your blackheads. This search was a very intimate act. Probably the first intimate contact lads had with another human outside of their own family. I was left out of this pastime, as I did not have any blackheads. I hadn't been long enough in Liverpool's smog to acquire the necessary build-up of pollution on my skin. Also I was a redhead and fair-skinned. So I missed out on the little acts of intimacy I craved for. Because of war rationing and the resulting effect of malnutrition, the powers that be had decided to give children free milk. We were each given a third of a pint of milk each morning. This had to be consumed before we were allowed out to the mid-morning break. Otherwise we might all die off and then there'd be no one left to do the work. As it was cold outside, the lads took their time drinking their milk. But the teacher in charge could not leave the classroom until he was assured that all of the lads had consumed their milk. "You're not having your milk Burton," Johnny shouted, "I only like it from the breast Mr Mulligan."

"What do you expect me to do? Go down to Lime Street and get you a wet nurse?"

On the bus from school I realised that I was a kid with all of the problems of the adult world on my plate. I had to listen to all the problems that Dad was having at work and share them as if I were his wife. But I had nowhere to air what I was going through at school. What was happening to me did not seem anywhere near as important as what was happening to Dad. Now as the bus approached Liverpool, I was certain I was heading for a new crisis, because that's the way Dad seemed to live, moving from crisis to crisis. No wonder my sense of security was radically undermined.

Corrigan had let Dad out of the Hall Green shop. Things were slack in the retail business after Christmas. He told him to get on with selling Corrigan's Cola on the road. He also gave Dad a room over one of his shops, outside of which we now stood, looking at the chickens on a spit in the window. God, I thought, what I wouldn't give to get me teeth stuck into one of them.

Inside of the shop, a middle-aged woman was serving behind the counter. We told her that we were looking for Mr Delaney the manager. "You must be our new guests," she beamed. Immediately Dad became suspicious. The woman could see that Dad was unsettled. She quickly reassured him, smiling, "Mr Corrigan has been on the phone talking about you two." "All good, I hope," Dad said laughing, always thinking that the axe was about to fall. "I'm Wendy. This must be your little boy Sean." "Smile, will you," Dad said, "you've got a face on you like the back of a turnip." "We're going to be neighbours," Wendy said, "I live upstairs. We all share the same corridor, kitchen and bathroom." Christ, is there no end to it, I thought. Still, as they said at school, "it's best to offer it up. These things are sent to try us." Sitting around the kitchen table, Wendy explained how she had locked Bonzo, her little white terrier, away in the spare room so as to give us time to get to know each other. Mr Delaney, the manager of the shop, lived off the premises. Wendy was the only person that Bonzo had any contact with. Meeting other humans would be a new experience for Bonzo.

Wendy generously shared her minced pork pie, which Mr Delaney the manager had let her have for half price. It had been in the window since the weekend, she told us. Dad spat it out immediately, saying that he got a bit stuck in his throat. Wendy instantly came to the rescue with a drink. "In the name of God," Dad said as he spat that out too. "What is it?" "It's water. Would you prefer tea?" "Tea, I wouldn't sleep the whole of the night if I had tea at this hour. If you'll excuse us," Dad said, "we've had a very busy day, haven't we Sean?"

Back in our room, Dad said "Did you hear her? Half-priced minced pork pies indeed; you'd need a sledgehammer to break them. If she comes back, just keep her talking. While the cat's away, the mice will play," he said. I didn't know what he was on about. The expression must have told on my face, because he immediately said, "I'm going downstairs to have a look around. I'll just take this," he said, wielding a big stick, "in case Bonzo decides to open his mouth." "He doesn't bite, does he?" I asked. "He won't be able to shite after I've finished with him."

Dad seemed to be gone for ages. Waiting upon his return always played upon my nerves and my fear of him getting into trouble and not being able to do anything about it. I was alone again in a room. Trapped. Waiting for Dad. I had been trapped in Capel Street in Dublin, then with the family in Inns Quay. Now in Liverpool I was trapped with him again. As far as I could see, there was no way out. I was another of his possessions to be moved around. Fed or not fed. Bullied. Loved. Laughed at. Laughed with or ignored. Whatever he thought fit. Sometimes I didn't have as much rights as a rag doll. I had fought against this for years but I always lost. Now I began to wonder if I could ever exist without him permanently possessing me. The only difference between God and my dad as far as I was concerned was that I could not see the former whereas I had the latter for breakfast, dinner and tea. Dishing out punishments or rewards as he thought fit.

When he came back he had one of the chickens we had seen in the window earlier and immediately I was thrust into a further state of anxiety. "But won't they miss it? They're bound to have counted them. Wendy's sure to know it's you." "That's why you'd better eat it all up," he said. "We don't want to have any evidence." Dad didn't seem to take things or women seriously. He laughed at women, especially those who he considered were past their prime, thinking that they were a bit simple. But I didn't think that there was anything simple about Wendy. On the surface, Wendy looked like an easy pushover. But I'm sure that she was a much different person underneath.

"What about the bones?" I asked. "They're for Bonzo," he said.

In the morning I had expected sparks to fly. But nothing was said about the missing chicken. I asked Dad for an explanation. All he said was the English were still shell-shocked after the war, especially the English women.

What I was to find out afterwards was that Wendy had covered up the whole incident by paying for the chicken herself. She was not going to give up the opportunities and prospects that a man and boy living alongside of her could bring for a mere lousy barbecued chicken. In a post-war Liverpool where her generation had lost most of their men in the war, Wendy probably thought that any price was worth paying to stave off her loneliness. So when Delaney the manager asked her about the missing chicken, she quickly said that she had taken it as a special treat for her new guests.

For the past few days I had drunk a lot of cola. My only friend at school, Wezzo, had drunk a lot of cola. There was cola coming out of our mouths, ears and arses. Dad had been all over Liverpool. Well that didn't take too long. Herr Hitler had seen to that.

As we walked up the drive from the school to the bus stop, Wezzo, frustrated at having spent another wasted day at school, was taking it out on me. "Where are you going with your life? What are you doing with it? You need money. So they tell you to go and earn it. Which is shit. There's thirty per cent unemployment in Liverpool. There always was and there always will be. You could try to nick it but you could end up in a nice little cell in Walton." Then he seemed to brighten up. "Throw away your satchel. Renounce your evil past and follow me. From this day forth you no longer will be a fisher of fish but a fisher of dirty old seamen."

So I was down with Wezzo at Liverpool Exchange. He had gone with this seaman around the side of the stadium. The plan was that Wezzo enticed the seaman to get friendly with him, then he was going to nick his wallet and make off with it, throwing it to me as I waited on the corner. I was a good runner so I could easily shake the seaman off. I'd meet up with Wezzo later at Lime Street Station under the clock. Nervously I stood waiting for the wallet as if I were a runner in a relay race waiting to receive the baton. But my concentration on the job in hand was totally shattered when I saw a Corrigan lorry drawing up with Dad driving. He said he was going on the road for a couple of days to see if he could shift some of the cola and off he went, just like that.

My thoughts were broken up by Wezzo running back up the alley, pursued by the seaman. I knew that he was a seaman as he was the steward who had served us on the SS *Munster* as we travelled from Dublin to Liverpool. Wezzo must have sensed that I was not giving my full attention to the scam. Instead of throwing me the wallet, he kept running, quickly outpacing the overweight steward. I didn't go to Lime Street Station to wait for Wezzo under the clock. I had no appetite for anything. I wound my way back to the rooms over Corrigan's shop. Wendy was storming around the place making everything shipshape. Wendy was one of those house-proud women who always cleaned up as she went along. You had hardly swallowed your tea before she taken the cup and saucer and was washing it up. Phyllis, who looked after me in Dublin when I was smaller, never bothered about washing anything up as long as there was another clean cup left in the house. And the only time we used saucers in Dublin was to give milk to the cat. Wendy was strict about folding and hanging up things. Shirts had to be hung on hangers. Things had to be put back in their place. "There's a place for everything and everything should be in its place," she'd say, as often as you'd say your prayers. I left the top off the toothpaste. You'd think I had committed the crime of the century by the way she lectured me. I tried to move away but she shouted, "I'm talking to you. I have not finished." She was a right Adolf Hitler in knickers. Phyllis wouldn't have given a fizz about a top on the toothpaste. That's if we had any toothpaste in the first place.

Dad was only gone a couple of days but Wendy was already showing her true colours. She was turning into a proper pain in the arse. "Don't do this, don't do that." I gave her one of my looks. "There's no need to look at me like that. It's for our own good. I don't enjoy admonishing you. We all have to learn." Feck you and your learning, I thought. But then I saw it all in a flash. It was as if she were a kid who had been given a new doll for Christmas. The only trouble was that I was the doll. She fussed over me. Hugging me, kissing me. Which really got on my tits. She was obsessed with combing my hair. I had a bit of hair on the back of my head that stuck up like a Mohican. It didn't bother me, I couldn't see it. But she couldn't leave it alone. She never gave me a bit of peace. "Oh my lovely beautiful boy," she'd say, pulling me to her breasts as she tried to feel up my arse. She got me up in the mornings at an unearthly hour. In Dublin, there was a point to getting up early. I sometimes served first Mass and got myself away from the rest of the family. But in Liverpool, there was no morning Mass to go to or family to avoid. So I'd linger in bed as long as possible. There was only school, which wasn't all that inviting at the best of times. Da may have had many faults but at least he'd leave me alone. That's if he wasn't in a bad mood. But Wendy invaded my privacy. She was always on about me washing. Threatening me with water. Water, in her mind, was the cure for everything. First of all she made me clean my teeth. A thing I'd never do voluntarily. You don't see cats or dogs standing in front of mirrors cleaning their teeth. And they all seem to have good teeth. Then she was always concerned about me having some kind of ailment or other. She'd look down my throat. Examine my head for nits. If I so much as had a casual scratch, she would check under my ears to see if I had any swellings. She looked in them for wax. She was always on about my nails. How I mustn't bite them. I must give up biting my nails. The only little luxury I had left in life was to have a good chew on my nails. It always seemed to steady my nerves. She looked up my nose for bogies. Next she'd be looking up my bum for shite. My instincts were proven correct when she asked when was the last time I'd been to the lavatory. Was everything down below in working order? What business is it of yours, I thought, what happens down there?

But things came to a head this particular evening, when I suppose a boxer would say I dropped my guard. "Tea is ready," she called. "Right kiddo," I said as I came out of the bedroom. "Have you washed your hands?" "Sure have amigo." "Let's see," she asked. "No you haven't. Go and wash them now. And don't lie to me. Well-bred people do not sit at the table with dirty hands." Yeah. Yeah. Yeah. I thought. Listen to Her Master's Voice. "You have to take personal responsibility for your own appearance and behaviour. Otherwise we will all have a state of anarchy, we will all be anarchists. I have not been through a war making sacrifices so as to let the likes of you behave and act like an anarchist." You'd think the bearded old cow had fought the war single-handed.

Each night over her cocoa, she'd give me her sad story. I'd never met a woman up to then who didn't have a sad story. If you weren't careful they could grind you down with all their misery. Women and religion could have the same depressing futile effect on me if I didn't stay on full alert. Wendy was a proper wallower. When she wallowed she wallowed. Before she began her performance, she would arrange herself as if she was preparing for a part at the Liverpool Playhouse. And I, her audience, would be trapped on the other chair to listen.

"Of course, if circumstances had been different for me," she'd say in a theatrical manner, "Derek would have been in that chair instead of you." Yes, I thought to myself, Derek got off lightly. "But the war ruined us all." You could have heard her in the gods at the Liverpool Playhouse the way her voice carried. "Ruined. Ruined us all. But I will not stay ruined. I will not live life like this. Like the phoenix I will rise again."

After having a good wallow, it seemed she'd cleared the air. So then she'd turn into a proper bitch again. I went into the bathroom and ran the tap, counting to ten. It was there that I resolutely decided that if I ever married, I would never marry a house-proud bullying woman who was obsessed with cleanliness and as moody and as unpredictable as Dad. My trouble was that I was at the mercy of people's moods. As the tap ran, I looked at her knickers and bra hung out like imperial flags. They were no different to what I had seen Phyllis air on the line in Dublin, only they were much bigger.

"Well, let's see those hands." I held them out. "No, young man, this will not do. You are going to have clean hands if I have to wash them myself." "They are bloody clean," I said. That was it. I had dropped my guard. "What did you say? I am asking you what did you say?" I was for it now. I stood staring into space. My body rigid, avoiding any eye contact with her. "I'm waiting."

"I didn't say anything," I said. But she couldn't leave it there. That's what I found out about some people. Once you showed any remorse or apparent weakness, they were in with both barrels blasting. "You're a wild boy. It's no wonder they call you lot the wild Irish. But I'll tame you." And once you've tamed me, I thought, you'll go after Dad and tame him and make his life as miserable for him as it had been in Dublin. With her clean hands and smelly breath from all the Woodbines she smoked, she was the wild one, I thought, as I looked at her dagger-eyed. Then she took me by the ear to the bathroom, which made me yell out. Once someone has a good hold on your ear, it's nearly impossible to get out of their grip without losing half of your head.

"You had better have a bath," Wendy said, as she sat me on the bathroom chair. She then released my raging hot ear. "I'm not dirty," I said. "You don't have to be dirty to have a bath. Come on young man. You're not in Ireland now." She ran the bath.

"Right, in you go. Get all that dirty stuff off. Put it in the basket." I looked at her. Oh God, I thought, when I saw there was no lock on the door. The lads in Dublin warned me about English women. Once they found out you were Irish, all they wanted to do was look at your mickey. "Come on," she said, "there's no need to be shy. I've seen it all before. I was a nurse in the war. Seen one, seen them all." That still didn't mean that she was going to see mine. "Hurry up," she shouted. Then, thank God, Bonzo began barking. "I won't be a minute," she said, "get all that stuff off."

I was in and out of that bath before she had time to draw her wild Woodbine breath. I was changed and sitting back at the table by the time she got back. "What about your bath?" "I've had it," I said. "But you couldn't have been in there for more than five minutes." "I told you I wasn't dirty." "You're typically Irish," she said, "full of blarney with the gift of the gab. But no one with any breeding sits at the table without washing themselves."

"Sticks and stones can break my bones, but names can never hurt me."

"You're a nasty spoiled little brat. I shall inform your father when he comes back."

"He's not coming back," I said quietly.

"What do you mean he's not coming back?"

"He's gone off with a younger woman."

"What?" she asked.

"He's dumping his family." It was such a consolation to see her drawn disappointed sallow face. "Oh my God," she said, "your mother should be told about this immediately." "She's dead," I said. It was amazing how much pleasure I got out of shocking Wendy with my lies.

"I don't believe you." "It's true, it was in all the papers and on the radio. She was killed with all of my cousins. The lies seemed to be speaking themselves without any help from me. "What a terrible thing to say." "It's true. Éamon De Valera came to the funeral. We had a High Mass. A choir. And black horses that kept shaking their heads. They did Ahs, Ahs, which made everyone laugh."

"Oh my God," she said. "Can I be excused from the table, Wendy, I feel so tired." I left the table. If she tried to play the big I am with me, then she'd have to suffer the consequences.

But I had got myself upset. I am not a person who can laugh things off lightly. I was angry and disturbed. I tried to suppress my real anger, not allowing myself to give full vent to my frustrating situation. I had a nightmare. I was being followed by laughing horses. I was in a lift that was out of control. I was falling into hell. I was shouting for help. The next thing I remembered was that Wendy was holding me. She clutched me to her sagging breasts. She patted my head and kissed my damp forehead. "There, there, there. You must have had a bad dream. No matter angel, your mummy is here to look after you." She wept. "There, there, you poor little thing. I'm a poor little thing." She laughed as she smothered me with her breasts. "We are both poor little things, poor little things," she said, rocking me, "who have lost their way. Dear Derek. You must learn to love. Don't be afraid of love." She stood up and dropped her nightie to the floor. She had a triangle of dark hair below her belly button. A kid at school in Dublin had told me that he had read on the lavatory wall of the Capital Theatre down in Lower Middle Abbey Street, that someone had written on the wall, that when he put his hand up this girl's skirt, that he felt a mound of hair. I didn't believe him at the time. Men had hair around their mickeys, that was to be expected because they shaved. Since women didn't shave, it was a shock to me that they had hair down there. She climbed into bed beside me and we slept together like an old married couple. I was used to sleeping with Dad, she didn't seem much different than him. Except that she had bigger tits. She farted just the same as he did when she snored.

She must have been trying to make up to me in the morning because she brought me a cup of tea in bed. But there's nothing I hate more than drinking tea or reading the newspaper in bed. So I quickly got ready for school and left without even saying goodbye. My outlook on the world had been shattered once and for all by this hairy horror on that night to remember. I sat on the bus trying to console myself. What if she were some kind of circus freak? We had all heard of the bearded lady at the circus although I had never actually seen one. The other women on the bus didn't look as if they could possibly be like her, so I relaxed. I decided that she must be the exception to the rule.

Chapter 6

The fear of the atomic bomb diminished our lives considerably. The effect of the last war and a forthcoming one loomed all over us daily. North and South Korea were fighting over their issues. Many of us did not have much notion of planning for the future. The teachers themselves were divided into two groups, those who believed in discipline and those who didn't give a damn. They thought that an atomic war was imminent, so why bother inflicting any more hardship on the kids. Some would say, it's all a chaotic mess, a joke made on mankind by a sick omnipotent being. Many of the teachers, with the backing of the Head, held onto personal discipline as if it was the saviour of all mankind and us kids. Copying what they had done in the forces, they would frogmarch the young boys around the corridors and the school playground.

The Head liked to think of his staff as his own squadron. As he entered the staff room, some of the staff rose to their feet as a matter of respect. "At ease men," he'd say, "nice to see you all turned out ready for the battle ahead." Some creep of a lay teacher would say that we were getting there slowly Headmaster. Then the Head would launch into one of his diatribes. "I dream of a day when all of the respective disciplines harmonise; a day when you have nothing to do but to catch up on your backlog of marking." This was a firm hint that they were not marking the boys' work quickly enough.

"Unmarked work is work half done. Leaving the boys in a fog of uncertainty." He'd say he had complaints from parents about the unmarked work. But then this parasite of impeccable timing would be saved from any further contact with the staff. The pips would go and the poor bastards of teachers went into the trenches of their classrooms. "Man the pumps. Put a brave face on it," as he passed the buck and repaired to his office, counting down the minutes to his coffee break.

On the way out of the staff room, an old rusty corrugated teacher, who had seen and heard it all before, and believed that the bomb would explode at any moment, was heard to say to a student teacher, "Remember, when you're in the classroom, you're on your own. There's no SOS. No backup. It's nigh impossible to teach anything. So the best bet is let them organise themselves. Join in with them. Otherwise you could end up like him." Along the corridor came a teacher goose-stepping, followed by a single file of boys who gave the Nazi salute behind his back. It was bizarre. The poor bastard was living in 1939. He had a breakdown in the war and was sent home. He can't accept that the war's over.

Anything I seemed to do got the thumbs down. In class, I had written an essay and I was told, "It's dealing with the past. It's sentimental, it's nostalgic." "But it happened Sir." "It's of no interest to anyone in this country." "Why not Sir?"

"Ireland is a little place with a huge inferiority complex, tucked away in fairyland. What you want to do is concentrate upon where you are now." Brother Ronnie, an Irish Christian Brother, seemed to have all the answers.

"Ireland has done nothing for you," he said. "If she had, you wouldn't be here in this country. Living among the English. You'll never succeed in this country if you bring Ireland with you. I'd like to know who's fuelling you with all this romantic nonsense."

Maybe it's because I was homesick I thought, or because I was finding out things about the birds and the bees that was proving alarming and driving me back to past areas of security.

"There's nothing romantic about 1916, Sir. When they strapped the wounded James Connolly to a stretcher and shot him."

"Forget where you've come from," Brother Ronnie said. "Unpack your suitcases." "You don't ask the other boys to forget where they come from, Sir."

"Then go back there." "There's nothing there Sir."

"Then I think it's self-evident what you should do."

"What's that Sir?"

"Write about the present. Write about a dramatic event that's taken place at your new home."

Oh yes I thought. I could write about Wendy. Talk about the blind leading the bloody blind. I was thirteen years of age and I probably knew more about women and life than this celibate man would learn in a month of Sundays. If he knew nothing about women, what other areas were there that he hadn't got a clue about? Like a lot of schoolmasters, he wasn't slow in setting himself up as an expert on things that he hadn't got the remotest idea about.

You could write about digging the garden, finding a body in it; or your summer holidays when it rained every day. Or an unexpected discovery you made. This man has second sight, I thought. Does he know what I discovered last night?

Or write about what you'd like to be when you grow up. Here I was on firm ground. "I'd like to be myself Sir," I said. "You can't go to an employer as yourself. They'll want to know what value you are to their business and the community at large." I gave him one of my looks. I thought of what Dad had said to me. There's no such thing as a good job or a good boss. All they want to do is get as much out of you as they can for as little as possible.

"There's the pips," Brother Ronnie said, "I've enjoyed our little chat. Get your milk. Forget the past and unpack those suitcases. Baggage will eventually wear you down."

I told Wezzo what had happened with Brother Ronnie. "You should keep mum with that prying bastard." "Why?" I asked. "In the war, they used to say idle gossip costs lives." "The war is over." "Not where those bastards are concerned. It all goes down on your report." "What report?" "They keep a report on everyone. So they can exonerate themselves for teaching you nothing. That lazy fucker does nothing for us because we belong to a Beta group. Nothing is expected of us. If you were in the Alpha class, you would be working from the textbook. He wouldn't be asking you about finding bodies in the garden. Otherwise your parents would be up to him complaining. He's got it all worked out. He knows who to look up to and who to look down upon. He ducks and dives. He's an expert at looking after number one. All of these Christian Micks are in it for number one and fuck you for coming a poor second. I know, I've got a brother becoming a priest. He gets everything showered on him. Nothing's too good for him when he comes home now. The *Echo* is not good enough for him to wipe his arse with. Me mam goes out and buys him a soft toilet roll."

I took my time getting back to our digs. I was not in any hurry to see Wendy again.

"Something will have to be done about you, young man. Out at all hours."

"Nothing is going to be done about nothing," I said. "Now, if you don't mind, I'm going to bed alone." I emphasised alone. "You should have some respect for your elders," she shouted. "You should have respect for me." "What do you mean?" she asked. "The way you behaved last night." She stood there looking at me. The balance of power had changed. How quickly the mighty can fall. When you've got something on them. And nothing is more dangerous than the loudest whisper. She was shit scared that I'd tell Dad if he came back. When I mentioned that I'd go to the Social Services if she did not leave me alone, she began to creep and crawl about me. There's nothing I hate more than whimpering. She couldn't do enough for me. It was then that I wished that she was more like her former bullying self. Then she took the violin out. "Do you know what kind of life I've had? Do you know how I have suffered? It's not easy being a woman all alone." I knew that. But I couldn't afford to feel sorry for her. She broken the boundaries once. "Your father and you are my only hope." "Don't whine." I can't stand whiners, I thought. Then Wezzo came into my mind. Nothing can be done about it. It all happened before we came on the scene. Then she played on. "Anything I do or say is only for the best." I'd had enough.

I had been through her Liverpool Playhouse days too many times already. "I'm going to bed," I said, "nightie night." She said, "God bless." She was old, miserable and horrible. But what could I do about it? She was as ignorant as a pig but it was her prejudices that I couldn't stomach.

Chapter 7

Dad came back from his travels as if he had never been away. He could always forget when it suited his purpose and he could remember whatever he wanted to if he needed to throw something up to win a row. I never knew where I was with him. He harboured things and brought them up on the most unexpected of occasions, land-blasting anyone in sight. Even if Dad forgave, he never forgot, if that's possible.

All Dad had on his mind now was the new direction he was going in. He had another plan. The Communists always had a five-year plan. The Fascists had plans. The danger of having a plan is that all other plans are scrapped and thrown out of the window as the new plan is implemented. Dad had no luck with the sale of the cola on his travels. He found it impossible to sell the stuff at that time of year. But when he returned to deposit the cola in the warehouse and was getting ready to face old Corrigan's wrath, he had a bit of luck. He bumped into Jim English, who was one of Corrigan's most respected, loyal and trusted employees. Jim was in overall charge of the warehouse. Nothing came in or out of the place without Jim's say-so.

"Bugger me," Jim said. "I thought you were going to move it. I haven't got any room in the warehouse for that cola." Dad could see that Jim was angling for something. "But what am I to do with the cola?" Dad asked. "You could say you sold it," Jim said. "But if I sold it I'd have to have forty-seven pounds. I haven't got forty-seven pennies." "If you tell Corrigan you haven't sold the load, you'll lose your job and rooms." "I still couldn't see what Jim was getting at," Dad said. "Do you know what he said then? His daughter is getting married soon and he wanted half of that cola at the reception. And I thought there were crooks in Dublin. He put up the forty-seven pounds and I can pay him the twenty-three pounds ten shillings when I get on my feet." It was all joy and jubilation when Dad went to see old man Corrigan. Dad was paraded before Corrigan's sons, William and Michael, like some Roman who had returned from butchering the Persians or the Gauls. Dad's reward wasn't a villa on the outskirts of Rome but it was nearly as good. Corrigan gave Dad the use of a little MG car so that he could go travelling on the road in Liverpool and the surrounding Merseyside area.

Next evening, Jim said to Dad, "I've got a couple of cases of butter here, one for yourself and one for my Mrs. Just drop off half the load at my house," Jim said. Butter wouldn't melt in Jim's mouth. But he knew that they could get ten pounds a case for it on the black market.

So each Friday, after Dad had listened to the ranting and ravings of Herr Corrigan, he would collect two cases of butter from Jim. They fitted nicely into the back of Corrigan's two-seater MG. Five quid for Dad, five quid for Jim and nothing for Corrigan. Not a bad income when the weekly wages Corrigan paid were barely seven pounds. Dad would say that if they don't pay you then you have to fine them. "You've got to fine the bastards," he'd say. "It's not that Corrigan hasn't got it. But he thinks that like the Egyptians he can take it with him. So you have to fine them. Fine the bastards," Dad would say in self-justification. Demonstrating to me that he wasn't a real thief deep down. He only nicked because he couldn't live on what they were paying him. A real thief will nick for the sake of nicking anything that's not nailed down.

As well as butter, soon there was chocolate, beef, ham, eggs, tinned fruit, tinned biscuits, everything Jim needed for the wedding reception, all transported in the back of the little MG. It got so bad that Jim's wife began to send things back. "We've already had half a dozen tins of Ye Olde Oak Ham!" Then, the day before the wedding, Corrigan called Jim into his office. "I'd like to give you a present for your daughter, a tin of cream crackers. They should go down well at the reception," said old Corrigan. Jim was nearly reduced to tears by the old man's generosity. "What did he want?" asked poor worried Dad, who thought the game was up. "He gave me these crackers," Jim said. "Bugger me, they're rejects. I wouldn't give them to the bloody dog. Better take three butters tonight."

Dad thought that he would get an invitation to the wedding as they were all thieves together. So he bought a flashy American type suit, the type of chequered affair that would be worn by Bob Hope in one of his Road films. He also bought a flat green hat in Burton's the tailors on London Road. Dad, childlike in his flashy music hall attire, waited for an invitation. But no invitation arrived. No matter how much stuff Dad delivered to the house, he was never allowed to cross the threshold, either before, during or after the wedding.

Dad was trying to infiltrate a different social structure from what he had experienced in Ireland and America. But these Liverpool Protestants and atheists did not socialise with Irish Catholics. No matter how much he helped them in thieving for their weddings or funerals. Dad felt hurt about being excluded. He could not take on board how closed the society was, closed to outsiders like ourselves.

"They're funny people, aren't they? They never drop their guard for one minute. Not like us Irish. We have the door open and a welcome on the mat for everyone." I worried terribly about Dad's dubious dealings. There was always the problem of getting the knocked-off gear into our room. Wendy had eyes on her like a hawk, Dad had to be very careful when and how he took the stuff into our room. He couldn't leave the stuff in the car overnight because he was afraid that it would be broken into.

"That's the trouble with Liverpool," Dad said, "it's full of thieving bastards." Normally he brought the stuff through the side door while Wendy was still working in the shop. This particular evening, Dad had an extra-heavy load on board, three cases of butter, three of chocolate Penguins and three of Wagon Wheels. He was late coming home because Corrigan's son, William, had been hovering around the loading bay. And Jim and Dad couldn't get the stuff into the MG. By the time he did get home, the shop was closed and Wendy was in the kitchen farting about. Dad couldn't take the risk of taking the stuff up to our room.

"You'll have to take her out to the pictures," he said. "No," I said, "I'm not taking her out anywhere, you take her out." "I'm

82

a married man." Then Dad looked at Bonzo, who was standing by the door wagging his tail. "I've got an idea," he said. Immediately Bonzo went and hid under the settee. Dad took a brush up and went after Bonzo. "Come on, you bastard. Come out and take it like a man," he shouted. Bonzo barked for all he was worth. This got Wendy's attention. "What is it Bonzo?" she asked. "Is it business time?" Wendy asked Bonzo, as his nose appeared from under the settee. "I'll get your lead." Wendy took Bonzo around the block while Dad unloaded the gear in our room, on the door of which he had now fixed a sturdy lock.

Like Dad, I had a plan of getting my hands on some money. It was impossible and demeaning having to ask Dad for cash each day. I remembered that he had been the same with Mam. He loved to control the purse strings. Power for him was all about what he had in his pockets. Like a real Irish peasant farmer, the last thing Dad ever parted with was ready cash. If I were to survive, I had to have my own income and become independent of him. The boys at school got their weekly pocket money come rain or shine. Wezzo always had money. So I hit upon the idea of lining my pockets by opening up my own tuck shop at school. I set up my pitch behind the gym, although it was an out-of-bounds area to juniors such as myself. This was where the hardened smokers and older boys congregated. I sold to Lower and Higher Fifth Form boys. I didn't let anyone in my class know of my business venture. There was always the risk of them informing the school authorities. I knew I was safer with the older boys. They were not as naive as the younger ones. The ones who assembled behind the gym for their morning smokes were deviants like myself.

It went. Wagon Wheels, Penguins, even Corrigan's cola, all at knocked-down prices. The first day I had sold out in less than ten minutes. These growing lads were always very hungry and seemed addicted to sugar. The third of a pint of milk they got each day was hardly enough to fortify them between morning and lunch break. The next day I brought in double the amount of gear. By the end of the week, a queue had formed around the front of the gym even before the pips went for the morning break. This alerted the prefects, who were down on me like a ton of bricks. There were more people queuing around the front of the gym than were in the senior playground.

Long, an Upper Fifth prefect, told me in no uncertain terms that I couldn't open up my own tuck shop. He confiscated all the stuff. He told me that the Head was going to hear about my shenanigans. He made me turn my pockets out and took all the cash I had. Back in class, I thought I'm in for it now. I've lost everything. He's going to tell the Head. I'll get it both from the Head and Dad. Why was I so daft as to think that I could get away with such a scam?

We had Brother Ronnie next. "Now boys," Brother Ronnie said, after we had said a prayer for wisdom and enlightenment. He waited until we all had blessed ourselves. But I wasn't listening to Brother Ronnie; I was waiting for some kid to knock on the door to say that the Head wanted to see me. "This is going to be a special lesson," Brother Ronnie said. The boys all shuffled in their seats and sat up straight folding their arms, hoping that there was a film or some other special treat in store.

"Today is Tony Long's mother's birthday. You may have come across Long. He's one of the Upper Fifth prefects. A man to keep clear of," Brother Ronnie said. All the lads laughed. "Well, his mother has kindly donated some chocolate biscuits to the staff. As I am watching the waistline, I've decided to award a Penguin and Wagon Wheel for the best composition written during this lesson. A composition on why you have a special relationship with a particular saint." I couldn't believe my ears. I felt like shouting out that they are my Penguins and Wagon Wheels. But what could I do? I suffered in silence.

I was to get to know Long very well. He was a great man for feathering his own nest, a born again criminal. You can never hope to meet better than that in your life. I heard later that my Penguins and Wagon Wheels had landed up in the staff room and the prefects' room, compliments of his mother. If the truth were known, he probably didn't have one. And if he had, she would probably have disowned him.

As I waited for my bus that afternoon, who should come along but the prefect Long? As cool as daylight, he said that if I wanted to bring any more stuff into school, it had to go through him. For his handling fee, he'd take half. This was worse than the protection rackets I'd seen in films. But the problem was that I was no Marlon Brando. Then my bus came by. I thought that I had to be careful with this bloke. He was not someone you could afford to muck about with. He held all the cards in the school. He played them how it suited him best. I half feared him, half admired and respected him at the same time. A bit like I did with my brother, Val. Maybe I was looking for a surrogate brother. Perhaps I missed my brother's advice and protection. I could always spout off about things to Val, things I wasn't clear about. Now I was like an only child, just me and Dad. I missed not having my brother Val to talk to. I always knew that he was there, that he'd be on my side. Any advice that he gave me was meant for my best interest. Now my only confidant was Wezzo. But we didn't appear to be going in the same direction. Anything we did was always done for a laugh. We were like a pair of confidence tricksters who'd always bottle out, were violence or anything really serious to raise its ugly head.

There were other directions to go in. But how was I to find them? It was funny how Long and Val were the same age. So I did a thing that I couldn't rationally explain to myself. My decision-making was coming from somewhere deep inside of me based more on instincts than on rational reasoning. I wrapped up some Wagon Wheels and Penguins for Long and got a kid to leave the package outside of the prefects' room. A few days later, Long stopped me in the corridor. He must have been like all of us lads at school, short of cash.

He gave me his stamp album. He wanted to sell his collection off individually. I suppose as a senior prefect, he couldn't go around the school selling stamps. So he used me as his lackey, giving me a small commission on all the stamps I sold. Now I was making contact with the lads who literally ran the school. I had access to the prefects' room. Why I wanted to cross over from my side of the track was a mystery to me. Wezzo certainly didn't want to. His unreserved loyalty rested with the firm core of no hopers, the defeated in the Beta group.

There was something in me that wanted to find out what their world was like. As I went on my stamp-selling duties, I had access to the whole school and diplomatic immunity because I had the protection of the prefects. One of the lads I was to become mates with on my sales trips was Hughes, who was in the "A" stream, a class above mine. He had more street cred and contacts than anyone in the Beta group, so I hung about with him.

We still had the trouble of storing the gear in our room, especially if Dad came home late from work. Then Dad would have to engage Wendy's interest as I slaved up the stairs with the loot. He would be suave and debonair with her. I didn't care. He could have her. She could have him. He could learn the hard way as far as I was concerned. But it all blew up with Wendy because of the state he left the kitchen in. When we first moved in, Wendy had taken it upon herself to cook for us. This gave her the opportunity to get to know us better, especially Dad. But she still behaved as if there was full wartime rationing in operation. "You'd put more on a mousetrap than she'd put on a plate," Dad said. So, on the odd occasion, when Wendy was occupied elsewhere, Dad would cook us an enormous fry-up.

We were used to grubbing for ourselves in Dublin but not too bothered about doing the washing up. After the meal, there would be pots, pans and crockery left all over the kitchen for Wendy to wash up when she had finished work.

She cleaned the place up a couple of times but eventually she saw red. She had it out with Dad. But she was no match for him, not when it came down to the brass tacks of rowing. Dad would pull out all the stops in an argument, as in the hidings he gave me. He was like Rocky Marciano, the heavyweight boxer in the ring. He did not keep to the Marquess of Queensberry rules. Dad would say and do anything to win. But Wendy was a street fighter as well. You had to be in order to survive in Liverpool. She threatened to go to Corrigan, make complaints about things missing in the shop since we'd moved in. I got fed up listening to both of them rowing. They were like two dogs fighting over a bone. So I decided to put an end to it.

"Don't threaten my dad," I said, as I went into the kitchen. "We all do things we wouldn't like other people to find out about." Wendy left the room. "What did you mean by that?" Dad asked. "Nothing," I said.

So we were quickly down to the local Catholic church bemoaning our lot to Father Devaney. Dad was hinting that he was suffering from sexual harassment from this woman. Father Devaney, a born again bachelor, probably suffered mortification from his housekeeper. He gave us the name of a St Vincent de Paul man who had rooms to let in his big house. He had recently lost his elderly mother so he was probably lonely for a bit of company. It sounded perfect, Dad said. "There you are Sean, God never closes a door but he opens a window." "There's just one catch," Father Devaney said. Feck it, I thought, there's always a catch. "The St Vincent de Paul man has just recovered from TB." This put the fear of God into Dad. He had seen too much of this contagious disease in the west of Ireland. It wiped out whole families in a matter of months.

I went with Dad to meet the St Vincent de Paul man. This spick-and-span man was nice to us. His hair was plastered down with Brylcreem. It was as flat as a pancake. He wore a suit and collar and tie. He looked as if he was dressed up to go out. On his lapel was a Pioneer Pin denoting that he didn't drink alcohol. This did not do anything to enhance his standing with Dad. He never trusted those who lived their lives dying of thirst.

The room was clean and polished, but it lacked the homely touch that a woman can give to a place. The man was keen to accept us. He offered to make us tea, which Dad declined. He said he'd be up all night if he drank anything this time of the evening. But the truth was he was terrified of getting TB from the cups. Dad, who could be such a bully, now showed the cowardly side of his character. He left the decision as to whether we should take the rooms up to me.

"What do you think?" he asked me. What do you want me to say, I thought. I felt so embarrassed in front of this poor second-generation Liverpool Irishman. If I said that I didn't think the rooms were suitable, then I was treating him like a second-class citizen. "He's the governor," Dad laughed. I am when you use me as a shield to hide behind, I thought. "What he says goes."

"Oh I can see that," the St Vincent de Paul man said forcing himself to laugh. I took the cue from Dad. "I suppose we'd better think about it," I said. "Oh yes," the man nodded. I can still see the look of disappointment on his face. "There's no hurry. When God made time..." he said. I looked at the photo of his mother on the mantelpiece. Mam used to say that some of us are like ships that pass in the night. I felt even more lonely for seeing the loneliness of this man.

Outside of the front door, I was furious with Dad because of the way he had compromised me. He, being the crafty old bastard that he was, said, "There's no real cure for it. They say he's cured but how do they know? They don't have to go and live with him. They don't have to drink out of the same cups and eat off the same plates. I didn't like the red blotch on his face. I'd never forgive myself if you caught anything." I was coming to be of the same mind as Shakespeare. There is no evil but ignorance and all the trappings of it were embodied in this man who walked before me.

Chapter 8

Someone told Dad that the council were duty bound to house us. So we waited for hours in a packed stuffy office to get an interview. If we didn't have TB when we got there, the odds were we would have it by the time we left. Eventually, we got an interview with a very negative, over-worked council clerk.

You have got to have points, she kept saying. You have got to have twenty points minimum. As soon as she found out that we had just come from Ireland, she exhibited her anti-Irish hostility. "We've got people born and bred here on our waiting list." It was obvious that she was getting enormous pleasure out of painting a graphic picture of our hopeless predicament. "We've been through a war," meaning Dad hadn't. "We lost a lot of our people in the war," she added. "Many Irishmen and women were lost as well," Dad said. "There is a chronic shortage of housing. I am just here to allocate houses to deserving families who have a sufficient number of points. Fill in the appropriate forms and we'll be in touch." "Is that by telegram, telephone or telepathy?" Dad asked. The clerk was taken aback by Dad's sarcasm.

Outside the office, Dad said that they did not want us in this country. "That's the rock bottom of it; no one wants us here." And no one wants us in Ireland, I thought.

We were now looking at cards in newsagents' windows advertising accommodation. Non-smokers and non-drinkers particularly welcome. "They want fecking rent-paying corpses in their rooms," Dad said. All of them were adamant that no Blacks or Irish need apply. Dad got round that one by pushing me forward in my school uniform. I lent us respectability, dressed as a scholar from a well-known, semi-public school. The snobbish appeal of the uniform seemed to weigh heavier with them than my dad's strong Irish accent. We took an address off one of the cards advertising a room to let. The landlady had peroxide hair and she was dressed up to the nines. Her rooms were on the ground floor so that she could keep an eye on all the lodgers. Our room was on the first floor at the back with a double bed, a table by the window and two chairs. There was a communal kitchen and toilet on our floor. She read us a list of rules, which went in one ear and out of the other. Dad had to wash the stairs down once a week, the ones that led up to our floor. Dad agreed. It was Hobson's Choice. All the time we were there in the house, there was always a strong smell of boiled fish.

The first evening I came home from school, I opened the front door to be confronted by an enormous Alsatian dog. I was terrified. I had to pass it in order to get access to our room but I had no intention of losing my arms or legs. So I stood out in the street until about half six or seven when Dad got back from work. When we went into the house, there was no sight or sound of the dog, just a strong smell of boiled fish. At eight o'clock there was a knock on the door. The landlady said, that according to the rota, it was Dad's turn to do the stairs down.

Dad could be horrible to me and he deserved a lot of what he got, but the sight of him kneeling on the stairs with bucket and cloth was so embarrassing, shameful and hurtful that I have had to keep those shameful moments locked away in my heart for years. Poor Dad. Poor me. Poor peroxide landlady, who was so consumed by the rota that she lost all respect for another human being. When I came home from school the next day, the dog was back in the hallway. So I had to stay out in the street for nearly three hours waiting for Dad. "The bitch," Dad said, when there was no sight or sound of the dog as we entered the main door. "She's doing it on purpose to keep you out. I'll see her." "Don't, Dad," I said, "I bet she has that dog ready to turn on you." "You might be right there," Dad said, settling down. There are some bitches of landladies in this world and we always seemed to come across them. So we had to look around again for somewhere else to live. A week or so before the Queen got the crown on her head and her feet under the table at Buckingham Palace, we had our annual Sports Day. It was a great swell affair, a real display of all the school's sporting achievements of the past year.

The stage of the school hall was packed with prizes contributed by the parents. Dad had not given anything. I suppose he could not really give a case of butter. That would have been a peculiar prize to give to the winner of the hundred yards. Anyway eighty per cent of the parents were much better off than Dad or the boys of my class. The well-off parents liked to show their gratitude to the teachers and to the school by giving pretty expensive stuff, canteens of cutlery, electric kettles and so on. Around the running track were placed dozens of different-coloured flags. The cricket pavilion was done up, the tables, laid with white tablecloths, were groaning with displays of sandwiches and fancy cakes. Tea was being served for parents who made further voluntary donations towards the school funds.

His Worship the Mayor and his bow-legged wife, decked out in chains of office and looking like prize shire horses, stuffed their faces with triangular-shaped sandwiches of mustard cress and cucumber.

The boys wore white flannels, white shirts, school tie and straw hats. Even the best of the lads could be squeamish about exhibiting their parents. Lots of jokes were made by lads trying to link parents to their offspring. Mum cussing was very prevalent at our Sports Day.

There's so and so. Look who's over there. Oh how are you? I've heard so much about you from Richard. Do drop around. Promise, you simply must see our new fridge. It lights up. When you open the door. Fancy. How is Steven? Oh he's doing well. I'm so pleased he's made such a recovery. Doing marvellously well at Cambridge. Yes. He went up there for an interview and came back with a Cambridge accent. Do come and have some strawberries and cream. What a delightful day. Beautiful, isn't it?

The tea tents and beer tents and a host of other Cavalier indulgences speckled the playing fields. England's battles have always been won on the playing fields.

The elite athletes and those with connections, like my mate Hughes, used the gym changing rooms where they had access to the showers and toilets. The changing conditions were chaotic. Normally the changing rooms in the gym could cater for seventy boys. But there were hundreds who wanted to change. So the spill over had to be put in the cloakrooms where we normally left our topcoats. I was thrown in with the riff raff.

I would show them, I thought, as I changed. Little did they know that I was one of the best runners on the Quays in Dublin. I had got my photo in the Irish press, winning a race in Croke Park in front of thousands. Everyone always said that I was a natural and that it was in my genes to run. As the no hopers mucked about, I changed. I felt disgusted by their lack of purpose and idiotic behaviour. They joked and laughed, that's all they'd ever do, joke and laugh and take the piss out of everything. They were afraid of committing themselves to anything in case they failed.

Dad arrived in the suit, the one that he had bought for Jim English's daughter's wedding that he wasn't invited to. He looked like a Yank in his gaudy outfit. His loud check suit stood out against the more sober attire of the other parents. Talking like the owner to the jockey of a potential National or Derby winner, he said, "Well let's see what you can do today. If I had had these opportunities when I was your age, I would have won everything and anything that was put in front of me. The Doyles are great runners. I don't want to see you let the good name of the Doyles down." Another time he'd tell me that the Doyles had brains to burn. He assured me that he had always been the top of his class as well as the best runner in the whole of County Mayo. With the inherited running ability and the brains, I didn't have a thing to worry about. All I had to do was switch on any of these talents and out they popped.

To win a race, you've got to focus on the event. It's no good standing on the starting line thinking about your Aunt Fanny or looking to the crowd for inspiration. You are on your own. You have got to focus. Blank out everything. But I couldn't concentrate on the race, not because I was overwhelmed by the whole atmosphere. I couldn't give of my best over the hundred yards because I was dying for a shit. There was a queue for the boys'. When they called for competitors for the heats of the hundred yards, I was in a queue, behind a load of blokes waiting to go into the cubicles. A hundred yards is a long way to run when you're thirteen years of age and you're dying to have a shit. Especially if your brash dad has made the effort to get to the event to watch you.

It would be nice to say that on my first school Sports Day, I won my heat, went onto the second round, qualified for the semi-finals and went on to win the final. It would be nice to say that, but I can't say it.

Hughes won the hundred yards. I came last in my heat. Long won the steeplechase, which delighted his parents. Peel won the long jump. The senior boys had all the track events stitched up for themselves so that each won a title. The old Mafia system was in operation on the playing fields as it was within the school. How could one break into it?

Dad went silent in anger at my performance. He was behaving like a Trappist monk, his eyes looking into the distance, disgusted by the fact that I existed and that I was his son. I decided to break the ice, I couldn't stand being ignored. As the announcer called for the competitors, I asked if I could go in for the consolation race. "You are a fecking consolation," he said, walking away. I stood there. I cried. I shut out all the colour, joy and excitement going on around me. You'll never call me that again. Never, I thought. The crushed have no reason to be alive. They have no family or friends. They can't do anything for anyone, especially themselves. That's how I felt on my first school Sports Day. To add insult to injury, Dad came back to me with his box camera to take my photo for posterity. I haven't got the photo now, but I can still remember the contents of the photo. This little kid standing under a tree alongside the long jump pit in white shorts, vest, pumps, school blazer and skullcap, hardly able to see as the tears welled up in my eyes, listening to Dad shouting, "Smile, you bastard, smile."

Chapter 9

We had to look around again for somewhere else to live. As a temporary measure we moved to a room over Mrs Ward's shop. I think Dad was letting her have butter on the cheap. Her son was doing his National Service stint but he was home on leave the day we arrived. Actually he was polishing his boots. He told me that he had been polishing them for eight hours a day for the past few weeks. They were still not up to the required standard demanded by the army. He demonstrated to me what spit and polish meant. He had been selected to stand on the Coronation route in London. He told me rather cynically that the Queen would never see him as she passed along in her horse-drawn golden Irish coach or know the hours he spent polishing his boots.

"Still," he said, as he spat on his boot, "it's better than being in Korea or fighting the Mau-Mau where the sparks are flying against our boys. The Chinese are the ones I fear most. They screech and play out-of-tune bugles as they attack. If you're captured, you'd be better off dead. They give you Chinese torture. Drip water on your head. Drip. Drip. Drip. Eventually it splits your skull. They brainwash you," he said, as he polished and listened to 'Far Away Places' on the radio.

It was in Mrs Ward's house, on a freezing cold wet June day, that I saw my first television. It was a black and white set packaged in a large oak cabinet that was taller than me. It had a nine-inch screen. The presenters were very posh. They all spoke in the received English accents of the time. The presenters wore dicky bows and monkey suits. I'm told they even wore similar gear on the radio, when they presented the programmes.

I saw the Princess Elizabeth being crowned Queen of England and practically everywhere else that the sun shone upon.

"That Duke can't be a proper man at all," Dad said, "I'd never let my Mrs be crowned Queen while I had to stand two steps behind her looking like a proper latchico. There can only be one captain on the ship. And I've yet to see the day when that's a woman. A penniless Greek, isn't he? Do you know he's had to take her surname? Windsor. Imagine getting married and you have to take the wife's name. I expect she'll have him washing out her smalls tonight." I was annoyed that Dad, supposedly such an Irish Nationalist, took so much notice of the Royal Family. Fuelled by newspapers and gossip columnists, he was fascinated by them. He couldn't believe that a country was daft enough to support such a lot of hangers-on. "They'll never have to work again," Dad said. "They'll never even have to wipe their own arses. It's not a very fair world son, now is it? How would you like to meet that Queen of Tonga on a dark night? Janey, there's eating and drinking to be had there."

Mrs Ward didn't see her son because the Queen's horse-drawn golden coach went by so quickly. We hardly saw anything on the little fuzzy nine-inch black and white screen.

It rained cats and dogs all day. All the street parties were cancelled. The fancy decorated tablecloths on the wooden trestle tables looked eerie. They blew in the empty streets under a canopy of bunting. The whole scene looked frightening because of the absence of life. It looked like a disused film set. In organising street parties, the older people had tried to bring back the wartime neighbourly atmosphere.

But the whole day was a washout. Kids like myself stood indoors waiting for the rain to stop. It rained well into the dark of the night on this most miserable of days. A day that seemed to promise so much but ended up giving so little to the ordinary people. The only good thing about it was that I got a free mug at school with pictures of the Queen and the Duke on it. There was never a dresser to put such ornaments on, so I used it daily for years.

Misappropriation of other people's property never seemed to deter Dad from attending church regularly. It was at one of these church meetings on a Sunday, after a week of fleecing Corrigan, that we came upon our next accommodation with the help of a Father Spencer. Catholics stick together, Catholics help fellow Catholics; it's a wonderful Catholic world. So we met two more Catholics, who we expected to treat us as we would treat them. We landed up in a semi-detached near Queens Drive. "Mum, everyone calls me Mum," this little woman told us as we arrived with our loaded cases. "This is my daughter Winnie," said Mum. Winnie had a beard like the Chinese leader Chiang Kai-shek. The beard was light and fair but still long enough to make many a South

Korean feel proud. Winnie had had a pretty hard time. She was Mum's stepdaughter by one of her previous marriages. Mum, who was over seventy, had just put her last husband away. That was her seventh. He had lasted less than eighteen months. She was now on the lookout for someone else. She'd meet these old boys mainly through the different churches. She was Ecumenical long before it became the fashionable thing to be, visiting all the different denominations. When she found that an old boy had a couple of bob and a weak ticker, she'd marry him then feed him up. Her cooking featured lots of chips cooked in fat, streaky bacon, meat pies, pasties and bread and dripping. He would be dead in next to no time.

On our arrival, Winnie took a shine to Dad. She thought that Dad was a widower. She couldn't go to church directly with Dad and me, as because of Mum's unspoken rule that any unattached men were her concern and out of bounds for Winnie. So when it was time to go to Mass, Winnie would leave the house a good fifteen minutes before us. By the time we set out for church, she would be waiting behind some corner, hidden like a Panda car, so that she could walk with us to church. As soon as Dad realised this, we began to make detours. Then we would hear Winnie's thundering shoes charging behind us, the poor woman's beard blowing in the wind as she called after us to wait for her. One Sunday, Winnie wore a gigantic hat in church. It must have had a diameter of twenty foot. Green, it was, dark green with black around the edges. Winnie made her way up to Communion. My dad belted me in the ribs, whispering to me to look at Winnie's friend. She had an identical hat. Both of these rival spinsters were determined to get a man. So they used the aisle of the church as if it were a catwalk. Other women in the church wore a headscarf or the older women wore little dark hats.

I think I laughed more in church than I laughed in the pictures at that time. Like all good Catholics, we were the last into Mass and the first out. At the back of the church you stood a better chance of getting out and not having to put anything on the plate at the collections. "Come on," Dad said, as the priest turned towards us and said "*Ite, missa est.*" "Come on, let's get going. Before Winnie puts her foot on the gas." It was a good walk up the hill back to the house.

"Mr Doyle, Mr Doyle," we could hear Winnie calling. As the nervous excitement welled up inside of me, I could hear the boom, boom of her shoes as her pace increased. "Come on, come on," Dad would shout. "Step on it. She's catching us." By this time, I could hardly walk for laughing. We'd hurry into the house and sit by the table panting. Moments later, Winnie would arrive, hardly able to get her breath. She'd slump against the door, green hat hanging off her head at a comical angle.

"My word, you do walk fast Mr Doyle." Still trying to get her breath, she'd ask, "Didn't you hear me calling?"

I was so doubled up with laughing that I had to stoop under the table as if I was doing my laces up.

The months had gone by and it would be Christmas in a week's time. We were upstairs in our bedroom when we heard a hell of a row going on downstairs. They were at it; screaming, tantrums and banging of doors. It was a real surprise to me. I'd seen plenty of rows in my time in the tenement flats of Dublin. But I did not expect that type of behaviour from these respectable people. Suddenly we heard this almighty roar and a voice proclaimed, "I'm not having any more of this." Dad looked at me. I looked back at him. We never said a word. We stood there in our tracks. Too nervously excited to breathe or move in case our noise might cause any disturbance to them. Then another roar shattered the silence.

"I've had enough." It was dear sweet little Mum. The very merry seven times widow of Peter's Parish. A cupboard was banged. Then, seemingly after an eternity, a door was banged. We both relaxed and shook our heads. Christmas Day came. We sat down to dinner with Winnie and her loose chattering teeth. Mum was poker-faced and tight-lipped. She was anxious that not too much of the turkey would be used. We had got a turkey free, compliments of Jim English, Corrigan's most loyal and respected employee. Dad sold it to Mum for thirty bob.

As Dad was the man of the house, he had the place of honour at the top of the table. He did the carving. That was Mum's first mistake. Mum had managed her house throughout the war. During which time she could probably have made a meal out of a potato and have enough left over to make chips for supper in the evening.

Mum's idea was that the turkey should last the Christmas and the New Year celebrations with soup from it for most of January. Well there was a leg for me, a leg for Dad, two wings to Winnie plus the parson's nose. There was a bit of breast to Mum. Then Dad gave me some breast. He had some himself. After a few minutes, it looked as if there had been a vulture at the table. Just bones and the inside looking out at you. We ate with relish. Winnie ate with relish, including the parson's nose. But Mum didn't touch a thing. She sat there turning all the colours of traffic lights.

"Not a bad bit of turkey," Dad said. Winnie was licking her lips like a pussycat.

We stayed with Mum for a couple of weeks after Christmas. Until one morning, "I can no longer have your son or yourself in my house. You must leave." These words had become as familiar to me as hearing the weather forecast.

I think that one of the main reasons for getting the boot arose from the fact that Dad and myself used to get up very early in the morning and literally raid the kitchen cupboards. Mum had not yet become so sophisticated a landlady as to lock the cupboards up at night.

"Oh God. Don't Dad," I'd say. "She'll know, she'll miss it." "Don't worry," he'd say, pouring a double portion onto my plate. "We can blame Winnie." But Winnie knew what we were up to. One morning when she came into the kitchen, we had a spread out on the table that looked like one of Henry VIII's banquets at Hampton Court. "Excuse me," she said and went out again. A couple of minutes later, she returned, more composed. "Have some breakfast Winnie," Dad said. "Come on, pull up a chair. Make yourself at home." Dad poured her out an enormous helping of cornflakes and emptied half a bottle of milk onto them. "There you are." He winked at me. "That'll do you good." "Oh I don't know. What will Mum say?" she pleaded. "Never mind Mum. I'm just going to bring her up those in a moment," he said, pointing to another dishful. I nearly fell off the chair laughing.

But the fact of the matter was that Winnie did begin to eat more while we were there. She began to come out of herself. She became more radical. She began to bang the cupboard doors herself. Once or twice during the last days, we heard her shout back at Mum.

The night before we left, Dad got a duck buckshee. He had cooked it in one of the ovens in the grocery warehouse. "God bless you Mr Corrigan," he said, as he tore the duck apart, sitting on the side of the bed. Once again we ate with relish in this post-war rationed England. So did a lot of people. It was just a question of knowing where to thieve food. As Dad finished part of the duck, he would throw the bones onto the top of the wardrobe. This had me in hysterics. He began to ape Mum. "Winnie, Winnie, come up here this minute. I think there's a dead duck behind the wardrobe." "Oh let me see, silly." "Don't call your mum silly. There, I told you. There's been a duck in here." He nearly had me choking to death on the bones. Next morning, we had one of Corrigan's lorries to move us. Mum stayed in the kitchen as we were leaving with packed suitcases and boxes. She didn't even come out to wish us goodbye. She had not forgotten the turkey or the big breakfasts I suppose. Winnie came out into the hall to see us on our way. She smiled bravely, wiped a tear from her eye and in a jolly hockey stick fashion said, "Take care chaps." She shook us by the hands and then rushed back into the kitchen to bang some cupboard doors. What were we but ships passing in the night? I never did know Winnie's or Mum's surnames, but I believe that we did some good. Winnie would never be the same again. She had lived in a hell with Mum, afraid to stand up to her, but now she was beginning to answer back.

It would soon be a new year and who's to know what 1954 would bring, I thought as I climbed onto the lorry.

Chapter 10

I stood with Stan at the bottom of the garden outside of the Summer House while he searched for a key from seemingly hundreds he carried on a steel ring like a Victorian jailer I'd read about in history books or seen in black and white films.

Our possessions lay in bags in front of me, dropped there by the Corrigan lorry we used to move from Mum and Winnie's up off Queens Drive. We had sheets and blankets that had never been to the launderette, dirty towels, shirts, vests, underwear, saucepans, socks, plates, kettles, Dad's best sharpest knife, DDT, Epsom salts and a tin of Andrews liver salts. We had everything in those bags but money, Dad used often to say. We also had a statue of St Jude, Dad's favourite saint. St Jude is the patron saint of hopeless causes so it was no wonder that Dad and him should be sort of half-brothers or at least best mates. The poor saint, at times I felt sorry for him with what he had to put up with from Dad.

Stan turned a key and we were looking into a small hall. There would have been more room in a confessional box over in Adam and Eve's in Dublin. "I'll try to find a light. You get your stuff in."

He tried various switches but nothing was working. "I'll have to get some bulbs," Stan said, slamming the door behind him.

I stepped inside through the hallway to where the kitchen was. It was about the size of a Hammond Lane matchbox. To the right was the bedroom, which was no bigger or better. I looked around and accepted that I wouldn't be doing any interval training in this place. In the dark I could rummage around the kip in two minutes.

In the kitchen there was a table, a couple of chairs and a sink in the corner with a makeshift of a cooker. In the bedroom was a mattress on a double bed. When would the day ever come, I thought, when I wouldn't have to sleep with me da. The floor was concrete and at the top of the hall was some sort of stove. All that was missing was an embroidered picture saying, 'Home sweet home'. I wondered what time Stan would be back with the bulbs or with whatever lighting I was to have. I searched through the bags for the radio, realising too late after I had found it that I couldn't use it as there was no electricity.

I had to wait until Stan came back so I had no alternative but to make up the bed for myself, hoping and praying that it was bug-free. I put lashings of DDT on the mattress and then I got in between the blankets after making sure that the Yale catch was down on the front door.

I began to get warm and feel comfortable. I was tired after all the old nonsense in school during the day. I was drowsy and falling in and out of sleep when I heard someone at the front door. It might be Dad, I thought, so I sat up in bed, but the steps went away. On the note, he had said that he was going to Manchester looking for work. He said he badly wanted to change his present job, travelling for Corrigan's the grocer, but I didn't altogether believe him. He had lied to me before when he went to Blackpool to sell Corrigan's Cola, now he might have gone again.

I lay in the dark and heard the sounds from outside. Music from Radio Luxembourg was blaring away from the house at the top of the garden then disappearing because of the erratic radio airwaves. A bell sounded and then I could hear a couple arguing and then a baby began to cry as the man was screaming at the baby and the woman. At least they were not lonely but what a price to pay for not being on your own.

I would have to be careful or I could end up in a situation like that. I tried to get comfortable by wrapping the blankets around my shoulders and then I must have fallen into a deep sleep.

In the morning I was awakened by the birds in the garden and the light streaming through some French windows I had not noticed in the previous evening's darkness.

The concrete floor was freezing so I quickly got into my shoes. I couldn't believe my eyes when I looked around for the lavatory. Surely to God he hadn't rented a place without a bog. Next it would be without a roof. So I had to make do with having a piss in the sink. I was in a dilemma, I had to wait for Dad to come back because he didn't have a key, but it was cold in the Summer House, probably colder inside than out. I decided to go out.

I had two shillings and a bus pass. I half-heartedly thought of going to school, at least I would get a dinner there, one of Kate's specials. I badly wanted to have a shit, so I had to go out.

Making sure that I had the key in my trousers pocket, I shut the door behind me and went out of the garden, which had its share of junk in it, through a side exit to the garage where Dad had parked Corrigan's little MG. I turned left out of the garage and went down the lane, which ran at the back of the houses where overflowing bins waited to be emptied by the council.

I was totally focussed on trying to find a lavatory and from past experience I knew that I'd find a place to crap in the park, the only disadvantage being was that there wouldn't be any paper in those bogs.

On the way to the park, as if straight out of a film, I came across a church. Inside of the porch were books of the Catholic Truth Society and little booklets with lives of great people who had been made saints by the church. I wondered if I ever would be a subject for one of these pamphlets. A fat chance I'd have of becoming a saint in Liverpool, I thought. Copies of the Catholic newspaper, the *Universe*, were on display and thank God, just in time, an unlocked lavatory. As my brother Val used to say, that got a load off my mind. And thanks to the Archbishop of Liverpool and his diocese, I made use of the softest paper I had encountered since my arrival from Dublin. I decided against going to school but really I didn't have much choice as I knew that Dad didn't have a key to the kip. On my way back to the Summer House, I bought a bar of Bournville chocolate, a dark-cocoa type of chocolate, which was fantastic if you let it melt slowly in your mouth, a Fry's Cream bar and the *Daily Mirror*. They would keep me going.

Now that I was living on my own a lot of the time, I had to learn quickly to become self-reliant and self-sufficient. I savoured the immense pleasure I could get out of little things. For hours I sat there in the Summer House, wrapped in a blanket waiting for my dad. Waiting for Da had become the norm in my life so

I listlessly thumbed my way through the *Mirror* a couple of times, only stopping to concentrate on Peter Wilson's column. He was usually controversial on sporting matters, particularly in the fields of athletics and boxing. Once the *Mirror* had to pay Don Cockell the British heavyweight champion thousands of pounds compensation because Wilson had written that the heavyweight was an unfit untrained fat boxer with a sagging midriff. I tried to do the crossword but I found it too difficult. Cockell's people won in court by saying that he was not suffering from a fat belly but from extra-large stomach muscles. He demonstrated this for them by doing a huge number of sit-ups in the gym.

My solitude was broken by Dad knocking on the door. He didn't say where he'd been overnight and I didn't ask but he did mention that he'd been to see the Irish doctor about his varicose veins. He would have to go into Alder Hey hospital to have them done.

I knew that he was trying to take my mind off the fact that he'd been out all night by trying to get my sympathy. Then he showered his guilty generosity on me by putting bread, milk, tea, sugar, bacon, sausages and black pudding on the table. He got the pan on and then realised that the cooker didn't work because there was no electricity.

"I'll see that bastard Hardy," Dad said. It seemed that we rented the Summer House from Mr Hardy, who was a prospective Labour candidate and who was also President of the Labour Social club in Prescott Road where Stan was the bar steward. Stan did odd jobs for Hardy like collecting the rent from the eleven-odd tenants who lived in the house at the top of the garden.

I asked Dad where we were supposed to go to the lavatory and he said we had to go through the lady's kitchen at the back and up two flights of stairs to the second floor.

I didn't fancy going through someone's kitchen, as I'd feel embarrassed, as everyone would know where I was going and what I was going to do. Dad said that I had an alternative, which made me feel better until he explained it. I could go out of the garden side entrance, through the garage where he parked Corrigan's MG, turn right and at the bottom of the alley, turn right again past the phone box on the corner and then right again at the top of the road to the main entrance of the house.

"But we don't have a key to the main door."

"Then you'll have to ring the bell," he laughed.

"I'm not ringing the bell of the main door of the house every time I want to go to the lavatory."

"Then you'd better go through the kitchen," he said as he looked at my disapproving face.

"Oh don't be such a jessie," he said, "I'd give a penny to everyone who doesn't have to do it."

Dad came back with a bag of coke for the stove, warning me that she'd only use coke and that under no circumstances would she touch coal.

So with a couple of firelighters, the greatest invention ever made by mankind up to then, we got the stove going and with rashers, sausages, black pudding and eggs in the pan and with St Jude looking down on the pair of us, we had the fry-up.

You'd have to go a long way in Ireland to find such a hillbilly existence. But when we got the stove going full blast on a bag of coke that he had got for less than a couple of bob up in Prescott Road, you wouldn't call the Queen your Aunt as Dad used to say. With the rain creating a cacophony of sounds on the corrugated roof, we were as snug as two bugs in a rug. We were experiencing what some people pay hundreds of pounds to partake of on an outback adventure holiday.

We had our own Garden of Eden right bang wallop in the centre of Liverpool and we knew that we were different; different from those who were living in the house at the top of the garden and different from those living in Ireland or those in Buckingham Palace.

Chapter 11

Dad was always telling me his problems, which I had to discuss with him as an equal adult. His difficulties were overshadowing my own. It wasn't all plain sailing for me at school. As time went on I was finding it more difficult to survive. I was very unhappy at school and I was becoming unhappier by the day.

The Christian Brothers put tremendous importance on sport and PE as character builders. Games activities were becoming the worst part of the week for me.

They pursued sport with an almost fascist determination reminiscent of Franco and Hitler with their youth leagues.

In school, you had to do games on Tuesday or Wednesday afternoon, depending whether you were in the lower or higher school. We had lessons on a Saturday morning till midday, then in winter you either played rugby or ran cross-country or spectated in the afternoon. In summer, you either played cricket or did athletics. PE, army style, was done twice a week in the gym. In the summer, weather permitting, rounders was played as a special treat. I hated team games. You just became a cog in a wheel depending on other people. On a winter's Saturday afternoon, we were marched to the rugby fields, either as a participant or a supporter. The boys stood around as boys always do with hands in pockets, school blazers hanging off their shoulders and skullcaps sitting precariously on their heads. It was one of the many hundreds of school rules that caps had to be worn at all times outdoors. The first-years always wore their caps. There would be a few dropouts in the second-years. Fewer caps were worn by the third years. In the senior school, there would be regular purges on the fourth year when all kinds of threats, even of expulsion, would be issued if caps were not worn at all times. In the fifth year, the caps were placed carefully atop the boys' constantly combed hair and at all sorts of strange angles so as not to ruffle their hair.

The same cap that his parents had purchased for him in the first year accompanied each boy throughout his school career, eventually becoming faded and well worn and far too small; it looked like a skullcap as worn by a member of the Capuchin Franciscan order but nothing like a school cap. We learned to live by the letter of the law practising dumb insolence, not yet officially punishable in school.

It was a cold winter's Saturday afternoon. The visiting schools were waiting to be pulverised on the rugby field or else knackered on the cross-country track, when Cynthia came through the gate. The boys stood in fascinated silence as reverence, fear and respect were the order of the day. "She's the one, she's the one who does it," they thought. When Cynthia came to see the rugby our school usually lost. Everyone lost their concentration including the referee, who was a man who had given himself to Christ when he was eighteen. Probably the only woman he had ever known well was his mother. Cynthia would stand on the touchline, the cold damp winter breeze blowing around her skirt. You could guarantee the ball would go into touch a hundred times during the match and never more than five feet from where she stood. It was as if the ball was attracted to her.

The players would go in the line-out and half-heartedly jump for the ball but the bite had gone out of the game. Even the most dedicated of Catholic boys could not help but glance at her lovely well-developed figure.

Rugby, the most pugilistic game I have ever played, was meant to give a boy character.

"A great character builder, makes a man out of you, toughens you up, prepares you for the world as you learn to take the knocks," the house master said as we went on to play for the house cup. Coming off the rugby field, knock-kneed, I thought that I'd better go back on the pitch to try to find my ear among the blood and guts spewed up there during the game.

The scrum – now there's an invention. You're tucked in behind ten or eleven blokes with your nose up someone's arsehole while some gorilla of a kid is yelling, "Shove, heave, push for the school." There's a little kid in the front row whose rib cage is collapsing and out of the corner of your eye you can see the ball gone mad running away from the two teams. But you must remain still, keep your nose up this kid's arsehole and pray to God that he doesn't fart, until Gorilla shouts, "Break."

Gorilla loves the scrum, a paradise for a sadist. It's a place where you can push other kids about, beat and be beaten.

He's the type of bloke who could play a whole game of rugby and not worry where the ball is. In fact, he'd be just as pleased if the ball were left in the dressing room.

Flanagan was his name, a towering monstrosity of a boy who must have taken size seventeen shoes even in the first year. He was covered in hair and blackheads and had two cauliflower ears with scars over both eyes, a broken nose and missing teeth. And this was a game to make a man out of you? Before a game, when you played for the school, you normally got nervous. Most boys hoped and prayed that they would get a good game because they didn't want to let the school down. They wanted that little bit of luck so they might score a try.

But when I played, I hoped and prayed that I'd never get the ball because if I was that unfortunate, I had Flanagan plus sixteen others and the referee after me. I know you think I am confused. Surely Flanagan was on my side but that made no odds to Flanagan. He didn't know the difference. There was our school, the visiting school and Flanagan playing as an independent. So if I were unfortunate enough to get the ball, I'd drop it immediately and run like mad away from the oncoming herd.

To illustrate the point, on this particular day the game was in a stalemate situation with tugging and pulling in the scrum and blood vessels, arteries, hearts, lungs nearly collapsing when Flanagan got the ball. He began to tear down the pitch like a grizzly bear. Our rugby coach was shouting from the touchline, "Wrong way Flanagan, wrong way."

After an hour and a half on the field, when you put your foot down, the mud went right up to your knees. Caked in mud, I listened to all the half-wit savages recounting the merits of their game. I stood in the hot shower with the water dripping off me, wondering how much my character had developed during the time I had spent on the gruesome rugby pitch. Before you got back into your clothes, you had to go under the cold shower. The coach told us it would put hairs on your chest.

This particular Saturday, as Cynthia stood on the touchline, the game had gone very badly. The players were lethargic and I suppose each one was wondering if he were to be the lucky one to be picked out next by Cynthia. Halfway through the first half, Prescott came along. He was a dead ringer for Dean Martin. With his tie half done up and cap on the side of his head, he was singing, "When the moon hits your eyes like a great piece of pie, that's amore."

It was obvious that he was not interested in the thoughts or opinions of his peers, or indeed of the teachers, by the romantic way he escorted Cynthia from the game, leading her towards the woods, much to the relief of the Headmaster and the coach, who now got back to thinking about the match. Our team went on to score a resounding victory.

After the showers, the thirty boys plus the reserves and the team coaches went for tea and fairy cakes. Even at that time, I thought that fairy cakes were very appropriate.

All of life is a game of rugby or cricket or a game of poker. No, says the sage, all of life is a game of chess. No, not at all, all of life is Shakespeare or Jimmy Joyce. Someone else said that all of life was at the Pier Head. All of their lives might have been games of cricket, rugby, football, chess, poker, Shakespeare or Joyce, but mine wasn't. All of life for Dad and me was about a constant struggle to survive.

The sheer snobbery attached to cricket, and for that matter rugby, used to really get up my nose. "Well done James, bang-ho shot. I say, what a near miss." How can you have a near miss? You either hit it or miss it. "Hard cheese Johnson, bad luck Duffy; oh he's good enough to get his colours." "Natural ball player. That's the kind we want. If they've got the hips they can go a long way.

But we don't want serious types. Sport is sport. When you're on the field be a sportsman and when in the classroom be an academic."

"Bad thing to take sport too seriously, bad thing to take anything too seriously." "Couldn't agree with you more. Going to the Foreign Office you say. He'll do well there." "Of course it's a team effort there. If you're one of the team pull your weight, that's what your captain wants."

"Pull together. Tally ho. That's what life is really all about, a good captain, a good first mate, and a team game. It can be tough in the scrum but learn to enjoy the knocks."

Chapter 12

"There's a letter on the table," I said as Dad came in. I had gone into the house earlier through the kitchen to see if there were any letters for us. There were a number of them on the mat, all with Irish stamps. I recognised Mam's slanted handwriting on one of the envelopes and cursed.

"I'll put the kettle on the stove," I said. I didn't want to get the brunt of his anger and rage as he read it.

"It's been a bad winter and the children are down with colds. The kids want new shoes."

I could do with a pair myself, I thought, as Dad read on but I didn't say anything because I didn't want to put any more pressure on him.

"I've never seen the likes of this weather for the time of year since I can remember. They're threatening to turn the electricity off."

"It's different now when you have to pay your own electricity bill," Dad muttered. "When I was there no one would turn a light off."

"I saw Miss Wogan today and she said that I should go and see a solicitor. I don't want to. Please send a pound if that's all you can afford. People make big money in England. You must be raking it in. Please send something no matter how small. PS Maureen's left. Gone to live with your man who doesn't believe in God or go to church. I've not been since you left. Couldn't bring myself to pray. God forgive me. Please come back. I'm sure we would work something out. We'd manage somehow, others do. Forgive and forget."

But Mam didn't understand that things were worse for many of us in Liverpool than they ever had been in Dublin.

Dad threw the letter down angrily. "They think that we're made of money over here. They don't understand what the Irish in England have to put up with. They think it's all one big Billy Butlin's Holiday Camp over here." "Shall I put a few spuds on?" I asked, leaving him to read the death notices on the front of the *Irish Independent*. Each day he would go through them assiduously. It was like winning the Irish sweepstake when he found the name of someone he knew personally. It would bring back a load of memories of things that had happened all those years ago when they were young. It was amazing for me to realise that a whole lot of things had happened to this man before I had ever existed. So this exile, with the help of the front page of the *Irish Independent*, would delve into a well of Celtic nostalgia.

Dad might have been more interested on the deaths page this evening because he was going into Alder Hey hospital to have his varicose veins done. No one fancies going into hospital at the best of times but if anything did happen to him what would happen to me? Would I be put up for adoption like the kids in the house at the top of the garden who had just lost their mother?

It was as if he read my thoughts. "Don't worry," he said, "everything I've got will be yours. You'll be well provided for. You'll not be left like me on the scrap heap. I'll make a will tomorrow." "I don't want anything to happen to you," I said.

"You never know. When it's your time no one can do anything about it, not even the Queen herself."

What a cheerful notion to end the day with, I thought. There was no point in doing anything because everything ended up either in the graveyard or the crematorium.

The English sweep death under the bed and the carpet, but the Irish advertise it on the front page of the newspapers. Dad was still adamantly clinging to his self-pitying mood. I thought of Brother Ronnie at school and what he had said. Maybe he was right about us unpacking our suitcases and forgetting about Ireland but Dad would never do that. He wanted to get back at the narrow bunch of bastards who he felt had frozen him out. He said, "Now that I'm going into hospital I must write to the *Irish Hospitals Requests*." This programme was broadcast on a Wednesday afternoon from RTE.

It seemed that Dad was going to make the most of going into hospital and let everyone in Ireland know that he was having an operation. Anyone who was anyone listened to this programme as assiduously as they read the death notices in the newspapers.

He wanted to show them that he had not disappeared into the all-engulfing Liverpool mist.

I think that Dad knew the Irish in Ireland very well and he was aware as far as they were concerned, out of sight was out of mind, but he was not prepared to let them get away that easily. The biggest problem was what to request. I went for Johnnie Ray or Guy Mitchell. He wanted something traditional. Then I suggested what about 'The Garden Where the Praties Grow'. "No. No," he said, "something on the pipes or the harp, a lament."

Next day he bought a postcard. No letters were accepted by Radio Éireann as there were millions of requests. Everyone in Ireland seemed to be in hospital recovering from an operation. He requested Leo Rowsome on the uilleann pipes. He felt sure that no one else would ask for such an unusual request so he would stand a better chance of having his record played. If ever I listened to this programme as unfortunately I had to on a few occasions, it always struck me that a huge amount of people requested each record. Before a record was played, a litany of names was read out requesting the number, so it was no wonder that we never heard Dad's request.

Chapter 13

I eventually got out of having to play rugby by taking Hughes' advice. He told me that there was a chronic shortage of cross-country runners. I didn't know anything about cross-country running. As far as the school and everyone else were concerned, I was what was euphemistically called a scrubber.

"Come on Doylie, we've got to line up in front of Mr Lane," Hughes said. "He's Domingo's house master."

Mr Lane was the Corkman who had examined me in Irish when I first came to the school.

"*Conas ta tu Sheain*?" Mr Lane asked.

"*Ta me go maith.*"

"Are you going to run well Sean? We need all the points we

can get to lift the shield from Sefton."

"I'll do my best Mr Lane."

Then we heard Brother King, the starter, calling. "Right you lot, quieten down. And get into line, English." There were about sixty of us milling around the starting line, thirty from Domingo and thirty from Sefton House.

"I'm waiting, English," Kingie shouted.

"English is doing his Latin homework, Sir."

"Shut it Toal. That's an old one," Kingie said.

Brother King now spoke in a very stylised army way unlike what you would expect from a Christian Brother from Cork who hadn't been over here all that long.

"Now for the idiots among you who don't know the course, I will go over it once, and only once, so Robinson, prick up those ears and listen. I don't want you getting lost again this year and ending up in the unmarried mothers' home at Fazakerley."

"He went to see his mum, Sir," someone shouted.

"I'm waiting for you comedians to finish before I start."

"Why don't you shut it Robinson, and find yourself a bit of toast," someone shouted. "I'm waiting," Kingie said, "I can wait all day. I'm wrapped up, I'm warm. It doesn't bother me." They all quietened down. "Now that didn't take long, just twenty minutes of my valuable time. But I can tell you that if there is any more of this behaviour, it will be cold showers and Latin verbs for the lot of you."

"Please Sir," someone shouted, "I forgot to bring any soap."

"Boasting again, are we Dobson," King said sarcastically, "I can smell you from here and no matter how much soap you brought you'd still smell because you are just an awful smelly little toad." They all shut up now. No one else wanted a tongue-lashing.

123

"Now, go as far as the rugby posts and then go around the white lines on the outside, not the inside. Anyone caught running on the inside of the lines will be disqualified. If you are disqualified, you will have to run around the course every evening after school for the next week. I would also like to warn any of you who have taken it into their tiny little minds to skive off when they get into the woods and have a crafty little smoke, the woods are patrolled and a month of detention awaits those silly individuals. Just remember that just like in real life, you can all try but all of you can't win. That doesn't mean that you can't try. Some of you, if you tried from now till the end of eternity, wouldn't win, but that doesn't mean that you give up trying. I want to see all of you give of your best. I want to see you dropping exhausted from trying. Regan, if you don't settle down, you'll end up outside of my office with a dozen Latin verbs. The first eight boys to finish will go on to compete in the final trials against the two remaining houses on this course on Wednesday week. The last five boys to finish, Robinson, will be barred from cross-country and will report for rugby next week. Now, I will say ready and then I will fire the gun. Everyone will commence running after I've fired the gun, not before. Does everyone understand?" A chorus of yeses went up.

"Are you ready? Hold it, it's not worth a dozen Latin verbs." My aim was to get through the gates of the woods in a good position because once in the woods, the path was so narrow that everyone had to run in a single file. If you were in a good position, you could slow up the others behind you and then make a big break for the finish when you came out of the woods. I was nearly last getting into the woods after going around the rugby pitches.

These blokes were much faster and fitter than me but I was determined not to finish in the last five. The fear of being sent back to the rugby pitch was a powerful motivator for me. I used my elbows to get past kids who would not give way, eventually finishing well out of the bottom five.

I realised that I would never be a great cross-country runner but I still got to represent the school by a fluke.

Hughes was the best runner in the junior school and I used to go along to see him running. I got to know the other lads and they used to let me help out in the servery with the tea and cakes provided for the visiting teams after the race.

On this particular Saturday, one of the greatest days of my life, some of our team hadn't turned up to run because of flu or whatever, so they asked me to run for the school.

Imagine my pride and joy when I lined up in borrowed pumps, vests and shorts, representing the school.

I tried very hard but I couldn't cope with the heavy ground, while my fellow competitors just seemed to skate over the churned-up mud.

All I can say is that I didn't come last and I stuck at it. It was something to do on a Saturday afternoon and you did get a free cake and a weak cup of tea afterwards. Not much for a two-mile slog but I learned at a very early age that there's nothing for nothing in this world.

I would never be any good at cross-country running but I was mixing around now with lads from the upper school. It seemed like ages ago that Long had confiscated my Wagon Wheels and Penguins when I tried to open up a tuck shop. It was through Long that I got to become a member of the Afton Harriers.

Dad was having a clear-out before he went into hospital. He didn't want to leave any stuff in our gaff because he was afraid that it might be broken into. The place would be empty while Dad was in hospital as I was to be billeted out with Jimmy Burke and his family.

125

Dad's normal buyer was Mrs Ward, who had this mucky old corner shop. Dad said she was a witch who would steal the eye out of a needle and come back for the thread.

She never took the shutters off the windows of her shop. You could barely see your hand in front of your face in the shop. The single bulb gave precious little light. You had to thread your way through the boxes and cases to the counter where Mrs Ward sat. All of these boxes and cases lay there unopened. It was more like a warehouse than a shop. Like Jim, who was in charge of Corrigan's warehouse, she could direct a person's hand to anything they wanted as if by magic.

On the top of the boxes and cases were several cats who seemed to me to be more like guard dogs than the normal domestic feline.

Mrs Ward lived at the back of the shop; I don't think she had ever left the premises in thirty years, or indeed closed the front door.

She would buy all the cases of butter and boxes of Penguins that Dad could supply at a fiver a box for the butter and three pound ten shillings for the Penguins. But Dad fell out with Mrs Ward because she sold us a loaf, inside of which was a baked mouse.

Mrs Ward was afraid that Dad intended to take her to court when she wouldn't come up with a lump sum in compensation. When the solicitor asked him for a hundred pounds up front, Dad dropped legal proceedings and ended his business arrangements with her.

But there were always plenty of other shopkeepers in Liverpool who'd buy anything Dad had at a knocked-down price. They had to survive throughout the war, when those who weren't thieves before it began certainly were by the time it had ended.

One evening we went to see a Mr Evans in Green Lane who bought all of the remaining stock Dad had in the Summer House. Questions would not be asked if the place were broken into in our absence now that it was devoid of any loot.

After emptying the MG, Dad parked up outside of Alder Hey hospital. "I can't for the life of me understand people who spend half of their lives thinking about and arranging their funerals," Dad said as we sat in the car overlooking the hospital. He almost had me in tears.

He wasn't due to go in for his operation for some time yet but apparently he was going through a dress rehearsal. "Well, that's it son," he said, as my eyes welled up with tears. "That's where I'm going under the knife but I'm prepared to meet my maker. If anyone was ever prepared to meet their maker and look him straight squarely in the eyes, it must be me." It was enough to make any little lad confused with the different messages I was receiving from Dad and from the school.

Dad and his partner in crime, Jim English, had more or less cleared out Corrigan's warehouse and here he was saying that he was prepared to meet his maker. At school, the Christian Brothers were saying that it was a serious sin to steal and that the sin would not be forgiven until the stolen property was restored. So, added to the worry about Dad's operation was the fear that if anything went wrong, he could go to hell for all eternity because of all the cases of chocolate biscuits and boxes of butter he had nicked.

As I tried to bite into the Penguin he handed me, I was wondering if my collusion made me responsible for the loss of Dad's immortal soul. Instead of me filling my belly with it, according to the teachings of the Church, I should have been putting it back through Corrigan's letter box, endeavouring to get forgiveness for Dad.

So Dad went to Alder Hey and I went to stay at Jimmy Burke's as arranged. Dad had made friends with Jimmy Burke, who managed the pub opposite Corrigan's warehouse, for Tetley-Walkers. He would go in there to the empty pub at lunchtime to have a pint of mild and a sandwich he had made for himself, as in those days pubs weren't into selling food as they are nowadays.

On a day off school, Jimmy would let me sit in at the back of the pub as Dad had his couple of pints and sandwiches. They'd sit together talking of methods of making money.

Jimmy had three kids but he was living from hand to mouth. When Dad went in to have his varicose veins done, I stayed with Jimmy and his Irish wife as Dad didn't want me to be in the Summer House all on my own. Not that he ever worried that much about my safety when he was off gallivanting. Dad didn't know at the time that Jimmy tried to make his money on the horses, where he lost everything. One morning while I was getting ready for school, the bailiffs broke in and put Jimmy, his wife and children and me out on the streets. His wife and children were sent to the workhouse in Brecknock Road. Fortunately, I was able to move myself back into the Summer House. When I visited Dad in hospital I didn't let on what had happened to them. A few days later, I saw in the *Echo* that Jimmy had been found dead in the Salvation Army hostel. He was barely forty-three.

I often think of Jimmy Burke. He was a little man from somewhere way down the country in Ireland. He had come here to make his fortune and had ended up losing his life.

It's hard to know the impact that the demise of Jimmy Burke and the sufferings his family went through had on me.

Before Dad went into hospital, this bloke at work told him about the 'Penny in the Pound' scheme. They had their offices down by the British Home Stores in Dale Street. This scheme catered for people who had come out of hospital after an operation and were in need of convalescence.

It was a new post-war measure brought in by philanthropists who had been moved by the suffering of many working-class people during the war and who were determined to make some amends.

In order to be eligible for the scheme you had to be a fully paid up member and, as far as you knew, free from any imminent illness that would require hospitalisation.

You signed a form giving your word that you were in good health, but there are always exceptions to the rules, the unforeseen can happen. So, two weeks before Dad went into Alder Hey hospital, he went down to the 'Penny in the Pound' offices and signed up and joined up, paying them seven pence halfpenny.

The sum Dad paid into the scheme was related to the amount of his take-home pay and as his wages were seven pounds ten shillings he paid in seven pence halfpenny.

The following week he paid a similar amount into the scheme. Then when he went into hospital he was a fully qualified member of the fund.

Dad came out of hospital and went on two weeks' convalescence to Colwyn Bay, all for the handsome sum of one shilling and three pence in old money. People like Dad and others exploited the 'Penny in the Pound' scheme to the extent that eventually you had to pay contributions for at least twelve months and undergo a medical before you could avail yourself of the scheme.

On the second weekend I paid a visit to the nursing home, travelling on a luxury coach and feeling very grown up as I entered another foreign country, Wales, where Dad was recovering from his operation with twenty or so other blokes.

To my surprise and embarrassment, Dad had settled himself in as the resident comedian, known by everyone as 'Paddy'.

He made jokes about the nurses, doctors, visitors, bedpans and the food. Everything was up for grabs as Dad was fed lines, characters and incidents by an English bloke who he had paired up with. He had the other men, who were often stitched up after their operations, literally in stitches for the fortnight. I saw another side of Dad that I had never seen before as yells of laughter emitted from the men, who said that he should definitely be on the stage, that he was a born comedian.

Maybe Dad was a born comedian and actor who had a real gift. In this environment he could turn on a routine with quick-fire wit about things that surrounded him.

He was definitely a square peg in a round hole. Perhaps if things had been different, he would have been much happier and more fulfilled within himself. His feelings of frustration often turned inwards, causing him untold pain, and overflowed into unpredictable bouts of anger directed against himself and those close to him.

Dad didn't need a script. All Dad needed was a straight man, like this bloke in the home to feed him material; the quickness of his retorts surprised even him. Where did they come from?

Maybe the gods of mirth visited Dad and his pal during their convalescence at Colwyn Bay. Maybe they had followed them there from Knotty Ash, just outside Liverpool?

Mass was at eight on the Sunday morning. The man running the guest house offered to call me. As I knew that this was the only morning that the couple could have a lie-in, I acted in a very grown-up way for a thirteen-year-old, saying that I'd be able to get myself up if they lent me an alarm clock, as I was used to fending for myself.

But the Welsh air must have got to me. The man came into my room, highly amused, after ten, as I lay luxuriously under their lovely red eiderdown, snoring my head off.

The bed was so comfortable, with clean sheets and pillow-cases, a bit different from the ones in the Summer House, that it was no wonder that I enjoyed the comfort of the occasion and never heard the alarm clock. I wondered if I would ever live in a house like the one I stayed at in Wales. It didn't seem likely while I remained in Liverpool but I had no alternative but to return there reluctantly after my weekend break in Wales.

Chapter 14

Dad had survived the operation and enjoyed his convalescence but he went back to work as if he were about to face a firing squad. He had an instinct that warned him when trouble was brewing.

When Dad arrived at Corrigan's warehouse, the hatchet dropped. On the previous Friday afternoon, William, one of Corrigan's sons, had been stocktaking and found that several boxes of butter were missing. Dad was told by one of the men that Jim had pointed the finger at him, the most recent person to be taken on there.

They were no better than the creeps I was surrounded by in school. Pilkington, the company clerk, was waiting for Dad on his return to work. "Mr Corrigan said that I am to give you your cards." He handed them to him in an A4 used envelope. Dad told me he tried to get his holiday money out of them. He was entitled to a day and a quarter a month. He had been told to clear off or they would contact the police.

But the biggest shock of the day for Dad was when he went across the road to the pub to see Jimmy Burke.

"Imagine poor Jimmy Burke," he said, "and there was no hurt or harm in him and look what happened to him." So I let him tell me about Jimmy Burke making out that it was the first time I had heard anything about it. It made him feel better to know that there were others worse off than himself.

So Dad was out of work again. Apart from the shortage of money, Penguins and Wagon Wheels, it was nice to have him at home when I came in from school. I didn't have to get the stove going as I was no longer entering a cold dark Summer House but one that had some semblance of a home.

It's always nice to go home when you know there's someone there to greet you with a nice fire, a hot cuppa and some bread and soup. To chat and talk and listen to what happened to us in our respective days. It's not a lot to ask for but it's so blooming hard to get.

When I got in this day from school, Dad was peeling the potatoes, "you know son, you're never hungry if you have a spud in the house. A meal isn't a meal at all without half a stone of potatoes." So into the saucepan went half a stone. Not that these were anything like the ones we had back home in Ireland. "You might as well be drinking a cup of water as eating these," Dad said.

At home we always cooked the potatoes in their jackets. They were always lovely and floury when you drained them and then the jackets would break open and there you'd have the spud smiling at you.

In the Summer House we had two enormous plates that were stacked high with salad, tomatoes, beetroot, eggs, scallions and now we were waiting for the potatoes to boil. "Christ," Dad said, "you could live to be a hundred and some spuds would never boil. If I've tried them once with the fork, I must have tried them a thousand times but will the bastards boil? Those potatoes are just like the kettle, if you look at it, it'll never boil either. Well feck you then," Dad said, "if you don't boil do you think I'll give a damn, we'll have bread instead."

It was as if the potatoes had been listening. I tried them with the fork and they were boiled. In summer time we ate salads, steaks, bacon, sausages and eggs. There's no doubt about it, when it's anything to do with what's going on the table, we were never slow in coming forward.

In wintertime we had chicken, steaks, thick brown stews made from brisket of beef. You'd need a hammer and chisel to break through the layer of fat that had accumulated on the top of the saucepan after it had stood overnight. "You're like a lot," Dad would say when he'd see me turn my nose up at the amount of fat I had on the plate, "you need oiling."

We bought our meat from a butcher who managed this shop on Prescott Road. We went along after five on a Saturday evening when the *Evening Echo* was about to be delivered and the men were waiting around the newsagents with their Vernon's or Littlewood's coupons to see if they had come up on the Pools that week. With eight draws, the dividend could be as much as seventy-five thousand pounds.

For twenty cigarettes, the butcher would fill the bag with anything that he had not sold during the day. After getting our meat, we'd go to one of Scott's grocery shops where the little manager would give us all the left-over cakes and bread we needed for another twenty cigarettes.

This little man by the name of Higgins was a devout Catholic with a powerfully dominant Irish mother who put the fear of shite into him about women and how to handle them.

He had three women working for him and by all accounts they were three of the greatest witches that Liverpool ever produced and that's saying something when you're competing with the like of those from Scottie Road. When we'd get to his shop of a Saturday night, the shop would already be closed and the women would have rushed out on the dot as soon as the closed notice had gone up on the door, leaving poor old Higgins to take down all the current display items that hadn't been sold during the week.

He then had to sweep the shop up and get the place in some semblance of order for the Monday morning opening. Sometimes he wouldn't see his family until nine o'clock on a Saturday night although he had closed the shop at six.

He used to be relieved to see us and have a chat while Dad gave him a hand to clean up. I had an enormous holdall that I used for my running kit and many's the time in the dark winter's nights, I remember when he'd fill it right to the top with cakes and all sorts of things because fridges were a rarity in those days and the cream cakes would have gone off and be sour by Monday morning, so they were either for the dustbin or for us.

His working life was an absolute hell because of these three witches. One of them, Agnes, was a bossy old cow and she used to order him about like his Irish mother. Dad said he was afraid to go out to the back of the shop to have a shite because Agnes would be continually clocking him.

Many a night he would sit there talking after the shop had closed. I would be drinking a pint of milk and eating cream cakes after my cross-country race. The three of us would be trying desperately to find a solution to poor old Higgins' problems. "You see that row of tins," Dad said, "well, move them forward so they are on the edge of the shelf, use some pretext to get her to stand under them and then jump up and down on the floor. She will need her head stitched after that I'll tell yeh."

"I wouldn't let the cow ruin my life," Dad would say. "I'd put something in her tea. You want to polish that floor there and have it as slippery as the ice rink up in Prescott Road. She could easily break a leg on it." But poor old Thomas John Higgins was a mild-mannered man. He suffered in silence apart from the chats he had with Dad and he carried his cross to Calvary unaided. He probably comforted himself with the thought that it wouldn't last for ever but Dad wasn't that type of person. "Nip it in the bud," was Dad's saying, "nip the bastard in the bud," he'd repeat, "or it will hound you till your dying day."

Chapter 15

I had done a couple of runs with Long and Hughes when they decided to go over the West Derby cross-country course. It was more muddy than usual and I found it very difficult to keep on my feet. The other two seemed to skate over the ground, talking and laughing, leaving me for dead. I watched them move away from me over the country. Struggling and humiliated, I felt alone yet again. But I continued following the bunting marking out the route, attached to the barbed wire.

I was pleasantly surprised, as I was miles behind, to come across them, both deep in conversation, when I came off a very muddy stretch. They were at a gate that led onto the road and eventually to the changing rooms.

As we were out for a friendly run, it was not considered cricket to batter the hell out of one's companions. In friendly runs, it was understood that the stronger helped to encourage the weaker. So they had waited for me as I clumsily scrambled over the gate onto the road in a state of disappointment. After some good-mannered English smiling and pleasantries, we set off on the three quarters of a mile to the hall where we changed. Maybe because I was sure of my footing on the hard surface, I found myself really motoring. To my surprise, I had somehow got into another gear. It was exhilarating and I just had to let myself run. This was the first time that I had ever run fast enough to get away from Hughes. I thought my performance was a bit of a fluke. Hughes had done a tough session with Long over the country, he had got cold waiting for me at the gate.

Long took me out a couple of times again over the country where I was all over the place trying to keep my footing but once I got on the road again, I found my balance and I moved like a Rolls-Royce.

I tried to discuss with him what kind of training I should do but he tried to dissuade me by telling me that Hughes had it all going for him, that he was a natural and there wasn't a hope in hell of me getting into any races on the track as there were a lot of naturally good sprinters, middle- and long-distance runners who always dominated the track season. So I was trapped in a vacuum hoping that a miracle or something would happen so I might be selected. In fairness to Long, he did give me some ideas on the type of training I should do. The interval-training schedule he gave me was based upon a modified version of the one used by Zatopek, who had won three gold medals at the 1952 Helsinki Olympic Games. It involved running repetition, a fast one followed by a slow one, set over a selected distance. One day it would be repetitions run over a hundred yards, another two hundred, then four hundred and so on. Training schedules up to Zatopek's time were often a hit and miss affair. A few cross-country races in the winter, some wind sprints in the spring and you were ready for the track season, which began in May.

Zatopek brought a whole new scientific approach to training, imposing a will of iron on his body, training exceptionally hard throughout the year. Despite illness, self-doubts or domestic upheavals, the schedule had to be followed. Sometimes it worked but other times it caused injuries and total breakdown. This obsessive dedication was frowned upon by the school, the club and particularly by the PE department. In England if you had to work hard to get success it was considered ungentlemanly. All of this was to do with class. Athletics stemmed from the two major universities, Oxford and Cambridge. To be an all-rounder and win your sporting blue was taken in your stride; the Olympics a good opportunity to update the Continental Grand Tour. But now in 1954, because of the influence of the likes of Zatopek, things were changing. Commitment to training and winning was becoming the most important thing and I was to identify with that new wave.

Down under in Australia, John Landy, in his summer and our winter, was making weekly attempts to break the magic barrier of running a mile in under four minutes. In the States, Wes Santee was trying to make sure it would be a Yank to be first to break the four minutes.

Meanwhile in Oxford, Roger Bannister was training under the Austrian coach, Franz Stampfl, who brought a whole new scientific approach to training, which resulted in Bannister's stupendous achievement. Bannister broke the four-minute barrier in Iffley Road in Oxford in May 1954. This caught the imagination of the public and mine. I knew that in running terms I was living in great times never to be seen again.

This was exciting stuff for a kid to follow and it didn't leave much room for the pursuit of boring academic trivia.

So at lunchtime I'd leave the classroom with my carrier bag and go to the gym, where I changed. Some of the lads went home for their dinners while others had school dinners or packed lunch, but I ran on an empty belly. As it was pretty cold, I'd put on a couple of jumpers and go out to do my training over the rugby pitches, my breath white in the cold air, as if it were steam coming out of the chimney of a train. I ran gently along the lengths of a couple of rugby pitches trying to warm up. When I was sufficiently glowing, I changed into a pair of second-hand spikes that I had bought from a bloke for five bob. He was a bit of a high jumper and had bought the same pair second-hand from someone else who was a long jumper. To have a pair of spikes, even if they were for field events and not for running, increased my status among my fellow athletes. My second-hand shoes differed from running spikes because they had spikes on the heels as well as on the instep. I was very disciplined and I followed Long's schedule to the letter. If you don't discipline yourself then someone else will gladly do it for you. From an early age I took the bull by the horns and became the captain, first mate and petty officer of my own ship.

Today my training schedule was thirty lengths of the rugby pitch with a gentle trot back. To count the exact number of strides I had done, I would arrange my jumpers around the rugby posts to denote that I had done a block of five strides. I was to learn that by working at a training schedule over the whole of the winter months, I might stand a chance of getting results. A week before Sports Day, some of the lads would come out to do a bit of training. They were going to rely on natural ability and they cut corners, but I could see no other way of achieving success except through hard work. The ground was muddy and I slipped all over the pitch as I strode between the goal posts but I felt good. Even though I was supposedly within this institution of the school, out here looking at the lights in the school building, I was indeed a solitary mister and a real outsider. My lungs were burning as I tried to run and keep myself relaxed. At last I felt in charge of myself. I was glad to have got the twenty-five strides in. Another five and I was a training session nearer my goal. I kept an eye on the school clock, which looked out over the rugby pitches. I would have to hurry in order to get back in time for late lunch. Perhaps today it would mean that I would have to miss my cold shower.

I hurried along the corridors to the dining room past the hall, where most of the school sat for half to three quarters of an hour for library time. Inside the hall, the boys had already put their books away. Library books were used in times of leisure as a means of relaxation and entertainment but they were looked upon with a great deal of suspicion by the Christian Brothers, who censored everything that went into the library. The biology books were locked away and were only accessible to the senior sixth form. Novels and stories were not considered to be real books because they were devoid of facts and figures. According to them, this constituted the real knowledge. The school had a big science department. A career as a mad scientist was the model laid down for many of the lads to follow. You were considered a bit of a sissy if you studied arts in the sixth form. Science and religion were the macho subjects encouraged by the Christian Brothers. I could never make head or tail of physics or chemistry books.

I didn't set out deliberately to be a failure, no one ever does; but I was never capable of getting past the first page of those formidable volumes. Each day I would make a firm resolution to master the facts. Jack Webb, in the TV series *Dragnet*, used as his catchphrase, "the facts, all I need is the facts," but I could never remember the facts. Water, hydrogen, oxygen, carbon monoxide, carbon dioxide, blue and red litmus paper and what we mixed with them were all a jumble to me. Sulphuric acid, H_2SO_4, H_2O, are some of the jumbled formulae in the back of my mind. Physics and the pulley system, contours, glaciers, terminal moraines, V-and U-shaped valleys all left me totally cold. Some of the swots took to the facts like ducks to water and they mastered them with ease. My reading abilities were weak and I was not all that interested in books, as my own life was richer than anything I could ever find in a book.

Because of my association with Long and the fact that I ran for the school, I could skip out of the lunchtime library session.

My emotional and intellectual development was taking place under the disciplined physical training that I subjected myself to on the rugby pitches. I was more into Zen than into the Victorian Christianity that the Christian Brothers were spoon-feeding the boys.

A few latecomers were still in the dining room when I got there. A lot of the boys looked down their noses at the school meals but as my mam often said, hunger is a great sauce, so that's how I approached Kate's school dinners. After the lunchtime training on the rugby fields on my own, I was hungry enough to eat the side of a house.

The food wasn't cooked on the school premises. It was brought in daily in steel containers from the school dinner centre in Penny Lane.

As head dinner lady, Kate had the difficult job of portioning out the food. Some days she would have more boys to feed than other days because of lads being absent from school. She could never know exactly how many mouths she would have to feed. She was outwardly respected by many of the greedy lay teachers, who creeped and crawled to her so that they would get big portions, sometimes depriving the younger kids of their allocated amounts. A teacher's plate could be stacked up like Mount Etna while the kid beside him would have less on his plate than you'd put on a mousetrap.

The Christian Brothers didn't eat school dinners. They dined alone in their house, which was in the same grounds as the school, where they had a couple of women to do their roasts for them. Most of the Christian Brothers were big-bellied men but they hid this under the black soutanes they wore. It wasn't until you saw them in shorts and jersey refereeing a rugby match that you could be forgiven for thinking that they were seven or eight months gone.

I devised a way of getting a good helping of dinner for myself. I was at a school where everything involved a process of learning and surviving. After my training session I'd be one of the last in to get my dinner. There would still be plenty of food to go round because Kate would be holding back in case of an influx of latecomers. I'd get preference over those waiting for seconds, whom I called the Alms for Allah brigade. They would be bobbing up and down in their places with their hands in the air begging for food. On my arrival, Kate would know that there'd hardly be anyone after me, so she would sometimes declare "no seconds", and the poor buggers would have to leave me to have a grand feed.

After eating, I'd help her and the other dinner ladies to clear up the plates on the table. Although it was a strict rule to return all the plates to the servery, many of these lads had never lifted a plate in their lives. They were waited upon hand and foot by their mothers, as they would be by their wives later in life when they were in high-flying positions doing their mad scientific research.

So I'd help with the plates and stack up the chairs on the tables. I've never had a handout mentality and I expected to show my appreciation in practical help.

After lunch I'd be tired from all the training and Kate's big dinner always followed by a pudding of triple jam sponge with lashings of custard, made from a secret formula that I've never found to this day. So I'd settle down at the back of the class for the afternoon, oblivious to what was going on, dreaming, planning and plotting about becoming a great runner.

Chapter 16

Dad was still out of work so he decided to try something new. We were at the Labour Club, where the drinks were cheaper than in the ordinary public houses.

"Ladies and gentlemen," the Brilliantined man announced from the stage, "tonight we are very honoured and privileged to have with us a most unusual act. This lady doesn't dance, she doesn't play the piano or tell jokes."

"No but she'd give you a right pain in the arse," Dad said as he waited his turn to go on stage with his button accordion.

We had seen her last week and the week before, much to Dad's disgust for he knew that for the next fifteen minutes we were in for a session of piercing whistling until the ringing in Dad's head would keep him awake half the night. Dad pitied her poor husband and said that he'd be better off living with a canary.

They gave her a good hand but I suppose in a way they felt obligated as all the entertainment was free.

Mam had told me, after we'd seen a woman doing a similar turn at the Theatre Royal in Dublin, that women couldn't whistle and that she was convinced that the person on stage was a man dressed up as a woman. So I was determined to study this woman. With her fingers in her mouth like a pair of chopsticks and her tree-trunk legs firmly set upon the stage, her massive bosom heaved as she blew out riveting sounds that would have deafened the dead.

After the woman had finished her whistling, Dad followed her act by doing a melody of tunes on the accordion.

"They love an Irish tune," he said, "much better than all that fecking whistling."

Then I got up and sang 'The Wild Colonial Boy' accompanied by Dad on the accordion.

Everyone clapped and I was no longer a 'consolation' to my dad as he had told me I was when I came last in the school Sports Day race. Life was lovely and everything was hunky-dory in the world when I wasn't a 'consolation' to Dad.

Dad was going to go into the entertainment business. "What do people want in this country?" he asked me. "No, let me put it another way, what do Irish people want in this country?"

I thought for a good while before I answered, "Easy money, plenty of drink and a good fight!" "You've become a very smart Scouser all of a sudden making a stereotype out of the poor Paddy." I didn't want him to blow his top so I decided to be careful.

"What do they want?" I asked.

"When they come home from work, wash, shave and have the feed and put on their suits?"

They want to go out, get drunk and have a fight but I couldn't say that so I remained mum as Dad stayed in his hypothetical world.

"They want to be reminded of home. Do you know that there's not one of them that's not homesick."

"This is what I'm thinking of doing. Remember what I learned in America; well displayed is half sold."

Dad handed me a piece of paper that he had laid out and was going to have printed as a card.

Irish songs Melodies Jigs Hornpipes for all occasions
Births Marriages Deaths and Wakes.
Contact Big Stan at the Labour Club just off
Prescott Road near the Ice Rink.

Then Dad went into a positive litany.

"Do you know I've got a feeling in me bones that we'll never look back from now on?"

"If God only gives me a few more years until I have the family off my hands and pay the mortgage off. That's a heavy load around me neck. It would break anyone's back, seven pounds fourteen and eight pence a month. I'm just paying the moneylenders you know. They might as well enjoy it in this world for by Christ they won't have it in the next."

Dad was calling the wrath of God down on all moneylenders and I had heard others do so on their soapboxes down at the Pier Head.

"Remember what they say on Radio Éireann, if you feel like singing a song why not sing an Irish one? That'll be our way out. If it's not then I'm a Dutchman." So I sang:

Last night as I lay dreaming
Upon my lonely bed
I heard a voice from heaven
That told me Dad was dead

As I got up next morning
I found that that was true
That he was up in heaven
Above the skies so blue.

Dad gave a shudder and said, "You've got a fecking morbid side to you just like your mother and there's no mistaking that."

I had the job of putting the printed cards in the shop windows at two pence for each week.

I was fascinated by the other cards. Some advertised rooms to let with the proviso that no blacks or Irish need apply. There was a large woman's bike for sale alongside a card selling a medium brown second-hand suit, 'Worn only once by my husband before his fatal accident', along with a pair of nearly-new shoes size ten that needed a bit of renovation on the left heel. So in went our card with all the others. *Irish music for all occasions by the Shamrocks.* Dad had added under the address *PS if there's no answer, knock loudly as the bell is not working.*

Really there should have been three Shamrocks, but as there was only Dad and myself, we had to be satisfied with that.

Every performer will tell you that the secret of success in the entertainment business is practice. A well-rehearsed act stands a much better chance of success than one that hasn't been worked upon so Dad shouted, "For Christ's sake, sing up. I can fart louder than that."

"I'm at full blast as it is," I said.

"You'll be singing in front of hundreds of people."

"I'd be better off dead."

"You will be dead if you don't sing up. The mortgage in Dublin has to be paid and Hardy's waiting on the rent here, so less of the prima donna and let's get on with it."

"I can't sing wearing this dress. I thought that we were supposed to be the Shamrocks."

Dad had a thing about putting me in dresses. When we were together before I went to school, he used to put me in dresses because he said that they were less complicated for a little thing like myself to get on than trousers. Then when we were on the road back in Ireland trying to peddle the fish, he dressed me up once again to look like a little girl as I'd attract more attention. And now that I was thirteen and had just started wearing long trousers with turn-ups, he still wanted me to stand in front of hundreds in a dress. I thought this was a bit too much so I was drawing the line and putting my foot down.

"The Shamrocks don't appeal to a big enough audience. We need to be more commercial to tap the bigger market," Dad said. "It's a gimmick for Christ's sake, I've got to wear one too."

Dad had got the idea to dress up like Old Mother Riley and have me as his daughter Kitty. On the strength of their popularity, Dad had gone out and hired two dresses from a Jewish theatrical costumier in a street just above the entrance to the Mersey Tunnel. Old Mother Riley wore a grey wig and a three-quarter-length dress with laced-up black boots, which came well up past her ankles. She also had a black shawl, which she pulled across her back and shoulders as she became more irritated. It was then you knew, as you watched the toing and froing of the shawl getting faster and faster, that she was about to explode. Then she'd discard the shawl and shout, "Put your mitts up," as she danced around her opponent ducking and diving, shadow boxing the pomposity out of the person who had offended her. Sometimes she wore a hat with a black veil when the occasion required it, such as funerals or when she was up in front of the beak. Old Mother Riley was always getting herself into jams, with Kitty her daughter and her newly acquired boyfriend always coming to the rescue at the last minute.

The similarities between Old Mother Riley and her daughter on the screen to Dad and myself in the Summer House was uncanny. Kitty's role was to rescue her mother from all the half-baked schemes that she got herself embroiled in.

"Let me leave school," I said, "I'll get a job."

"How can you get a job?" he roared. "I can't get a job!"

"There's jobs for the likes of me because I'm fit and younger."

"I'm not old," he shouted. This seemed to be his greatest fear, to become old and not to be wanted.

"I didn't say you were old but they don't have to pay the likes of me as much as they pay a fully grown man!"

"You've got a good voice, you can milk them so sing 'The Old Bog Road'."

As they carried out her coffin down the Old Bog Road.

"Louder for feck's sake, louder," he shouted.

"No one cares about the Old Bog Road or having my feet on Broadway!"

"I can see a lot further ahead than you," Dad said. "Nostalgia will become the thing of the future for the Irish and their descendants scattered all over the world."

On the train to Manchester for the audition, Dad had an attack of last-minute nerves as the reality of the situation dawned upon him and he began to panic. "I think I'll make a list of the songs just to be on the safe side." Out came the pencil and on the back of an envelope, Dad noted down half a dozen numbers or so that he knew us both to be conversant with. "They should be enough to get us through the audition tonight. If we do, we'll make three pounds a night. For five nights a week, that'll be twice what Corrigan was giving me. We can start with 'When Irish Eyes are Smiling'," Dad said. "That can be our signature tune. At last we're on the road." I was getting irritated.

"I can't sing in the clubs, I'm underage."

"Stand back so they won't see you. You'll soon get older. I should have stuck to the music in America. We'll go over it one last time," Dad said. So, as the train raced towards Manchester, I sang

When Irish eyes are smiling sure it's like a morn in spring
It's the lilt of Irish laughter you can hear the angels sing
When Irish eyes are happy all the world seems bright and gay
When Irish eyes are happy sure they steal your heart away

"You sing that at the audition Sean and we'll be in the money," Dad said as the steam train drew into Piccadilly Station, Manchester. After a few different bus rides and getting the wrong directions, we eventually found the Emerald Club. It smelt like a place where old tomcats hung about. The manager was an energetic crisp dismissive type who was clapping his hands saying, "All right darlings," as we entered. The dark auditorium was filled with tables and chairs and there was a small stage at the top. The whole place stank of stale beer and cigarettes, which nearly turned my stomach. It could have done with a good airing but I suppose those who came to this club were not the outdoor types. The manager buzzed around the place as the different acts, who had barely begun their performance, were instantly dismissed by him clapping his hands and saying, "Don't call us, we'll call you. Next one, for my sins," he clapped.

Everything moved so fast we didn't even have time to change into our dresses. His lackey announcer said, "Doyle and son." "Thank God, not Dombey and son," the manager shouted. "Accordion and songs. 'When Irish Eyes are Smiling'. Ten out of ten for originality. Go on, prepare to weep into your glasses. Have they started?" I was halfway through.

When Irish eyes are happy all the world seems bright and gay

"Thank you darlings, don't call us we'll call you." "Next one, the comedian," the announcer said. "Hear the one about the Paddy in the concentration camp. Zee English will play in the west field. Zee Russians will play in the south field and zee Paddies will play in the minefields." "I like it," said the manager. "No, no, listen, wait a minute, hang on a mo. Did you hear the one about the Irishman who wanted to start a cider factory? He went out and shot four hundred woodpeckers." Ha ha, laughed the manager.

The manager knew what the Irish audience wanted. They didn't want Irish eyes are smiling or the old Bog Road. They wanted jokes, even though they were Irish ones.

"You get a funny lot in these clubs," Dad said, as we came back on the train to Lime Street. "The thing is that they don't really appreciate good music. When they come to this country they forget about being Irish."

It was Dad's idea to go into the entertainment business but when it came down to brass tacks he bottled out and instead of him being upfront, he put me there to receive all the flack. I was finding out that Dad had great imagination. The world did not cater for Dad's imagination, it only tolerated and negotiated with people who had their feet firmly on the ground. As the years went on, I was to meet many who had nailed or glued their feet to the ground and what did they get out of it in the end but a bank balance, which they were afraid to touch, and a load of regrets for being so careful and afraid, and never having had any imagination.

We failed abysmally in Manchester and for many years, I was embarrassed and ashamed to even think about it. But at least we went there and I have the memory to prove it, even if unlocking it still proves painful.

Chapter 17

As time went on, I was finding that I was desperate to have a guiding figure; Dad took little or no interest in me as I was growing up. My needs were changing and he was too busy trying to be centre stage himself.

So I had to fend for myself.

Dad never encouraged me to develop. He had no respect for O or A levels or going to university. In fact I was annoyed once when I asked him to help me with some algebra, which he dismissed as irrelevant shite.

Dad had an unhealthy distrust of books and education. He felt that there wasn't anything worth learning in books. People who read, in his view, were being neutralised by reading. They lived their lives through books, playing safe, mediocre people not originators.

How unlike Hughes' background was to mine. He was a scholarship boy who came from a Huyton council estate but unlike many of the other scholarship boys, he had an academic background at home.

There were as many books in his house as there were empty tins of Cow and Gate in our Summer House. One of his sisters had already completed her degree at university while his other sister was doing her A levels with the intention of going on to further education.

So Hughes was no stranger to the world of academia. He could converse with Long although Long was three and a half years older than either of us. Long intended to groom and coach Hughes to the very top. As Hughes and myself were both the same age and the best of mates, I tagged along behind, so Long took me over too. Long was like a big brother to me and he guided me by telling me what training to do. The triangle built up between Long, Hughes and myself had everything going for it but then disaster struck. Hughes got injured, so I was put in as a stopgap to run in Hughes' place in a trial.

All of my training was put to the test when I raced over two laps on a cinder track at Fazakerley. I was well back down the field on the first lap but at the bell going into the second lap, I pulled myself out of my lethargy and moved up the field on the back straight. Coming round the last bend, I was in about fifth position. The first three in the race would be selected to represent the Liverpool schools in Manchester, so I put a great spurt on coming up the home straight to finish third.

Long and Hughes were delighted. It said a lot for my achievement as all the other lads in the field were a year older than me.

I was on my way to Manchester, travel free on a coach to compete in the Lancashire schools half-mile championships. We had been there before with the Old Mother Riley act, which had proved a disaster but let's hope that the next visit would be more successful.

So off I went to the White City Stadium in Manchester but the journey proved daunting. Before I reached the stadium, I had to endure this posh lad sitting next to me whom I'd never met before, for the three-hour journey. And as I wasn't versed in the art of small talk, I couldn't cope with him. All he got from me were sullen reactions and half-smiles with which I tried to cover up my shyness and feelings of inadequacy.

My dilemma got worse when it was time for us to have our sandwiches. I had mine, which I had made myself in an Oxo tin. This fellow patted his stomach, saying that a spot of lunch seemed to be in order. I didn't know what to do when he produced a packet wrapped in greaseproof paper in which were sandwiches that had been cut into dainty triangular shapes like the ones we tried to make with our compasses in geometry lessons. I felt so undermined about my wedges of jam jaw-breakers in my Oxo box that I didn't bring them out.

To give him his due, he offered to share his repast with me but I declined because I didn't want to start titivating the taste buds in case I ended up biting his hand off. So I sat on the coach with my guts rattling as we approached Manchester. When he took his *Times* out and asked me what I thought five across and three down might be, I made out I was asleep.

I couldn't wait to get off the coach for my legs were as stiff as two planks after the three-hour ordeal. I wanted to go and see the huge stadium and the White City running track, which was three hundred and thirty yards of cinder unlike the standardised track of four-forty yards on which you had to do four laps to complete the mile. Circling the outside of the cinder track there was a turfed greyhound track over which hung poles on which lights were fixed. These were switched on at night when the dogs chased the hare from their traps, adding more excitement for the punters.

I was all uptight about going out on the track while Hughes and Long were having a great time mucking about in the stand. They had travelled down on the same train as Dad, unbeknown to each other.

In the arena, I think I felt like the Christians felt when they were being thrown to the lions, the lions on this occasion being my fellow competitors. I also felt doubly undermined because I knew no matter how well I did that I would be compared to Hughes. I was in a no-win situation. Hughes was the kiddie as far as they were concerned whereas I was his understudy and no matter what I did, when the star recovered from his injury, I would be quickly put on the back burner. So in reality, I was running two races, the one on the track and one against Long and Hughes in the stand.

I had to run a first-round heat to qualify for entry into the final, so I had to use the heats as a final because I couldn't take any chances on not qualifying. By sheer dogged determination, I held on to finish third, which got me a place in the final. I ran nine seconds faster in the heats than I had done in the Fazakerley race, which represented a seventy-yard improvement over the half mile.

I was elated with my performance but I was also shattered and drained. The tiredness really took hold of me when I realised that I would have to go through the whole thing again in the final in less than an hour and a half. "How are you feeling?" Dad asked. He was all dressed up in the suit he had bought for Jim

English's daughter's wedding, the one that he wasn't invited to. Dad never needed to be asked twice to dress up and to show off his fine feathers. "I feel very tired Dad, I feel shattered."

"Of course you're not tired. You don't know the meaning of the word," he said in his bluff manner. "If you had to work as hard as I've had to do then you'd know the real meaning of tiredness."

I should have known that I wasn't going to get any sympathy from Dad. I was left in splendid isolation with my worries about what if I didn't do well in the final. What if I came last? There'd be hell to pay then, I thought. I cursed myself for being so stupid, for making a rod for my own back. Why did I have to put myself on the chopping block?

My two pals were laughing and joking and having a great day out and me as miserable as sin with all the cares of the world on my little round shoulders. I hated the waiting between the heats and the final in this no-man's-land wondering what was in store for me in that arena in less than an hour's time. After the heats, all the dads, including my own, had repaired to the pub. Now they were back at the trackside. They were talking about their sons animatedly as if they were greyhounds or horses. Steel, a well-set young man who looked to me as if he was well into his thirties, was considered favourite. In the centre of the arena, the runners put on their spikes. Some wore white socks, others, like myself, stuck their bare feet into their spikes. I carefully did the laces up of my second-hand long jump or high jump spikes depending on which former owner you believed as to their past history. Immediately I undid the laces again because they were not tight enough. One of the many fears runners suffer from is that their laces will come undone during the race.

The final started on the bend because of the shorter three-thirty-yard track. The starter wore a red three-quarter-length coat and a black peaked cap, a bit like the master of the hunt. He carried two enormous guns, one to start the race with and the other one to be fired in the event of a false start. If you made two false starts, you were automatically disqualified.

The starter was not a man to mess about with. He warned us that none of us should have a foot over the newly whitened semicircle starting line, which was on the crown of the bend beside the steeplechase water barrier.

As we went to our marks, the starter had two officials check that our feet were behind the line and that we were in our correct starting lane positions, which had been determined by picking numbered straws before the race. This had proved to be quite a palaver as none of the competitors wished to be first to get the ball rolling, so there was a lot of good manners and "after you" in evidence before someone could be persuaded to pick the first straw.

With the fear of not complying correctly with the starter's orders and the fear of Dad's reaction, who had to pay a return train fare and entrance money, as well as the fear of letting down Long, Hughes and Brother Mac and with the tiredness in my legs from the heats, I was yawning non-stop and really I didn't know where I was until the starter's gun went off. The loudness of the bang knocked me back into the reality of the race.

I was last coming down the straight where I entered under the shadow of the main stand; Dad, Brother Mac, Long and Hughes sat there. This would be the finishing straight after we had completed two laps.

Around the bend I moved up a place or so on the nine-man field. I was always warned not to pass on the bend as this makes you run further as you are forced to run wide. But it's all right making rules in the changing rooms on what to do and not to do on the running track, but in the heat of the race the best and worst of us forget the rules and get on with it.

So down the back straight, I was seventh, consoling myself that at least I wasn't last. I then passed this lad going into the crown of the last bend, which made me sixth.

Down the finishing straight, into the shadow made by the main stand, surprisingly I wasn't aware of people watching me as all of my focus was on holding onto sixth place.

When I heard the bell indicating a lap to go, I wished that this was the end of the race instead of having to do a whole lap more with those three behind me. Another thing I was told in the dressing room was never to look behind you. For one thing, you lose concentration on what's going on in front of you, and if you do look back, you encourage those behind you to make a bigger effort to catch you up as they know that you are suffering.

Around the bend I was forced to run wide yet again to pass this kid. I was running further than those on the inside who were hugging the bend but I didn't care as I was getting there. Down the back straight, I was fifth. Fifth in the Lancashire School Boys' under-15s championships and them all a year older than me, Jesus, Mary and Joseph, I prayed, if I can only hold onto this. Around the top bend, I was still fifth, but I was shitting myself in case those four behind would come up on me. Then, up the long straight I went. It was now ninety yards to the finish on this long straight. Then I was fourth. They were spread all over the track in front of me. Dad said later that at this moment, some of the officials said, "Look at little Doyle, look at little Doyle go," which I'm sure made Dad stick his chest out and give that old Doyle swagger. With thirty yards to go, I was third, but in terrible pain. Everything ached. I was forcing everything out of my little body. I was now running wide across the track in an effort to get past the two in front but the more determined effort I put in, the more I tied up. Finishing third, I was disgusted with myself, which must have showed on my face, for when I met my pals they congratulated me, saying that all of the lads are a year older than you and look what you'll do next year. "You'll walk it next year," they said, as they clapped me on the back. Back in school, the Big Fella said, "I hear you got third in a race in Manchester." I don't suppose he'd ever been to Manchester in his life. "Yes," I said, throwing my shoulders back, "I was third in the Lancashire Schools' Championships." "Let's see your medal," he said. "I didn't get a medal," I said, "they only give medals to the first two." "You are a wanker, a fucking Paddy wanker," and he walked away delighted with himself and his few well-chosen words.

Chapter 18

I don't know which of the two types of letters from home were worse, those threatening Dad with the courts or the ones thanking him for sending some money. I was so powerless to do anything about the hopeless situation that presented itself. Any letter with an Irish stamp on it always turned me into a state of anxiety because I never knew what to expect.

"You shouldn't have sent all that," Dad said as he read from the recently arrived letter. "We need it, God knows we do but you shouldn't leave yourself short. Tommie needed a new pair of shoes. He's growing so fast that I've hardly bought him something new but he's grown out of it and I've been busy going to the hospital but the fares, they're a fortune now. I saw them putting some Christmas things in the window down in Henry Street. Christmas seems to come upon us earlier each year. I thought wouldn't it be nice if we were all together again for Christmas. I'm always praying at night for the time when we will be together again as one happy family, please God."

Dad threw the letter down. "It's a pity that she didn't try a bit more of the happy families when we were there instead of taking notice of everyone else. Send plenty of money over there and it's all love and kisses by return of post and now she wants to send your brother over as he's doing nothing but moping about for the three months of the summer holidays. Where are we supposed to put him?"

"I'm sure we'd manage," I said.

I wanted to see Val again for I was sure he'd take some of the weight off my shoulders. Having a one-to-one relationship with Dad was heavy going. "It can't do any harm," I said.

I went to meet Val at the Pier Head as Dad couldn't afford to miss a day off labouring. Nothing seemed to have changed down there. There was all the morning hustle and bustle, with men jumping on and off buses, and the tea stalls where I had tea when I first arrived two years ago were all still going full flow. The Mersey was as busy as ever with ferry boats on their way to Birkenhead and New Brighton at this early hour of the morning. The cormorants on the top of the Royal Liver Building were still about to fly off somewhere. They had been years now in that position and they still hadn't made their minds up in which direction to go.

I was thinking I would be able to tell Val that I had come third twice in two big races, first in Fazakerley and then in Manchester.

I hadn't won a medal yet but one day that might happen. I knew that none of the people I saw milling around the Pier Head

163

dodging the pigeons would have the chance to win a race as they were too preoccupied with having to earn a living.

It seemed that droves of cattle and people had been coming off the boat non-stop ever since Dad and I had landed. I felt superior to the new bloods arriving for at least I could find my way around Liverpool and I had learned to cope with living in England.

As the people continued to come off the boat, there was no sight or sound of Val. Perhaps he hadn't come over after all. It was a well-known fact that Val had a mind of his own. Then I saw him as he came down the gangplank in his relaxed swagger with no rush or hurry on him, typical of Val. He must have been one of the last off the boat. He went through the customs and it seemed ages for him to get through.

"I thought you hadn't come," I said.

We didn't shake hands as we were young brothers, the best you could expect from us two was a familiar nod of recognition or a pat on the back.

"I was giving a couple of tips to the captain," Val said. It was great to have Val here, he hadn't changed, still fearless, full of bull and good humour. "How are you kiddo?" He didn't give me any chance to make any acknowledgement, "and how's the ould fella? I expect he's not changed, not for the good at least, but he can take it from me that if he starts any of his Andrew Martining about with me that—"

"Val, give it a chance will you? Come on," I said.

"Hang on, I want to have a burn-up. If I can't have a burn-up every ten minutes, I'm a goner."

Like Mam, Val was addicted to the weed from an early age. The path was laid out before him and he had no option but to follow it. In Ireland then, you were considered pretty weird if you

164

didn't smoke. It was a way of breaking down social barriers if you could flash a twenty-pack of Afton, Players or Capstan in company.

Val had changed a lot in appearance. He had filled out considerably, becoming very sturdy. His hair was longer and he had sideburns. He had a black three-quarter drape jacket and Oxford bags. The legs were so wide that you couldn't see what kind of shoes were worn under them and he had a dapper suitcase the size of a Hammond Lane matchbox.

There was always a thing in our family about who was the tallest as Dad's side of the family were known to be shorter than Mam's. Many's the time back in Dublin, when Dad was out in the pubs and poor Mam was left to entertain us, we'd have measuring contests against the wall that had been marked from the last reading to see how much we had grown and who in fact was the tallest of all the siblings in the family. I sidled up beside Val and lo and behold, I was just that tiny bit taller but of course not as strapping or sturdy as Val, who was built in the Rocky Marciano mould.

I felt like cock of the walk with Val as I knew which bus to get and I could point out famous spots to him, not that he showed much interest 'cause he had the suspicion and natural fear of the immigrant who was entering unknown territory irrespective of what was on offer.

Right away I had a problem, which I aired immediately as we waited for the bus.

"You're not going to smoke in front of him?" I asked.

"I'll do what the feck I like," Val said, nodding his head.

Chapter 19

Dad never fully appreciated or realised the consequences that his leaving Ireland would have on the rest of the family. He didn't seem to understand the effect that the break-up of the marriage would have on the children. It was this lack of sensitivity that added to our problems.

Dad thought that he could turn the clock back as far as the family was concerned. We were there to be resurrected whenever it suited his purpose. Dad's problem was that he thought that the family was a static thing. He didn't realise that it was an organic unit, constantly changing so that when Val came over to work during his school summer holidays, sparks were bound to fly.

Val was now seventeen and a half, a heavyset lad with a pair of shoulders on him as wide as a door. As soon as I saw him I realised that he was not the type of person to muck about with and I was so glad that he was here for the summer. There wasn't much that Val didn't know or have an opinion on. He had a very scrutinising look that he'd give from time to time. It wasn't too comfortable when it was aimed at me. Val's eyes looked straight at the world, looking sadly, thinking but saying nothing unless he thought a response was worthwhile or his ground was threatened.

"Well, what do you think of it so far?" Dad asked.

"Ah, it's not bad, a bit like a graveyard only the corpses are walking."

"Well it's been responsible for keeping your belly full for a good many years."

Thank God Val ignored Dad and turned his attention to me by asking, "How are you kiddo?" I nodded, smiling in trepidation.

"I talked to the ganger man," Dad said, "he said that he might be able to fix you up with something."

"Doing what?" Val snapped.

"Labouring."

Val straightened his tie as he brushed his suit. "I don't intend to get my gear dirty in England," he said, examining his hand, "or my hands for that matter," he went on, going into the kitchen. He came back into the room with a pint of sterilised milk.

"You'll have to sleep on the floor for the time being. I'll ask Stan for a spare bed."

"As long as I don't catch anything I don't mind where I kip." After taking a swig from the bottle Val turned and nearly threw up over the stove.

"Do you drink this stuff?"

"When I can afford it."

"You mean you pay for it as well."

"No it grows on trees."

"Well it never was inside a cow, that's for sure."

"We don't have time in this country to be examining the finer points of food. We take what we can get and are damned glad to see it."

"I believe very much in the philosophy that you are what you eat."

"What in the name of Christ are you talking about? Will you shut up and let me read the paper?"

Dad was obviously losing his patience with Val and he barely landed. Val wouldn't let anything go with Dad whereas I'd swallow things so as to keep the peace. But the danger of my policy was that by letting things go they'd fester like a boil until they'd blow up in the most God Almighty row.

Val was like Dad and believed in nipping things in the bud. He was also like a proper barrack-room lawyer. At this point I wouldn't have said anything but Val went after it like a cat would chase a mouse. "The well-informed man," he mocked, shaking his head, "must keep abreast of current affairs. Of course it's all propaganda you know." Dad retorted, "I was reading papers before you were born."

"And a lot of good it's done you."

Oh God, I thought, I wish he'd stop.

"I'm very particular about what I read and what I eat," said Val.

It was evident that one was as bad as the other by the reply Dad gave him.

"But you don't give a shite about what you wear."

"This is what you call fashion," Val said, moving about as if he was in a fashion parade. "It probably wasn't invented in your day."

Val's long black jacket and Oxford bag trousers were unlike anything worn by Liverpudlians.

"You look like a proper Katie Whiteface in that outfit," Dad said, shaking the paper.

Katie Whiteface was the nickname Dad had given Val in Dublin because of his pale complexion.

Dad rattled his paper again realising that he couldn't out talk Val, so he tried a more conciliatory approach. So he said, "Sean and myself are going to see a James Stewart film tonight, *Bend Of the River*, you can come along if you want to." I suppose Dad was like a lot of Irish parents in that he treated all the children in the family as if they were the same age. In this instance, he was treating Val as if he were my age but Val was three and a half years older than me, nearly eighteen. "I saw that old film years ago," Val said, "I wouldn't be bothering my backside with it." Dad couldn't understand that Val wasn't an ardent film buff like himself.

"I wouldn't mind if I was in a film myself starring with a big mot, getting plenty of gyno for smiling at her."

"If you're not interested in films," Dad said, "perhaps you'd like to stay in and listen to the radio."

"Is it steam or battery you've got? I'm going out looking for a bit of talent."

"Talent," Dad said.

That was the first time a reference had been made to talent in Dad's company under this corrugated roof. Val had no hang-ups about women as he was living in a house full of them apart from my little brother. Val was used to women popping in and out in Dublin. At home and at school, I was surrounded by boys and men who lived in a world devoid of women and who actively disliked and mistrusted them.

"Where are the dance halls around here?"

169

I could see Dad was fuming. If I had said half of what Val said I'd be on the floor by now. But Dad knew that Val had done a fair bit of boxing up in Arbour Hill Club in Dublin so Dad stayed with sarcasm rather than resorting to the fists.

"Oh I don't know anything about dances," Dad said, "we are all far too busy here working earning money to send back to you lot in Dublin."

"Well that's your problem kiddo, but I've come over here to have a good time. You're only young once. Of course some of us were always old."

This drew a stunned awkward silence. "Can I have a key for the door?" Val asked, breaking the silence. As grown up as Val looked, I now could see that he had a lot to learn. If he knew Dad like I knew him then he would know better than to ask him outright for anything.

"Key?" Dad asked, amazed.

"Yeah," Val flippantly said, "it opens doors."

Val was reduced to a state of nakedness by the way the old man, who had waited in a room adjoining the maternity ward in Tuam when Val was born, looked at him. Fighting for his corner, Val added as an afterthought, "I don't want to be waking you up when I come in. I'm sure at your age you need your eight hours."

Dad was fuming. Val, I thought, don't keep on.

"Key to front door," Dad said, "I didn't have a key to the front door till I was twice your age," which wasn't true as Dad had celebrated his eighteenth birthday in Chicago in 1926.

I brought the tea into the bedroom. "There's a good lad Sean. Oh sure what would your da do without you?"

I was glad to make the tea and do little messages and jobs so that I could keep on the right side of Dad sometimes. But Val could see through me. "You'd make a lovely little waitress, little

Seaneen," he whispered when we were out of earshot of the old man. Oh shut up Val, I signalled with my eyes. "Sean knows how to make the tea, don't you Sean, not too strong and not too weak, just how his da likes it."

I felt embarrassed. They were both having a go at me because I wouldn't take sides, but how could I?

"It must be like working in a hospital for the incurables," Val whispered. "Look at the colour of it. What did you do to the tea leaves? Gnat's piss is stronger than this. With the sterilised milk and the tea, it's no wonder he writes those rotten letters back home."

Dad tried to change the subject by asking how the baby was, but now Val was on firm ground and he drove the point home mercilessly.

"Topping, just topping," Val said. "Crying every day for the father she never sees. There was another long deep hurt embarrassed silence, then Val stood up feeling very awkward. He was angry with his father but more so with the whole situation that he was powerless to do anything about.

"I can't stand any more of this tea. I'll have to get some air. I suppose the air is as bad as the milk. I'll see you later alligators." Dad was furious. You could tell by the way he was rattling the paper. He tried to read it but he was too upset to even go through the death notices and that was saying something. For Dad, the death notices had a fatal attraction.

"What kind of an eejit is he still?" He paused, gasping for words. "That's your mother's doing. Filling his head up with nonsense, telling him not to show the proper respect to his father. Did you ever see a bigger eejit in the whole of your life? I'll knock the corners off that bucko before I've finished with him."

Chapter 20

It was nice having my brother Val here with me in Liverpool. He'd take me to the Labour Club, where we'd have a few games of billiards and snooker, not that I could play on the full-length table as it was too big for me. It was no wonder that I found it hard to get a partner as I'd miss the easiest of shots. At the club, I used to meet what I estimated as worldly-wise blokes, a bit like the men I admired in the Western films. Many of them were doing their National Service and they all knew how to roll their own Rizla cigarette papers with one hand.

Luckily Stevie always took pity on me when partners were being sorted out as otherwise I would be the last one to be picked.

Stevie must have been about six years older than me. I could not imagine living another six years and being that old. Six years seemed such a long time away as it was almost half my life up to now.

He had a tattoo embroidered on his arm that said *'Mum and Dad forever'* encircled by an ugly-looking snake, over which he wore a gold watch. He had a ring on his little finger. He wore white socks. It was said at school that boys who wore white socks were virgins but I think that Stevie might have been an exception to the rule. He was years younger than Dad and he had a full head of hair, unlike Dad who was as bald as an egg. Oh, what I'd give, I thought as I watched Stevie play, to be able to press a button and turn into Stevie or someone like him, anyone different from myself. What I would give to escape the next six years and be where Stevie was now, looking, acting and behaving as if he didn't have a care in the world. I looked across the table at my brother Val playing. He was tough, much tougher than me, a much harder nut than me.

He'd handle anyone in this snooker room, National Service or not, and they knew it by the way he talked and by the way he walked and the way he dressed. He was proud of who he was. Compared to Val, I had no identity at all. I was invisible in the crowd whereas he stood out.

Although I liked being out with Val and the mates he met in the club, I vowed that this would be the last time I'd go there with him as it was impossible to get him to leave at a reasonable hour and getting in late always led to a hell of a row.

By refusing to come to the Labour Club, I knew that Dad was using a form of blackmail on me. I felt sorry for him that he was on his own in the so-called Summer House going through the death notices in the *Irish Independent*, probably wondering when would it be his turn to have his name in there. My loyalties were torn between Dad and Val but all Val would say was feck him, if he wants to be miserable let him be miserable. But that still didn't satisfy the guilt that I felt about leaving Dad so isolated. All of the people I came in contact with in Liverpool had family. Family was a mum and a dad, cat or dog, brothers, sisters, relatives. Since we had been in England, I had no one else to turn to but Dad. There was just Dad and me. When I tried to share myself between Dad and my brother Val, it seemed that things got worse. I tried to do alternate sessions. I'd go out with Val one night and stay in the next with Dad but either way I still seemed to end up miserable. When I stayed in, I kept out of Dad's way by staying in the kitchen, pretending to be doing a bit of washing and cleaning. Then Dad started winding the clock, getting ready for bed.

"He should be in by now." He was talking more to himself than to me. Oh God, I thought, now we're for it.

"He needn't think he's coming over here and doing what the hell he likes. Did he say anything to you about what time he'd be in?"

"No he didn't say anything."

Dad put his head around the kitchen door. He was already in his pyjamas. "Do you know what they call him out on the job?"

He was getting himself into a rage.

"Johnny Ray, would you believe it, Johnny Ray? Honest to God, he was out there the other day three o'clock in the afternoon, singing on the scaffold to the whole job as if he was at the London Palladium." 'If your sweetheart sends a letter of goodbye…' Honest to God, he stopped the job. I didn't know where to put my face. I've never seen such an eejit. Everyone is laughing at him."

I tried to pacify Dad by saying that Johnny Ray was a very popular singer but all this did was to get a further outburst from Dad.

"Johnny Ray, is it? Do you know what they call me? Do you know what I'm known as out there on the job? Johnny Ray's dad."

"I thought you liked Johnny Ray," I said.

"On Radio Luxembourg, yes, but not to be known on the job as his fecking dad. He's going to Hollywood to be a film star, another Clark Gable in the making and he's going to marry Marilyn Monroe and she's not even a Catholic. Imagine her being your sister-in-law. I think if he keeps on like this he'll get himself and us certified."

By this time Dad had gone back into the bedroom. He was banging the pillow, a habit he had after saying the rosary, which he did each night on his knees by his bed before he got into it, but the banging this night was more pugilistic than meditative.

"He didn't say what time he'd be in," he said, as he thumped away on the pillow. He was trying to make an egg-shaped hollow from the feathers in the shape of his skull to rest his head in for the coming night.

Then there was a knocking at the door.

"That'll be him now Sean," the old rascal said gleefully as if this was curtain-call time for a play at the Abbey. The drama was about to commence.

"Open the door, son," Dad said.

I opened the door to Val and warned him that the devil was in Dad in spite of five decades of the rosary and a final act of contrition.

"Ah feck him," Val said, "I fancy a burn-up."

"Where have you been till this hour?" Dad shouted from the bedroom as Val made his way down the short corridor. "I've got to be up for Mass in the morning."

Val was a bit jarred and unsteady on his feet as he stood at the bedroom door. "I'm not stopping you from your beauty sleep, I asked you for a key."

Dad began to bang the pillow again.

"You'd better watch how you talk to me mister. Now go to bed."

"Bed," Val exclaimed, "it's barely past midnight. I thought we could have a hand."

"Val," I whispered as I stood behind him, "you know there's nothing he hates more than cards."

"I won't tell you again," Dad said.

Dad fussed over the things on the little makeshift of a table he had beside the bed, not knowing what to say or do.

He blessed himself with some holy water he had got from a fellow in a pub who said that it was the genuine article from Knock. Dad had a woeful fear that once he nodded off, he would never see another morning. So each night he was kitted out with blessed medals, holy water and rosary beads ready to meet his maker.

As Val took his jacket off his mood turned sour, for he probably felt trapped and defeated and denied of having a good time or at least of having a few hands as was the custom in Dublin. Mam loved her game of cards above anything else. So he began talking, more to himself than either of us. "You old b*** you needn't think that you are ruining my life just because you're nearly in the grave it doesn't say that I have to climb in there after you."

"Val," I said, "this isn't going to get you anywhere."

Dad sat up in the bed supporting himself with his arms.

"So that's the way you've been told to talk to your father."

"Ah go and talk to your hole," Val said, turning his back on Dad.

"That's fine respect, I must say, fine respect."

Dad believed that while you were here in this world you should respect your biological father as if he was God the Father's direct representative here on earth. Dad expected blind obedience.

But Val came from a matriarchal household, which did not subject itself to male dominance either within the house or outside of it.

Little respect for father figures here on earth or in heaven was in evidence. Probably the heavenly link was made through Mary and the female saints and of course baby Jesus whom many believed hadn't been all that well treated by his own father anyway.

The general consensus of opinion among a lot of old ones in Dublin was that God the Father wasn't much of a parent to send his only son travelling all over the Middle East, always a volatile area, but then it had the Romans as well as the locals hanging around the corners with stones in their hands and pockets, at the ready to throw.

His Father had said that he had done all he could to keep things on an even keel and now frankly he was prepared to close the whole works down if things didn't improve on earth. So Jesus got on his bike and ended up with Mary and Joseph where he caused a lot of ripples and eventually turned things upside down. But he had to pay a humiliating price, which the old ones in Dublin thought was too big a price for a Father to ask of his son.

It was no wonder that sparks were bound to fly in Liverpool. I was embarrassed by all the heavy stuff, but Val, being older than me, was not as naive. He called a spade a spade, but like my mam, all I wanted to do was to keep the peace. Time and time again, she had been accused of not standing up to him, of allowing him to walk all over her. How many times had I heard it said that if you give him an inch he'd take a mile, but Val had no intention of giving him a quarter of an inch, particularly because of the way he had seen Mam treated.

Dad began to bang the pillow again.

"I'll tell you it's lucky I'm in bed or I'd soon show you how to have respect."

"Respect? What respect? You went off and left us all in Dublin."

Here I felt guilty, embarrassed and ashamed as at the time I was glad to leave. It wasn't till years later that I realised that I was set up to leave as Dad wouldn't leave on his own and Mam's health was being affected. I was the sacrificial lamb but like many children I spent a lot of my life blaming myself for my parents splitting up.

Val had a version and I had a version of what went on between our parents but who could say which of them was true.

As father and son, Val and Dad communicated their love for each other through anger, which wasn't doing my nerves any good.

I said, "Please Dad, don't say any more. What's the use?"

Dad tried to gang up with me by saying, "Sean and myself have got to be up in the morning for Mass so if you don't mind would you kindly shut your big mouth and get into bed?"

I was adamant about not taking sides. All I wanted was to make sure that there wasn't a row, which might end up in a fight.

But Val continued, "You forget I'm sleeping on the floor."

Dad sat up and said, "Where's your wages?"

By now Val was taking his trousers down.

"That's my business," he said.

"I suppose you've been doing the big fella in the clubs tonight buying everyone drinks."

"There's the money you old skinflint," Val said, as he flung the wage packet at Dad. It landed on the table where the Knock water stood beside other remedies that catered for coughs, chest pains, arse aches etc etc.

Dad grabbed the packet.

"That's better," he said.

Sitting up in bed like Queen Victoria or Florence Nightingale, who were both fond of the bed, he took the crisp notes out of the already opened pay packet. "Now there's three pounds for your keep."

"What keep?" Val shouted. "You should be paying me to stay here."

Dad took more money out of the packet.

"And then you'd better send home something to your mother. So we'll say another three pounds for her, then if I put three pounds in the Post Office for you, that makes nine pounds altogether. If I take two pounds to hold onto in case of a rainy day, that'll make eleven. So there's a pound for you and there's the odd change, four and two pence for the plate in the morning."

Chapter 21

Running gave me a freedom to express something in myself that I was searching for. When I ran alone I was tapping into another person inside of me who admired what I was doing.

By running, I could get away from the cynicism and failure that was manufactured in the classroom. There seemed to be contempt for the apparent naivety of any individual who was not prepared to surrender to the world of work or the pursuit of a career. Perhaps most of the lads did not realise until much later what the system did to them and how they sold themselves out. When I was out running on the rugby pitches, I was running as a free agent, I was running from within so my efforts were not directed in achieving specific goals like winning races or medals.

I was alone and I was experiencing a purity of detachment from the contamination that I felt existed within the school and among my fellow students and teachers.

Running gave me the freedom to get away from all of them and to explore something different. I felt that if what existed within the school was all the world had to offer, I did not wish to have anything to do with it.

So at an early stage, I realised that I was intrinsically motivated and rewarded. At the time I didn't know what intrinsic or extrinsic meant. I couldn't even spell the words but I did know that when I had a session of free running on my own, I was being released from the chaos of the world that they were browbeating me to enter.

Now I realise that my running was a way of escaping from myself and my own problems. I had to create another reality otherwise I would have perished within the system that as time went on I was less able to face. I was not ready to face up to the real things that matter in life, which deal with where we come from and where we are going and what in the name of God are we doing here in the first place.

That's why I probably liked Dan Dare. He was not bogged down by the mundane things of everyday life.

I used to listen to Dan Dare, pilot of the future, on Radio Luxembourg 208 metres medium wave. This particular evening I had to miss him because I had been selected by the school to run at an evening meeting at the Liverpool University Sports Grounds. It was a great sacrifice for me to miss Dan Dare. That was my fifteen minutes of listening time when I could identify with Dan Dare and believe that he would surely identify with me. I didn't tell anyone at school about missing Dan Dare in case they would think me too much of a baby.

I required suitable narrative to feed me as much as I needed food on my plate every day.

The previous evening Dan had got himself in a tight corner and the fifteen minutes ended with Dan shouting, "Hang on chaps, this could be a touch uncomfortable."

Naturally, it was important for me to know how he got out of this scrape but I also realised that he couldn't go on escaping for ever and that one day when he finally got his chips, it would be a night that I hadn't tuned in.

Long had dangled a carrot in front of me by saying that the bloke who won last year's Liverpool Schools' half-mile championships had got his photo in the *Liverpool Evening Echo*.

I would be running against lads a year older than me, who had run faster times than me. Some of them already had O levels and had their eyes set on getting a place at Liverpool University and having those grounds as their permanent training area.

I had to win and get my photo in the paper.

To be in the papers and on the radio, this was the thing haunting many people like me who could see the stars but didn't know how to achieve them.

Becoming humdrum was my greatest fear. What a shame it would be to go through life and not leave your mark on the world.

To be in the media seemed easy enough as Radio Luxembourg blasted out at me each evening. I had done more interviews on the mike with my empty sterilised milk bottle than Pete Murray the Radio Luxembourg disc jockey had had hot dinners.

What I would have given to be in a skiffle group like Lonnie Donegan, to lug my guitar on my back or my washboard about and be popular with everyone. Then I would have been able to put my fingers up at the whole establishment, but I was hopeless at music.

I felt honoured as I changed in the university dressing rooms, even though I had butterflies in my stomach. I realised that in order to win, I would have to make a tremendous leap forward. Up to now I had come third in each of my big races.

I was third in the trials at Fazakerley. I was third in the Lancashire Schools boys' championships at the White City in Manchester. I was third in a half mile at Pilkington's Glassworks in St Helens. Was I always going to be third? I didn't want to be in category 'C' all my life.

Some people went through life always coming second or third. I think that in the end they didn't want the responsibility of winning. Being second or third, you were still a member of the 'failed', comfortably part of what would inevitably be the majority. If you were a winner, you were a different kettle of fish. You were set apart and treated differently from the rest of them. I realised I was only holding onto my position because Hughes was still injured. Everyone thought even if they didn't say it that I was really Hughes' understudy. A second-class merchant not long landed on the Liverpool shore.

When we went to meetings, Hughes and Long always came to watch but it was always "how are you doing Hughes? How is the injury?"

There I was flogging my guts out but no one asked me how I felt. As far as they were concerned I was just a stopgap for Hughes. Even when I sounded Long out, looking for a bit of praise, he said that in his opinion once Hughes recovered, he would wipe the floor with everyone. He even said that he was sorry that Hughes was injured because he couldn't see him being beaten in any of the races I had been in. That was rubbing salt in the wound but I couldn't say anything. I just had to take it on the chin. It made me even more determined to show the bastards.

At the Liverpool University sports ground I lined up alongside competitors from eight different schools who had entered two runners in each event. So I stood at the start as fifteen other lads including myself waited for the gun. This was an evening meeting, which began at six. There wasn't sufficient time to run heats so they bundled all of us into one final.

On this luscious four-forty-yards grass track, my brother Val took a photo of me at the start on Dad's box camera. There was a bloke standing beside me, Williams was his name, who looked very embarrassed. He must have been six foot three if he was a day old. He was the type of lad us shorter kids would ask if it were snowing up there and then run a mile in case he got hold of you. And there I was, a little mucky round-shouldered kid of five foot three inches wearing my yellow vest and black shorts, neither of which had ever been to the half-crown bag wash.

Dad came along just before the race in his work clothes. He had just come off the building site after boasting to the blokes that he was shovelling sand into the concrete with that after work he was going to see his son running at the Liverpool University sports ground.

He gave his distinctive whistle and I waved back to him from the starting line.

I felt embarrassed because in his green faded gaberdine coat done up with a belt from a navy one and an old battered green cap on his head, he stood out from the other parents.

Dad had safety-pinned the lapels of his gaberdine coat together so as to cover his dirty collar and shirt. But in case the pins gave way, he stood with the palm of his left hand underneath his chin with the right hand free as if he was about to give his blessing to all of the swanky swaggering posh people who stood around him.

The race is memorable to me for the tremendous pain I felt in my legs. Earlier in the afternoon in the Summer House, when running the race over in my mind a thousand times and dreaming of victory, I had plastered my legs with Vaseline. For some unknown reason I believed that Vaseline would make my legs more supple. I think I equated going on the running track with going into a boxing ring, where Vaseline was always used in abundance to protect the boxers from cuts.

I got around the first lap suffering excruciating pain in my legs. I can remember my brother Val in his dark black drape suit on the inside of the track on the back straight at the top bend urging me on. I got to the bell in about fifth position with the crowd along the finishing straight cheering us all like mad. On the bend into the back straight, the pain in my legs subsided for a while. I chased the four in front of me, urged on by my brother Val, who was running faster than any of us in spite of carrying pockets of loose change, matches, lighter and cigarettes.

I somehow got around the top bend but the pain in my legs was now almost unbearable. Up the long finishing straight cheered on by the crowd I dug deep into any reserves I could muster. The noise was horrendous. There must have been a thousand people on the finishing straight.

Somehow I passed those in front of me. I don't remember crossing the finishing line, all I can remember is collapsing into my brother's arms and listening to him repeat, "You've won kiddo, you've won."

"Do your lap of honour, you deserve it," he said, as he pulled me to my feet. I jogged towards the top bend and then I heard Dad's whistle. I waved to him and he proudly waved back his tired hand after having had a hard day on the concrete mixer.

I realised bitterly that many sacrifices had to be made by

others in order for me to run. But it was worth it all to give the navvy proudly standing there a couple of minutes' pleasure.

I was champion of Liverpool and the whole of Merseyside. I had run faster than anyone of my age had run before over the half mile.

I'll never forget that summer's evening, Val in his black drape suit as good as or better than any of the other school lads on the university grounds, puffing away like a chimney of the Brighton Pullman Express.

This was the first time that he had openly smoked in front of Dad. Now both of them were exchanging cigarettes because they were so proud of me. All of the pain and training was worth it. We were bonded together by our success.

Long and Hughes congratulated me but not with the love and sincerity that Val had displayed. They were looking at me, re-examining me, probably thinking that we had better watch out for this Paddy.

Chapter 22

Nineteen fifty-four was a great year in England and Ireland and a great one for me. It was the year when things began to fall into place. I was fourteen. Everest had been conquered, which I loved to watch on the newsreels. Fuchs had got to the Pole, Bannister had become the first man to run the four-minute mile and in Ireland, de Valera was succeeded by Costello as Taoiseach. There was an air of hope and optimism about. The film *On the Waterfront* had been released and I had won my first major race.

The boys admired the willpower and independence that I had shown by going out determinedly training using the facilities, which were there for all to use but no one else did.

Not that the authorities wanted them to be used outside their normal allocated times; using the training facilities during the lunch break was deviating from the set pattern of the day.

There was a time and place for everything otherwise we would end up in a state of anarchy.

"Training through his lunch break, well that's the best I ever heard."

Kids like me were taking things by the scruff of the neck. We had caught the complacent authorities on the hop so we burrowed our way to freedom. I had got the boys' respect. The swots, the swanks and the swells all looked up to me but I was claimed by the deviant Beta class.

After taking the morning register, Mr Lane, our form teacher and the man who had examined me in Irish and was responsible for me getting into the school in the first place, called me up earnestly to his desk as if he was going to give me the strap.

All corporal punishment recommended by the lay subject teachers was given out by Mr Lane. The Christian Brothers carried their own straps and they could dish out beatings ad hoc there and then on the spot depending upon the state of their mood or liver.

Even at sea there was a book kept of the punishment given to sailors but not among those card-carrying Christians. As I approached Mr Lane's desk I thought that I was in for a dose of the strap. There was a hush in the class as none of the lads except bad breath Harvey and the Big Fella liked to see anyone get the strap. But I didn't get the strap.

Mr Lane could be a fiery Irishman and fly off the handle at the least provocation. Then at other times he was as gentle and kind as a saint you might meet out walking on the hills of Wicklow where St Kevin spent the best part of his days.

Mr Lane wanted to know in detail about how I had become Liverpool School Boys' half-mile champion.

I stood there nervously at his desk trying to make the run interesting telling the story of the race. I couldn't get into the intimate details that I had done with Dad, playing the race over to him a hundred times the previous night and him getting more excited each time as I told him the story.

But then Dad, to add a tinge of pepper to the race, would suggest some laws of probability by saying if this one had done that or if he hadn't gone off so fast then it could have all been a horse of a different colour. "But it wasn't Dad. You've got to admit that the best man won on the night." "I wouldn't say that. If that race was run a dozen times, I could see a different winner emerging each time. It was a bit of a fluke," he'd say.

It was really great the two of us sitting around in the chaos of the Summer House with something exciting and promising to talk about.

The running was an entity apart from the two of us, which could be taken out when things in other areas were going wrong.

The race would be run over again and future races would be planned and they would be run and won as we sat around the table even though they were still more than five or six months away.

"You are a credit to us all," our form teacher said as the boys passed my medal around the class.

When it came to the Big Fella's turn to look at the medal, he glanced at it and then sniffed, trying to get a cheap joke, but Wezzo, whom no one went up against in the class or in the school, took the medal off him and looked at it reverently. No cheap jokes were going to be made. Our Beta class was probably the worst class in the school and getting worse by the minute but it had produced the best runner in Liverpool over the half mile. They were all as proud as if they had won the medal themselves.

I suppose poor Mr Lane must have thought that he had one good apple in his barrel but how long would it be before it began to rot too?

Any teacher who came into the classroom that day was shown the medal and was given an account of the race by one of the lads. Even stuttering Horrie got his twopenny-worth in by saying that Doylie was going to be the new Roger Bannister. "Shut up," said another lad, "or I'll stand on your foot." This got a laugh as Horrie's old man was a chiropodist.

On the Friday evening, I made a special journey out of the Summer House to get the *Evening Echo*.

I was as nervous going up the road to the newsagents as I had been before the Liverpool Championships. I bought the *Echo* and I also bought a bar of Bournville, I would have bought a Fry's Cream as well but the money for the Fry's Cream had gone on the paper.

Outside of the shop I stood and counted up to ten before opening the paper but there was no photo. I searched through the paper but there was nothing. I couldn't believe it.

For a couple of days since the race I had gone around looking down on the world from dizzy heights. But now the sense of disappointment I felt was beyond belief. I had been so gullible as to believe Long, that's what really hurt. I wasn't a rebel at heart. All I wanted was to be accepted. I wasn't running for myself. I needed the photo to feel that I was somebody, so that I would be accepted and belong after all.

Chapter 23

No way was Val going to work for one pound four and two pence a week. He had had enough, he said as he packed his little case. "I'm getting away from the old fool. I'd murder the old bastard. He deserves murdering. The way he's treated Mammy and he's made a muck-up of all of our lives."

"Where are you going?"

"London, you half eejit, you can have a good time there. Why don't you come with me?" "I wish I were more like you Val," I said.

"Come on then kiddo, come with me. We'll buy new suits with the first week's wages and the pair of us will be great swanks beyond in the dance halls."

"No I can't do it. It wouldn't be fair to leave him on his own and I can't give up the things I'm trying to do here."

"There, I've left him a note so he doesn't have to send the law after me."

"I hope you haven't written anything nasty in it."

"Well I am off, if you're ever down Texas way look me up."

"I'll see you in Hollywood Val."

"That's a date. You can come to me and Marilyn's wedding."

"I'll walk out with you. I've got to see Stan about the sink."

I opened the door of the Summer House and went into the kitchen, where Dad looked around at me for a minute. On the table was a wage packet, a torn-open letter, probably from home demanding money, and the note from Val.

"What the hell do you think you're playing at? Why haven't you unpacked this stuff you little layabout? You think all I have to do is keep the likes of you."

Luckily Stan appeared in the doorway otherwise I'd have been in for a hiding.

"What's to do, Mr Doyle?" Stan said.

"This fellow was to clean the kip, I'm out all day and he won't lift a hand to help."

"I'm not your wife," I said quietly.

"What did you say?" Dad said, turning on me. "I'm not here to serve the likes of you. I keep you."

"In fine fashion in this dump."

Stan tried to intervene. "Now steady on."

"You are a bloody madman. It's no wonder Val has gone. Ruined your own life, now you want to ruin mine."

"What did you say?" Dad said as he rose from the table to hit me.

"Steady on Mr Doyle," Stan said, "he's only a lad."

"He's a little cur."

"Mr Doyle, he's only a kid. Come on, leave it, life's too short," said Stan.

He half-heartedly pulled Dad away from me.

"Now what's this you wanted to see me about?"

"The sink is blocked up."

Stan unblocked the sink from underneath.

"Put the kettle on," Dad said.

I didn't chance my luck so I obeyed.

"Pooh, this hums a bit," Stan said, as he unblocked the drainpipe. "Cor mate, has someone been piddling down here?"

I started to laugh and trying to suppress it made me want to laugh more. Stan left and now I was all alone in the world and at the mercy of this religious hypocrite and a cowardly old pig.

A couple of days before, during and after the race, I was his pride and joy but now he took one calculated look at me and slapped me contemptuously in the face. Slaps not punches. He saved the punches for my ribs and kidneys but he concentrated mostly on the guts, which sent me sprawling across the room. In his calculated madness he was sane enough to know where to administer the punishment in case I had the marks and evidence to use against him. He shouted about killing me for insulting him in front of a stranger. He hit me again and again, cursing my brother as well.

"Now get that lot straightened up," he said pointing at the room, where everything was in a terrible disorder with bags, clothes and all kinds of stuff all over the place.

He put his jacket on and went out, banging the door behind him.

I got up as best I could and ran some water in the sink. I bathed my face and had a look in the mirror. My face wasn't too bad, though my lip was swollen. I stared into the mirror at this unhappy face as the tears welled up in my eyes and wondered what was the purpose of it all.

I cleaned up as best I could, swearing to myself that I would get out, that I would get away from the mad bastard before he killed me, but where could I go?

I had no money and the friends I had at school had little or less than myself, but the worst thing about it was the shame I felt.

How could I go and tell anyone that my dad had beaten me up? I knew that I was making excuses for myself for not moving out. Inwardly I knew that I loved the old unpredictable fool. He could be decent and great fun at times but he was like the weather in his moods. I always had to be on the lookout, which shredded my nerves. He was angry because Val had walked out on him and Dad felt that Val had little or no respect for him. If you respected Dad, you were supposed to stay there to be kicked about whenever he was in a bad mood. Dad had hit me this time because he wanted to give Val a good beating. He wouldn't raise his hand to Val even if he had still been there because he knew he'd get it back from him, and he would never have hit me either if Val had been around.

I could go back to Ireland but my mother was just as bad in her own way. She wheeled and dealed and she had to in order to survive. She had her own agenda and to hell with anyone else's. There on the table was a letter from home, which had further exacerbated the situation. A letter from my mother demanding money at once otherwise she was threatening to take him to court. I didn't mind Mam writing the letters to get it out of her system but I only wished that she never posted them. It's no wonder he flew up in the air after doing a whole day of back-breaking shovelling and then coming home to the Summer House with nothing in it but a mess and unpacked suitcases and having to face the fact that the apple of his eye had walked out on him.

I reasoned with myself that if I wanted to get out, that if I really wanted to get away, there was only one thing to do and that would be to take the first step, which would always be the hardest.

Take the bull by the horns, make a clean break, pack a few things now and travel light. It would be tough at first but eventually I'd get on my feet. I didn't have any fear of falling on my face. I thought that I had done that already.

Using a rational decision process upon my convoluted family set-up did not seem the answer.

And then there was the English Schools' championships next year. I desperately wanted to qualify after the hours of hard training I was doing. Why should I sacrifice all that?

Then there were my exams. I could only take them if I was still at school, not that I had much chance of passing them.

Long had got a handful of O levels by getting a doctor's certificate so why not me? But who could trust what Long said? Val didn't like him. He thought him a snob and said that I was gullible to expect anything from any of them. But where would I go? Everyone headed for the smoke and London but where would I get a place to live let alone a job.

Then there was Dad. He'd kill me if I left. He'd probably come after me and swear blind that I should be put in care because there was nothing he could do with me.

Or I might end up in the missing column of the *News of the World*. I'd hate to give the Big Fella and bad breath Harvey, who were avid readers, the satisfaction of being in that paper other than on Joe Blink's sports page. No, viewing the whole situation, I decided that the best thing to do was to grin and bear it and ride it out. Hold on in, keep quiet and be patient. Rome wasn't built in a day, as the Paddy says, to which his colleague replies, "I don't know, I wasn't on that job."

If I wished to succeed I would have to be quietly determined and persistent to get where I wanted. I was learning that I had to work on long-term goals and be prepared to work for months and months, even years, without getting any rewards.

Because of this attitude I was moving away from my father and most of my schoolmates, who were living on short-term rewards. They were all back and belly and they needed instant satisfaction. A new outfit to wear today, a full belly and what did the morrow matter? But you never really developed that way. You would never dig deeply enough to escape from the way they had moulded you. Zatopek, in his book, *The Marathon Victor*, said that it was necessary and possible to change yourself in order to fulfil your potential. So I continued to try to tidy the place up. I didn't know what time Dad would be back but I had got used to living in a waiting vacuum for him and for some alternative form of life. I made up the bed for myself and in between the blankets, I began to get warm and feel comfortable. I was tired after being beaten up and a hard day's training. All the other old nonsense in school could take it out of you as well.

I lay in the dark and listened to the usual sounds, which were familiar at this hour. Radio Luxembourg was blaring away from the house. The couple were rowing as usual with the baby bawling in the background. I listened hard as if I were a priest behind the curtain in the darkened confessional. It was comforting to know that other people were having trouble like myself. Then I heard him coming in and he was whistling. He always whistled when he was in a bad temper so I moved to the edge of the bed, right up close to the wall, and pretended to be asleep. In the morning I was awakened by the birds in the garden and the light streaming through the French doors. I could hear him whistling in the kitchen and then I heard him banging the front door. He must have woken up half the neighbourhood with the force he put into the banging. I quickly got dressed.

In the kitchen, there was a note on the table. There was no dear or anything on this one. The first part of this note gave instructions. Don't forget to get some milk. We're low on sugar and bread and get yourself something for your dinner. There were two half crowns left by the scrap of paper.

There were notes of necessity and notes of dire business. How different were these correspondences from those of Evelyn Waugh to his son, Auberon, or Winston Churchill to his son, Randolph, or Kingsley Amis to his son, Martin. They didn't have to worry about getting a quarter of Lipton's loose tea because it was cheaper than the packet or a bottle of sterrie or a quarter of Spam.

There was a PS on the scrap of paper indicating that diplomatic relationships had been restored.

"I'll see you outside the Boaler at five thirty. The programme starts at five forty five. There are two main features so there's bound to be a lot of people so you'd better get there early to get a place in the queue."

Dad didn't like going to the pictures on his own and he didn't fancy the whole of the night sitting in the Summer House looking at me and the four walls.

Good, I thought, he's bound to be in a good mood after going to the pictures. That was Dad all over. There'd be nothing said about the beating-up, not until the next flare-up when the whole past history of misdemeanours would be thrown up again.

Now he'd probably buy me an Orange Maid, the ice cold drink on a stick, and we'd get fish and chips on the way home and things would be back to normal again for a while. I might as well make the best of it. Make hay while the sun shines as the man said.

Chapter 24

During the track season, which ran from May to the middle of September, we used Crawfords' grounds where our running club had the use of the playing fields.

In this company, jobs were passed down from generation to generation, so as far as Dad was concerned, you'd have to be a proper suck-hole to work for such an outfit.

When Dad first arrived in Liverpool, he had tried to get a job in a similar company but after being turned down, he consoled himself by calling them a lot of arse-licking crawlers spending their lives working for next to nothing and tipping their caps to their betters.

Once a year, the Crawfords employees were taken out to the

playing fields for their annual sports day by the coachload. I suppose it was all to do with a healthy workforce.

Sefton Harriers, the running club that I belonged to, had somehow got the use of changing rooms in the basement. In the winter we'd do a run on the roads from the clubhouse of a Wednesday evening. In the summer we'd have use of the grounds where a grass track was laid out for the Crawfords employees. After training, we'd have a cup of tea from the canteen and biscuits by the wagonload. You could get as many as eight water biscuits but alas no cheese, or four Rich Tea for a penny. Opposite the canteen was the television room. This was the second television set I'd ever seen, the first being in Mrs Woods' when I watched the Coronation.

Here I saw Chataway beat the Russian Vladimir Kuts in 1954 at the White City in a new world record for the three miles. The race was on live and the room was packed as at this time very few people had televisions in their homes.

I can still hear the older men shouting, "Come on Chris, come on boy," as if Chataway had been their own brother. The red-haired Briton raced over the last of the twelve laps, stride for stride, against the barrel-chested Russian up the long White City straight.

At this time there was tremendous anti-Russian feeling in the country because the Cold War was at its height and the media got all the political change out of Chataway's victory that it could.

I suppose it was better for them to be fighting each other on the running track than throwing atomic bombs at each other but still it amazed me to see such patriotic fervour. Most of the men in the running club had been in the services during the war or had done National Service. I realised that I was the product of a far different culture. I had never had any contact with military institutions.

After the race was over, I went out with the pack into the night air feeling elated and ran and ran myself into the ground through the dark roads, imagining that I was Chataway passing Kuts. I identified with him easily because I was a redhead as well.

When I came back after my run, I quickly changed. I didn't have a shower because the race on the box had made me late and I knew that Dad would be anxiously waiting for me at home, so I said quick goodbyes to the blokes who were casually changing, still talking about the race that they had seen, and without being under the constant pressure that I seemed to be.

I jog-trotted from the club up the lane to the main road, turning left at the top towards Hall Green, feeling like a hunted animal, my heart in my mouth because I had never been this late before.

At Hall Green, I waited ages for the bus, getting myself into a terrible anxious state. It made it seem worse to see people roaming around the place without a care in the world, not knowing what I was going through.

Eventually the bus came along but by then I had resigned myself to getting a hiding.

As I went through the back garage to the Summer House, I began to take in deep breaths. Inside the side door to the garden, I could hear and see people in the house going happily about their business.

There was a light in the kitchen, which meant that he was in, so I resigned myself to the fact that I had to face the music.

As I entered the corridor, Dad shouted from the kitchen, "Did you hear about the race?"

"That's why I'm late, I watched it on television."

"Oh don't worry about that, I heard it on the radio. Isn't it great to think that one day you could be running on that same track. That would be something to tell them back in Ireland. Take him with you," he said, referring to me, "and make a tramp out of him as you have done to yourself. They were the last parting words your mother said as we were getting ready to go to the North Wall for the boat to take us to England. But we'll see now who is the tramp," Dad said, smacking his lips.

In fact, Mam never said that when we were parting. These words were said much earlier by Mam's father when Dad had first taken me away from the family. We were living in Ballindine then in Mayo. They had made an impact on Dad and he now believed it was Mam that had said them.

I was used like a football between my two parents. Whenever they separated, I was always the one taken with him. Sometimes I felt like a hostage held by a very unpredictable captor.

Mam had been left to struggle in the shop in Dublin and to take in lodgers to make ends meet. Bringing up the other four children was no easy matter for her.

My brothers and sisters probably thought I was the spoiled one that I was getting everything while they were getting nothing. Little did they know that I was having as hard a time as them in Liverpool. No one was giving me any handouts, either in school or on the running track or in the Summer House. The trouble with living with my dad was that I was the only one to get the blunt of his wrath and anger. If I had been in the rough and tumble of a family I could have hidden but being the only one around, I was continually in the firing line.

Dad was so moody that I never knew where I was with him. One minute he could be the kindest man in the world. He couldn't do enough for you. He'd be living in my pocket and the next he could flare up and beat the daylights out of me for the most innocuous of reasons.

Coming home was always a worry. I could be punched for

being five minutes late and another time I could be hours late and nothing would be said.

The unpredictability of the man did not make for a secure or happy life or engender further happy relationships, as the damage done by him in those formative years was beyond repair.

He could be very generous but I felt that I was earning everything he gave me, that there was a price tag on every scrap of food on my plate.

I don't think he had heard of Pavlov but he was a real behaviourist. The trouble was that I wasn't a dog but that didn't make him less of a control freak.

I had to be careful to let him know that I always agreed with him, for to disagree with him was tantamount to a total breakdown of the relationship, that is if one could call it a relationship.

He had no idea of a child's needs or requirements. A child to him was like a little doll that could be beaten, bullied or loved on any whim that took his fancy but the doll had to forget any former treatment when it suited him. I suppose some parents' behaviour towards their children reverts to the way that they were treated themselves as children.

There used to be a radio programme on at the time with the catchphrase 'the answer lies in the soil', which always got a laugh, but I think the answer lies with the grandparents.

Get to know them, research them out, and you'll know what to expect from your own parents.

My grandfather on my father's side was a dictatorial type with short red hair and a shorter temper. He ruled his children with his fists until the day came when he was no longer strong enough or fit enough to dominate his sons when one of them stood up to him and from then on, the five foot three, well set up bully was sat in the corner.

203

Would that be the road I would be forced to travel down, I wondered, as I tried to relax after getting myself in such a state about being in late.

The next day on top of the bus on the way to school, Chataway's picture was all over the front page of the *Daily Express*. I felt one with Chataway as I went to train on my own that lunchtime. At last an athlete and athletics was more popular than soccer or any other sport. My dream was that perhaps one day I would take Chataway's place.

Chapter 25

I got off the bus at the bottom of Stanhope Street in Chinatown by the underground toilets. We had moved from the Summer House in Mr Hardy's garden. Our landlord would not fix the galvanised roof. It had begun to let in with the first rainstorms after the freak baking-hot summer of 1955.

I went up the steep steps, enclosed by railings on both sides. I was surprised that these railings had not been melted down for armaments during the war. The key to the front door was as big as a mouth organ. The Victorians believed in building everything big, including Liverpool Cathedral, under whose shadow I stood as I manipulated the key in the sturdy lock. I went in through the heavy black oak door but no matter how quietly I tried to close it, Bobby and Nellie always began barking. I tiptoed along the corridor by the landlady's dining room, past the main staircase to our room at the end of the passage.

I unlocked the door and once inside, immediately re-locked it, throwing both the keys on the unmade double bed. I placed a bottle of sterilised milk with a packet of firelighters on the crowded table alongside unwashed dishes and half-finished meals.

We used newspapers as our tablecloth, which might be changed every month or two during one of our 'spring cleans'. Invariably we had Irish newspapers. We bought them a day after their publication in Dublin, at the Liverpool Central Station paper kiosk. The Irish papers were brought by boat across the Irish Sea so if there was bad weather, Dad could be starved of news from home for two to three days. The newspaper seller at the Liverpool Central Station was a typical Liverpudlian piss taker.

One evening when Dad went to buy his *Irish Independent* after work, the newspaper bloke said in all seriousness that there was a terrible run on the papers that day as Bing Crosby had died. So Dad who wouldn't normally buy an *Evening Echo* purchased a copy. He searched through for news of Bing Crosby's death, to no avail. When he came home, still mystified, he asked me if I had heard about Bing.

"He's having you on Dad. They're always having everyone on in Liverpool. That's what Liverpudlians are, first and foremost, proper mickey takers."

I was fortunate enough to learn at an early age that if I didn't do it myself, it wouldn't be done. So as I was captain, cook and chief bottle washer on board, I took the electric lead from the back of the chair by the bed that acted as a bedside table. On it were the alarm clock, the ash tray, radio and electric lead that Dad had placed there in the morning after removing it from the ceiling holder so that he could insert a bulb in order to get some light to get ready for work.

I then put the lead in my left-hand trouser pocket and, standing on top of another chair, I took the bulb out of the light socket and put it into my right-hand trouser pocket. Then I inserted the lead into the ceiling socket, fearing all the time that I might lose my balance and fall off the chair, for I have never had any head for heights.

I turned on the switch by the door and gave the radio a couple of minutes to warm up. You either had light or music but it was impossible to have both at the one time during the autumnal months. I had invented my own disco with pop music blaring from the radio and me dancing madly in the dark. After a couple of minutes I tentatively tapped the plastic brown set, trying to get rid of all the interference and crackling. Then I held it up to my ear while I moved the dials around like a safe-cracker, hearing many foreign stations jabbering away.

Suddenly I got flashes of an optimistic self-assured BBC male weather forecaster, but knowing that this radio had a mind of its own, I left it to warm up a bit more while I attended to the ashes in the grate.

Then I tore up newspaper from the stacks that were at the side of the bed, twisted it tightly in knots in the centre, allowing the ends of the paper to remain loose so that they would light easily and take the flame into the hard core of the tightly knotted newspaper. Formerly, the fire had been a swine of a thing to light but by the holy of holies, I had discovered the greatest invention that God, man or the devil ever presented to Planet Earth and I don't mean the wheel or ice cream.

With a box of firelighters purchased for one shilling and three pence and a box of matches, you'd have the fire going in next to no time. Without them I would often have to spend hours after returning from school trying to light the wet and damp bundles of wood.

The corner shop sold wood, but it was always damp from the build-up of condensation in the shop. All the time I lived around there, the old woman who owned the shop never removed the shutters, thus starving the place of fresh air.

She had countless cats that pissed on the wood, so sometimes when I lit it, the room smelt like a tomcats' convention and then the object of the fire, which was to heat the room, was defeated as I would have to open the window to get rid of the smell. But the firelighters didn't come for nothing. I always ended up having to beg from Peter to pay Paul.

If I wanted to buy firelighters, I had to sacrifice my bar of Bournville or my Fry's Cream. Dad considered it girlish to use firelighters when there was wood about. He always had the fear of me turning into a bit of a sissy, so I had to hide the evidence.

Then I put my coat on and opened the *Irish Independent* to hold it up under the crowded mantelpiece where there were old letters from home in Mam's slanted handwriting demanding money. I held the paper in front of the fireplace to get a draw on the chimney and read the headline:

DAD WARNS IRISH SCHOOL BOARD

It amazes me that I never burned the house down when I tried to get the draught on the chimney. Many a time the paper caught fire, nearly setting alight all the junk on the mantelpiece.

Once I got the fire going, that was the housework done as far as I was concerned, and with a couple of coats or blankets at the bottom of the door to keep the draught out, I settled down with Radio Luxembourg and the Jack Jackson show.

If the room was really cold, I'd pull the wooden shutters closed on the window, but this was only done as a last resort as I was afraid I would find something lurking in the recesses. And when they were closed shut with the great big steel bar across them, I felt as if I was a prisoner in a cell, unable to see the stars in the heavens on a clear cold frosty night.

This window overlooked the yard, which backed onto the Chinese laundry. The chimney of the launderette gave out puffs of smoke just like you'd see at the Vatican when they announced the name of a new Pope. We had 'Habemus papam' as a daily event.

I opened the door to the kitchen area, where we had a gas cooker alongside the cold-water sink and a marble worktop.

Before people had fridges, this area was used as the larder. Food was stored on the cool marble top in gauze-covered wooden containers to ward off flies from festering the meats. On the left of the kitchen I opened another door, where steps lined with an iron hand railing led down to the yard where the lavatory was, sharing a wall with the launderette.

As darkness set in, we'd use a candle to light our way down the steps. Holding on to the iron railings while carrying a candle in the other hand, trying to keep it alight in spite of the howling wind that visited us uninvited from the Mersey, proved a pretty risky business. You could easily trip arse over bollocks, landing in a humiliated heap in the yard. I often thought that I saw things in the dark. I wouldn't say that I believed in ghosts but then again I wouldn't say that I didn't either. As long as they left me alone, I'd leave them alone for as far as I'm concerned, if they do exist, ghosts are just poor restless souls. There might have been a lot of them around where we lived, close to the Liverpool docks. Maybe poor fidgety haunted characters who couldn't rest walked through the dockland fog looking for a passage to some other port where they could settle their grievances and find peace after an eventful life.

I didn't think that these ghosts would do you any real harm, not like banshees, whose wail always brings death with it. These are a completely different kettle of fish with their lice-ridden heads and rotten teeth, ready to put the blink on you for the hell of it.

I've heard of them out in the country parts of Ireland, howling on dark nights trying to get their mitts on you. But ghosts, I think, are like a lot of people in so far as they're in the wrong place at the wrong time.

All the same, I didn't think that there was any point going down the steps upsetting any passing ghosts or straying banshees, so I followed my big brother's advice that he used to give me when I'd wake up during the night at home in Dublin. "Save it up till the morning kiddo," and that's what I did all the time we lived in Stanhope Street.

Our landlady was a frail little woman who had lost her husband Jim during the war, but she was convinced that he was still sailing the high seas as a merchant engineer and that he would be home any day.

So some mornings she got breakfast ready for his homecoming. "Jim's coming this morning," she would say to Bobby and Nellie. The two dogs would be sitting at the table in front of the finest cutlery and Delft you'd ever hope to see, all collected by Jim on his travels over the seven seas.

Dad had his eyes on the cutlery but alas the dogs had their eyes on Dad. The house felt eerie, it was like a disused film set. It had been full of life and energy at one time. Now that the film had been made and the cast dispersed, a strange aura hung over the once-beautiful china, furniture, carpets and curtains.

Our landlady, Mrs Coats had been left behind when the middle class moved out of the inner city after the war. Now the area had fallen into a state of disrepair and was full of immigrants such as us. Stanhope Street was in the middle of the Chinatown district of Liverpool.

Mrs Coats had lost all her family so Dad and I were now some of the last few whites to live in the street.

One of the big hits of the show *My Fair Lady*, which came out at the time, was 'On the Street Where You Live'. I kept quiet about where I lived at school and about the fact that my parents were separated. Lads would often take the mickey out of me asking what bus I was taking home because we had moved so often.

When I came out of school, I could be heading north, south, east or west, depending upon which way the wind was blowing, and the outcome of the last confrontation Dad had had with our current landlord. My lips were sealed about where we lived as they were about whether Mam was alive or dead, whether I had sisters or brothers and what my dad did for a living.

In my Jekyll and Hyde existence, neither occupant knew the merits or deficits of the other. Only when I would be able to bridge these two narratives would I find my own voice.

Living in Chinatown, I got a cosmopolitan outlook on life, unlike many of my contemporaries who lived in the leafy suburbs in fear that one day immigrants would come to live alongside of them and devalue their property. It certainly knocked any racism out of me when Dad took me to sit at the back of the local to watch the Westerns on the pub television. Unemployed West Indians watched avidly the conflicts between white American lawmen and whiskey-drinking Native Americans. They drank, laughed, cursed and excitedly jigged about as they witnessed the treatment meted out by the white man to those whose land they had stolen.

I could see that they were not really all that different from the men that I had seen back in the cattle market in Gilsen's pub in Dublin, except for the colour of their skin. I knew that the one thing they had in common with the men in Dublin and the Native Americans on the television screen was that they were all shackled together by their poverty and low expectations.

Mrs Coats knocked on the door and asked me to come along to see her husband Jim yet again. She said he had just arrived home from sea. This angered and frightened me. How was I expected to cope with this poor woman who could not accept the fact that her husband was dead? It's difficult enough to handle the finality of death even if one is imbued with some kind of religious faith. It amazes me how people with no belief in the afterlife can cope with the termination of a loved one.

Most people would have had a corpse to weep over, but poor Mrs Coats had nothing but a telegram telling her that her husband had been lost at sea. There seems to be a need in us to see the departed one and know where they are buried or cremated, for at least then we know that they are at peace and not wandering all over the place like Lee Marvin in the film *Paint Your Wagon*.

Mrs Coats had a photo of her husband Jim in full Merchant Navy regalia, taken in 1941 on the SS *Ulysses*, the year that James Joyce died. Bobby began to bark on seeing me. I felt helpless and frustrated because I could not reach into this woman's world, as indeed I couldn't communicate with many of those whom I came into contact with. I tried to excuse myself and went back to our room.

Why should it be, I thought, that this frail little woman, who probably had never done any harm to anyone in her life, should come to this. In her dress, apron, slippers and glasses, she was less

212

than six stone of confused suffering, but she raised her long arms and, spreading the web of her fingers across the air, she looked like a concert pianist from the Philharmonic Hall across the road in Hope Street. "Jim, Jim," she called out as I left, "he was here a minute ago."

Chapter 26

After twiddling with the dials for ages to get the radio cleared of all the static interference, I finally got through to Radio Luxembourg clearly. Dad came in complaining that he had been all over the place looking for work and that there was nothing out there but miserable, impoverished Liverpudlian faces. He threw *The Universe*, the weekly Catholic newspaper, in which I got many a write-up because of my running exploits, onto the bed and immediately changed the station from Radio Luxembourg to Radio Éireann. This made me see red after all the time I had spent trying to get the station and the reception just right.

I gave him one of my looks. My mam used to say, "If looks could kill, we'd all be on our way to the cemetery."

"There's no need looking like that," he said, "I want to hear what's going on in Ireland. And anyway it's my radio," he added as he twirled the dials. Typical, I thought, he's just like a kid. If he's not allowed to take all the free kicks, penalties and score all the goals, he takes his ball, puts it under his armpit and goes home.

I tried a different tactic as some lunatic rattled away in Irish on the radio to himself before the main news in English came on. "They've got St Therese of the Roses and Frankie Laine due to come on at any second on Luxembourg." These were Dad's favourites. I sang a bit of 'Rawhide', but all to no avail. "I'll listen to what I want," he said as he dug his heels in deeper.

My temper was getting the better of me and I just couldn't let it go. I wanted to have some rights and I knew that I risked a walloping by trying to demand them.

I was at bursting point with anger and I had nowhere to go but out the back and down the steps where I might bump into a ghost or two. Left with no alternative, I spoke my mind.

"What do you want the Irish news on for?" I asked, implying that only a half eejit would be interested in what was going on in such a backwater, when the latest and greatest record releases could be heard by just moving the dials. "It's always twenty-four hours behind the English news," I said, shaking my head at how ridiculous his behaviour was. "Yesterday in Parliament and last week in the Dáil," I sneered.

"You're getting very English, aren't you? Well, you can cut the ties with your own country but I never will. And I want to hear the news."

"I suppose that you can't help being old-fashioned and living in the past."

That did it. He turned on me.

"Who's old-fashioned? I'm as young as you any day, you fecking little guttersnipe."

On the radio they were saying that there would be a ground frost tonight in the east. I tried to make light of it all by saying, "Listen, Dad, there'll be a ground frost tonight. We'd better cover up the spuds."

"Why you little sneering brat," he said. I thought I was going to get it but I was saved by further interference on the radio.

"Fix that," Dad said.

"Oh I can't touch your radio, Father," I said.

"Fix the fecking thing," he shouted.

I took my time twiddling the dials until on came Frankie Laine singing 'Rawhide'.

"Damn and blast you, I want Radio Éireann," he shouted, pushing me away from the set. He began to twirl the dials but there was a terrible lot of interference.

"Perhaps there's something happening over there."

"Get the fecking station," he said, giving up with the dials.

I went back to twiddling them saying maybe the Micks have taken over the Post Office again and the radio station into the bargain.

"You're developing a very cheap low type of Scouse humour."

As I continued to move the dials, I said, "You brought me here Dad."

"Not to make you like them," he retorted.

As I got a fix on the radio, it blared out the Irish National Anthem. I stood to attention for the 'Soldier's Song' but I soon stopped fooling about as Dad bent over with pains in his belly.

"Light a candle, will yeh."

"It'll be like High Mass here if we light any more candles."

"I want to have a shite," Dad shouted.

"Why can't you wait until the morning like normal people?"

"I've never been normal and I've no intention of starting now," he said firmly.

I paused for a bit and sniffed. "I hope there's no one down there," I said tentatively.

"What do you mean? We're the only people in the house besides Mrs Coats and the Chinese opposite in the launderette."

"I have found chopsticks down there in the morning."

"Are you saying that they come across the barbed wire?" He paused. "Why don't you come down with me?"

"I'm not going to the lavatory with you Dad." It's bad enough having to sleep with you, I thought, coughing and farting all night.

"Well by Christ, the next place I live I'll have an inside lavatory."

"Welcome to the twentieth century. Right, which do you want, *News of the World, Mirror, Universe* or *Irish Independent*?"

"I've got respect for my arse."

"Right Monsieur, one *Irish Independent* opened at the death notices. One candle. One box of matches and God bless all who sail in her."

"If you hear me shout out, come down, and open that window so you can hear me."

"Don't worry Pater," I said, as I opened the window, "you won't go before your time. None of us ever do. Everything was preordained before we were even thought of. Now you are going down the steps tonight in the dark to do your business as part of the grand overall plan."

"I don't know what those latchicos with the white collars put into that head of yours above in that school, but they have a lot to answer for." Dad went out of the pantry door into the pitch-black night saying to leave the door open as well just in case. I watched him going down the steps with the *Irish Independent* under one arm while protecting the flame of the candle with the palm of his other hand. Then I shut the door to the main room and twirled over the dial to Radio Luxembourg, turning it up high. Standing by the open window, I mimed to Doris Day's 'By the Light of the Silvery Moon'.

Then it was as if all hell broke loose. It began with Dad shouting to throw him down the matches as the candle had gone out and me shouting back that he already had a box.

Dad roared. The noise started the dogs barking. Mrs Coats unlocked her basement back door and the dogs were out in the backyard barking madly at Dad, who could be heard shouting over the din, "Come here you bastards and I'll throttle the pair of yeh."

I stuck my head out of the window and shouted down, "Mrs Coats, Mrs Coats, it's my dad down there powdering his nose." Mrs Coats called, clapping her hands, "Bobby, Nellie, come here at once, you've made Mummy very cross." The barking subsided and I pulled the window down and turned the volume on the radio down as Dad came in, banging the pantry door.

"We might as well be out in the Middle East," Dad said, referring to the Suez conflict, which was raging in the press daily. "But I'll tell you one thing son, if I live till tomorrow, I'm going to get a bucket."

Chapter 27

D ad went to the Latin Mass as defined by the Council of Trent of 1545–1563 as often as possible.

Like a lot of the congregation, while Dad was at Mass he would recite his rosary in isolation from the priest and the rest of the assembly, on his knees with the crucified Christ dangling from his beads.

Dad would say the 'Our Fathers', 'Hail Marys' and 'Glory Bes', using a five- or seven-decade rosary depending upon how long the Mass was going to take. Like runners, so with priests, there are fast and slow celebrants of Mass. Padre Pio, the Capuchin friar, took hours to say Mass, but miraculously it seemed no longer than half an hour to those present.

In St Patrick's, the priest would say the Mass in Latin with a little help from the altar boy, who would make the responses in the language of Ancient Rome on behalf of the congregation.

There was little or no contact between the priest and the congregation but for the distribution of Communion, blessings and the '*Ite, missa est*' at the end. I found going to Mass a very harrowing experience. When it came down to the serious business of trying to get to heaven, it was as if everyone, including the priest, was intent on looking after number one.

There was little sense of community or encouragement within the renovated building, which had once been a music hall.

Dad didn't seem to give a hoot as long as he got into heaven himself. In fact, he wouldn't have been slow in making out a list of those he considered didn't deserve to be there. The priest stood with his back to us. I thought he was praying for his own soul and probably for a good silver collection, trying not to get too irritated by the relentless coughing from the congregation. The Liverpool smog and the damp air coming in from the Mersey, along with the dismal tenements they had to live in as they waited on a place from the council, meant that bronchial troubles were the norm.

Dad liked to receive Communion as often as possible for by receiving it, he felt that he was storing up bags of grace for himself that would guarantee him a much better spot in the next life.

Dad was convinced that heaven was no different from earth apart from the weather. It would be a class-ridden region with private and council property. One had to have the required number of points through the acquisition of grace in order to guarantee an excellent seat at the captain's table and a good view of the floor show.

Dad's faith was his greatest consolation in a world where he often felt crushed. Companions such as baby Jesus, Christ on the Cross, God the Father, St Jude and any new up-and-coming saint recommended by the old ones were pitting their wits against the world on his behalf like trade union representatives. So was it any wonder that when he came out of church, he squared up his shoulders and strode off with the Doyle swagger? Confession was always important to Dad. He believed in having a clean slate and he boasted to me of the small penances he got in Confession, putting himself in a good light.

Dad's attitude to Confession was a bit like the former Conservative Prime Minister's approach to Question Time in the House of Commons. When asked how much should be divulged in a reply, he said that one should never reveal anything that is not already known. To be fair to Dad, he had inside knowledge of the clergy and the matter-of-fact workings of the church. He had an older sister who was a nun in a French teaching order in Bromley, Kent. He was on great terms with her and he considered she was the equal, if not the better, of any priest or nun alive. Sarah, his sister, known as Mother Patrice in her order, had come from a modest village in the west of Ireland to be a language teacher in a posh French order. He felt well equipped to be on talking terms, if not on first-name terms, with any clergy he came across.

Dad's sister had told him that a lot of them in the convent were no better than the laity in so far as all they wanted was a cushy life. Many of them joined up because they got the best to eat and drink with a roof over their head, no bills or mortgages and hardly anything to do. It's no wonder that Dad never had a hierarchical approach to the clergy. He considered that there were many roads to heaven, which were not automatically controlled by them. He was a man ahead of his time in seeing the laity on a par with the clergy.

Dad was in another way unlike many of the congregation who went to Confession, as he enjoyed having long chats with the homesick priest. He could appreciate that the priest was as exiled as himself and perhaps instead of ministering, he would have been happier labouring. I thought at times that if the positions between the priest and Dad were reversed, both parties would have been much happier.

The parish priest was Father O'Dwyer, a heavyset, red-faced Tipperary man who was a decent enough old stick. He would have Dad in the confessional for an hour or so, talking about how he was missing the hard rewarding work of saving the hay back home in Ireland. He'd reminisce about when he was a boy on the land or would discuss with Dad whether Dev would ever get in again or did he think that Tipperary had any chance of making the hurling final this year.

A man called Durkin had a shop right opposite St Patrick's Church. He used to go on drinking bouts. These 'benders' could last for days on end. Then he'd go off it just as suddenly as he had gone on it. Father O'Dwyer asked Paddy Durkin one day why he didn't come across the road to Mass. "I'll go, Father," said Durkin, "if you'll come over and mind the shop for me!"

Father O'Dwyer went off laughing, knowing full well that Paddy Durkin was setting him an impossible task; he was the only priest in this poor parish of St Patrick's in Chinatown.

Although Dad attended Confession, Mass and Communion as often as possible, I don't think that the piety he exhibited in St Patrick's ever seeped into his daily actions.

He never considered that leaving my mam, sisters and brothers to fend for themselves in Dublin might be wrong. I suppose that in his mind the circumstances justified his actions and as far as he was concerned, it was always someone else's fault.

He believed that we were in a different category from the married or singles who came to this country. We were unusual at that time in being a single father living with his son.

I think that the rest of the family back in Dublin hoped that if Dad had a dose of England, it would cure him of all his old nonsense. One day he would return with his tail between his legs. But the further along the road Dad went, the more determined he became to show them in Ireland that he could survive and make good under the English masters. When he got miserable depressing letters from Mam, he would gloat over the fact that she was suffering, not allowing any of the circumstances to penetrate upon his being.

The letters made me so miserable and forlorn that at times, I wanted to hide them from him and stop any further communication between them, because they were both intent upon hurting each other.

Mam had written in letter after letter the turmoil she was going through, both spiritually and physically. She had stopped attending Mass or receiving the sacraments, which according to the laws of the church meant that she was living in a state of mortal sin. Unlike Dad, she considered it hypocritical to attend the sacrifice of the Mass with so much hurt and hate in her mind, heart and soul.

It seemed like water off a duck's back to Dad. He appeared to be able to divorce the actions of his everyday life from what was expected from him by the Church with total equanimity.

Dad's sister, the nun, played an extremely influential role. She always took his side. As she was an inner member of the Church, she had probably discussed the situation with Dad and assured him from her elitist standpoint that he should go on attending Mass and receiving the sacraments, as none of the break-up of the marriage could possibly be her little brother's fault. Fuelled by his sister, Dad would argue that those buckos with the white collars could not possibly know what a married man had to put up with. The philosophical pundits at the Pier Head invariably attacked the Church as regards her wealth. This always put me in a precarious position because I was unable to defend the Church's policies on collecting money.

The bishops were always squeezing the parish priests for more money to send off to Rome, where they were trying to make a name for themselves with the cardinals in the hope that one day they would land a red hat themselves. A good fundraiser in any organisation will generally rise quickly to the top. But the likes of Father O'Dwyer didn't have a lot. These men lived in genteel poverty in their parishes and saw nothing of the great treasures that were being continuously built up in the Vatican.

I suppose it could be said that Dad had once harboured the seeds of a vocation. He often said that when Mam died, he intended to enter a monastery. When Mam, who was in continuous bad health, was told this, she said "God help the old bastard, he might go before me, but I can't see myself entering a convent." She had laughed as she took another drag from her Gold Flake cigarette.

Dad despised those that he saw at church wearing the Pioneer pin, denoting a pledge of total abstinence.

"Look at the bastards," he'd shout, "they're dying of thirst."

Dad's attitude to the Church was bound up with politics, nationalism and, strangely, the fight to preserve Ireland's pagan past. He celebrated the old traditions by playing the pre-Christian music of the Druids on the uilleann pipes.

Dad was born in 1908, the year of the Irish Universities Act, which saw the foundation of both the National University of Ireland and Queen's University, Belfast.

Between the time of my father's birth and his adolescence, the first flight across the English Channel took place. Ford's Model T came off the production line. The *Titanic* sank. Archduke Franz Ferdinand was assassinated at Sarajevo, leading to the outbreak of the First World War. There was gun-running in Howth and the Easter Rising took place in 1916, leading to the Anglo-Irish war, which lasted until 1921.

The Black and Tans were sent to Ireland and soon after that a bunch of IRA members came to Dad's village in the west of Ireland, looking for his older brother John, who immediately fled to America, never to return again. Where he got the fare is still a mystery.

In Mountjoy Gaol, Dublin, the bishops in league with the government would not allow the clergy to administer the last rites to the condemned revolutionary leaders. It was not until a Capuchin friar from St Matthew's in Church Street took it upon himself to go against the bishop and the government that the men got the last rites. By the time Dad was seventeen, he had been steeped in nationalism.

He followed his brother to America, to the land of the free, and celebrated his eighteenth birthday in Chicago, finding for the next six years that there was nothing for nothing in the land of the dollar.

I don't know where he got the fare to go to the States in 1926, perhaps his brother John had sent him a ticket?

I was getting mixed messages from my parents, church and school all the time. I became totally disillusioned with the inconsistencies that I saw around me. Sunday became a day of unhappiness, full of sulking and hate for me. I had no alternative but to get up and attend Mass with him like a devoted son, without so much as a drink of water inside either of our stomachs, as fasting was obligatory before receiving Communion in those days.

On this particular Sunday, I was in a more rebellious mood than usual and becoming more uncharitable than ever. I did not want to queue up behind these doleful people who had pathetically accepted their lot and were hoping for a better life in heaven. My main concern was whether I would win my next race.

As the bell went for Communion, Dad asked me if I was receiving, to which I replied that I wasn't feeling too well. I was furious and nauseated by the whole loathsome situation. I felt the whole service was pointed towards a celebration of death, when I was fighting hard in my youthful exuberance for the celebration of life.

Nothing else was said about me not receiving until I had finished a huge fry-up of a breakfast back in our room in Stanhope Street.

"Well I'm glad you have recovered your health," he said as he removed the empty plate.

"You weren't well enough to receive the body and blood of Christ but you ate a hearty breakfast."

After that, any other time I went with him to Mass, I went up and received and crossed my fingers asking God's forgiveness for I meant to imply no disrespect but what could I do? I had to keep the peace at home and stave off the Lord's wrath for the last day when the bugles are sounded.

When that day comes, Wilde, who is buried in the same tomb as Ross in Paris, is supposed to have said "Let's pretend not to have heard it."

I found going to Mass a hardship and it would be only a question of time before I lapsed and finally collapsed. But that didn't mean that I wasn't still an emotionally indoctrinated Catholic. At the Pier Head or Hyde Park Corner, I would find myself defending Catholicism when I heard it being attacked by hateful fundamentalist Bible-punchers. The proof of the pudding is in the eating. In moments of crisis many of us revert to the religion we were brought up in.

I remember being taken down to the operating theatre on a trolley and thinking to myself, "Ah God, I might see you soon and I hope it's a welcoming smile you give me."

Chapter 28

When Dad was out at the pub or at the rosary at night I would sit by the fire and look at the pictures in books, which had been lent to me, of athletes and boxers and of the heroic deeds that they displayed when winning. It was my way of dealing with the boredom and the isolation I felt in Liverpool during the winter months.

I would study the content of the photo for hours, trying to get into the mind of the athletes or boxers, and find out what they were thinking and feeling as they struggled to victory. I wondered what was off the frame of the picture. How they arrived at the venue, who was there and what happened after the victory.

I was trying to guess the background story to the photographs. Did their father, mother, wife or girlfriend come to see them? What kind of transport did they use to get to the event? Did their lives radically change after the victory and what did it feel like for them to see pictures of themselves in newspapers and books?

When I did eventually get my photo in the paper, I had a great sense of disappointment. I could not believe that the picture of me on the sports page of the *Mirror* made little or no difference to my everyday life.

Other people in my isolated situation might have read books to woo them away from their loneliness. My problems with school made me a reluctant reader, so I used the pictures in the books to fill up my imagination until boredom set in. Then I would pretend that I was the victor in the picture. I would play out interviews with another character I had invented, a tough-talking American newspaperman.

I would be the reticent victor, bordering on shyness, exasperating the newspaper reporter, who'd call me a dumb son of a gun because I refused to give him a sensational story. I would use an empty sterrie bottle and speak into it as if it were a handheld microphone.

Another time I would stand in front of the mirror and practise my arm action as I drove them faster, my face grimacing as if I was in a tight finish, trying to win a race, and I would practice my victory salute. Come to think of it, I was a bit of a dab hand with victory salutes. I had studied Hitler's wave, which he made with the right hand. I always covered my lip with the index finger of my left hand when I did that one.

The Russian, Vladimir Kuts, had the very best victory wave. He looked great as he crossed the finishing line. After seeing Kuts winning the European 5000 metres wearing black socks,

I astounded my teachers and fellow athletes by wearing black socks, which I pulled up to my knees, while out training. To be influenced by a Russian Communist was risking ex-communication in this Catholic school.

As I watched the flames dance in the fire, I would dream about the time when other boys would read books about me, which was slightly ironical as I couldn't read all that well myself, but I expected them to take great delight in how I had won six gold medals at one Olympic Games. How my performances had stopped the Games and the ovation I received was so spectacular that the commentators had wept at the sight of me lapping runners in the 5000 metres. Ron Clarke of Australia was to do this, years later at the White City in the AAA's championships.

It can't be denied that I was my father's son when it came to aiming for the stars. At other times in my mad moments of dreaming, I was a boxer identifying with the social injustices suffered by inarticulate men who fought their way out of the gutter.

With a grimacing face expressing agony into the mirror, I would be caught by a left hook from my invisible opponent and knocked flat on the unmade bed, which was never made up until we were about to get into it.

As I stretched out on the bed in agonising pain, the referee would begin to count, but not until between six or seven would I begin to shake my head and try to clear my eyes as I tried to come back to some kind of consciousness to comply with the audience's screams for me to get to my feet.

At the count of nine I would struggle to my feet as the referee looked into my eyes, and put my gloveless hands up to defend myself as he told me to fight on. I gave a definite nod, certifying that I was in the best shape of my life as my invisible opponent came from the neutral corner towards me.

I could duck and dive, sending rights and lefts into my opponent's body. In my lonelier moments I would imagine myself being taken from the ring after being knocked down by the great heavyweight champion Rocky Marciano. It wasn't that he really hurt me but as I fell I bumped my head on the floor, causing a fracture of my skull. Blood trickling from the side of my mouth and ears, the St John Ambulance Brigade attendants stretchered me from the ring, down through the gangway, through the hushed cigar-smoking spectators. As they carried me through the gangway, a choir of angels led by Mario Lanza could be heard singing the Ave Maria. Everyone in the auditorium cried silently for the greatest athlete ever known, as the stretcher ascended slowly towards the roof, which miraculously opened to the starry blue heavens above as the St John Ambulance Brigade attendants stood speechless.

Then I would tire of the charade, wondering what kind of insanity I was suffering from. Mam always said that we had all inherited madness from his side of the family. I often wondered when the symptoms might express themselves without me being conscious of the fact.

I never got a buzz when I went to see the film *Billy Liar* because I had been living a Walter Mitty existence for years myself.

At quieter times I would dream as only an adolescent can, in terms of black and white, of God's understanding and pity on my plight. Sometimes He talked to me, not that I would swear in a court of law that I had heard voices – my schizophrenia never developed to that extent – but I listened out for directions as to the purpose of my life.

Perhaps it was being hinted at, that is if God ever hints, that I should give up my sporting life and enter a monastery to spend the rest of my days in penance and prayer. I was soon put off that

231

notion when an older lad at school, who thought that he might have a vocation, left school to enter a monastery. He was back among us before the end of term because he said the friars in the monastery were even greater bastards than you'd ever find among the Christian Brothers.

One of my most pleasant fantasies was to be invited by Roy Plomley to select the eight records that I would like to have with me on my desert island. Mine would be Bill Haley, Elvis Presley, Eddie Cochran, Buddy Holly, Duane Eddy, Fats Domino, The Platters and Mario Lanza singing Ave Maria. Besides the Bible and Shakespeare, which books would you take? To which I'd answer something by Steinbeck. And my luxury item would be a towel. Growing up in a large family in Dublin, I always ended up trying to dry myself with the wet end of the towel and any morning that Dad took it into his head to shave, he dried his face on the towel and then blew his nose on it. This drove me into apoplexies.

But apart from complaining of my deprivation in the towelling department, which would be a justifiable case at The Hague, I can see many more good reasons for taking a towel as my luxury item on a desert island. I could wear it as a dressing gown after I had used it all day to sunbathe on. I could wear it as a turban or use it as a pillow. I could barter with it if I met any friendly natives and I could light a fire with it if any inclement weather set in or to alert a passing ship.

It was pretty difficult for me to get out in the evening. I had to report my every movement to Dad. Eventually I said that Hughes' mother had invited me around for tea. This idea had been hatched in Lewis's record department, where we spent Saturday afternoon when we were not racing, having a free listen to the latest records.

It was normal practice for Dad and me to go out to the pictures every Saturday night. I was fed up with the routine. I could see it going on until I was a hundred and one or more. I wanted to go to a dance with people of my own age. I was in a terrible dilemma, as I felt very selfish leaving Dad in on his own while I was out enjoying the bright lights. Guilt-ridden, I suggested that he go to the pictures as usual.

"No, no, that's all right," he said, rattling the paper in temper. "Don't mind me, I've got some things to do and I can listen to the weather forecast," he said, shaking the paper with such ferocity that I thought the letters would fly off the page. "You enjoy yourself."

I sighed a sigh of relief but then he dug the knife in deeper and took away any good I might have felt by asking in a sly diminutive way, like a supposedly slow-thinking farmer in the west of Ireland might ask, "And what time do you think you'll be in?" I could feel the shackles being tightened.

"I suppose I'll be in by ten," I said tentatively.

"That's very late to be eating tea," he said, looking at me over the paper. "What time are you starting tea?"

"Seven," I murmured, cursing the fact that I had allowed myself to be subjected to this inquisition in the first place.

He enjoyed his cat and mouse sport of making me hover, so the loveable old rascal continued.

"Well, you won't be eating tea for three hours," he said delightedly, with an air worthy of a barrister in court. "From what I know of the English, you won't be eating for half an hour either," he said, nodding his head as he cocked his left eye.

"That's one thing about this country, when they ask you to have a cup of tea, they mean a cup of tea," he stressed, trying desperately hard to ally himself with me and to make certain that I knew who buttered my bread and who the real enemy was.

233

"Don't be in late," he said, "behave yourself and remember who you are," he whipped out as if he were a disgruntled priest handing out penance in the confessional before he administered absolution.

After getting myself as presentable as possible and constantly arranging and rearranging the knot on my tie, and trying to instil a Bill Haley on my quiff, I stood at the door with one arm as long as the other as I waited for him to cough up some money for my fares. In spite of rationing myself on my usual intake of chocolate bars for the week, I still did not have enough money for admission to the dance and my bus fares.

But now he seemed to be oblivious of me and all his attention was taken up by some world-shattering news item in the paper. I coughed, reluctant to ask outright for fare money, while I prayed for the day when I would be solvent. I eventually succumbed, and asked Dad could I have some fares please. He looked up from the paper blankly as if I was some kind of an apparition standing in the room.

Dad viewed me very complacently, smiling as if he had all the time in the world, "God, son," he said, more to himself than to me, "this takes me back a couple of years, I remember when I was your age." He sighed pleasurably as if he was glad that time and all the old nonsense of dressing up and having to go out was over.

"It doesn't seem like yesterday since I used to stand at the door waiting for the old fella to give me a couple of bob before I went out. God, time flies, how it flies."

Jesus, I thought, if he keeps on much longer, I won't bother going out at all.

"There's no doubt about it," he said, "time flies." He then put his hand in his pocket and gave me five bob.

"That should be enough, don't spend it foolishly. It's not easy to come by."

"Thanks Dad, I'll see yeh."

"Have a nice time," he said, as he went back to the paper-rattling again.

It was wet and wintry, the type of night when anyone with an ounce of sense would have been satisfied to sit in front of the fire and listen to the radio, but what sense do you expect to see from fifteen-year-old youngsters who are determined to go out wenching. There were five of us altogether, two girls and three blokes, and I was James Mason, the odd man out without a girl. It was my first real dance, apart from the Harriers' Christmas Social. The one we were going to now was full of people of my own age, not fuddy-duddies or old codgers like we had at the Harriers' Social.

"It'll be all jiving," Hughes had said.

"I've never jived," I said miserably, realising that there was another thing that I was useless at. "I know nothing about jiving."

In his house, when his mam and dad were out at the pictures, Hughes showed me the basic steps of the jive.

"There you are," he said, letting go of my hands. "There's nothing to it. Just one, two, and back."

We felt pretty embarrassed by the whole thing. I don't know why because girls hold each other's hands when they dance and no one ever says that there's anything peculiar about that.

On the top of the bus on the way to the Cricket Club, I sat on my own behind Hughes and his girl. She was peculiar looking, a blond giddy type who was taller than Hughes and as thin as a rake. I kept my opinion to myself, but the more I looked at her, the less I could understand what Hughes saw in her.

In front of them was Herbie Maxwell, a bloke from Hughes' class, to whom I took an instant dislike. He was playing the big I am because he was with a good looking blond girl.

"How much have you got on you?" Hughes asked, in the downmarket accent that he turned on any time we were out socially.

"Well, with fare and the entrance, one and six," I said.

"I've got about two bob. Let's put it together and we can get a bottle."

"What about Herbie Maxwell?" I asked.

"He won't," Hughes said, "he doesn't like the taste of sherbet."

After getting off the bus, we went into an offie to get a bottle of cheap wine. Outside the shop, Hughes raised the bottle to his head.

"Drink it down as fast as you can, then it will affect you quicker."

Herbie Maxwell said, "I'll see you inside," as he chaperoned his girl away. "I've come to dance, not to stand in the street watching a pair of winos."

I took a swig from the bottle and drank a good few mouthfuls down like Hughes had shown me. Then I passed the bottle to Hughes' girlfriend, but she wouldn't touch it, and she gave it to Hughes.

I felt quite confident, so I smiled and asked her what her name was. She didn't look as bad now as when I first met her.

"Here," Hughes said, handing me back the bottle.

"Get stuck into that, and I'll get stuck into her. Give us a kiss our Sylvia."

"Oh you're getting drunk," she said, pushing Hughes off.

I took a deep swig from the bottle and started shouting, "I feel great, I feel fucking great," deliberately imitating a Scouse accent.

"Here, give us that bottle, you poxy bastard," Hughes said, pushing our Sylvia off.

He drank deeply from it as our Sylvia looked on, feeling rejected because of the bottle.

"Give it here," I said, pulling the bottle from his mouth. "Leave some for me, you thirsty bugger."

"There you are," Hughes said. "Finish the fucker off. I feel fantastic. Here, our Sylvia, give us a French kiss. What colour drawers are you wearing?"

"What shall I do with the bottle?" I asked as I drained it.

"Here, give it to me," Hughes said.

He took it and threw it up in the air as we all ran for the dance hall to the sound of the exploding empty bottle on the pavement.

The dance hall was packed but we got a little corner to dump our coats in and it wasn't long before I was jiving away confidently in the darkness of the hall with our Sylvia and Hughes, who kept shouting out, "Christ, this is the life, I feel great." Hughes began to jive furiously with Sylvia, yelling at the top of his voice, "Arseholes, arseholes." You couldn't really hear him very much because of the noise of the music. Herbie Maxwell was the only one on the floor moving sedately with his girl. He looked a proper prick in his suit, being more kitted out for a wedding or a funeral than a dance. After the jiving had finished, Herbie came over.

"Don't think much of this," he sniffed, as he took an immaculate handkerchief from his top jacket pocket and dabbed his brow.

"It's fucking great," Hughes said, "fucking fantastic, all those arseholes dancing."

"You're disgustingly drunk," Herbie Maxwell said. He ignored me. "Excuse me," he said to his girlfriend, "I'm going to the cloakroom."

"Have one on me," Hughes said, "and don't forget to pull the chain," he scoffed.

The music began again as I stood looking at Herbie Maxwell's girl, who had a fine well-nourished body, unlike Sylvia who looked a proper skinny lizzie. As the music played on, I squared my shoulders, hitched up my trousers and said, "Do you fancy a dance?"

She considered it a moment.

"Come on," I said, pulling her hand, which felt remarkably cold, "you can only die once."

We rocked and ripped it up until our legs ached.

The tempo changed to a quieter slower dance, more the type of thing that they did at Billy Martin's Dancing Academy. I pulled her into me. Although I was hot from the humidity of the hall and the excessive madness of our dancing, her cheek was as cold as the mountain stream, that they used to say in the cigarette cinema advert to plug menthol fresh cigarettes. I pulled her in close to me again. I could feel her firm breasts on my chest, which made me very protective and proud to be able to shield her from a hostile world. As I squared my little round shoulders, we floated around the room, as if there had been no yesterdays or tomorrows.

"What's your name?" I whispered.

"Shirley," she said.

"I've got a cousin Shirley," I lied, but it was something to say. "She's lovely, just like you," I added.

"I bet you say that to all the Shirleys you meet."

"Come to think of it, I do," I said pulling her closer.

"Are you always as charming as this?" she asked, making me feel that she was not in the least impressed by my blarney.

"Only when there's an R in the month."

"ORR," she said.

"What's an ORR when it's at home?"

She was laughing at me. I pronounced my Rs with an Irish accent.

As the dance ended, Herbie Maxwell came over with his handkerchief in his hand like Louis Armstrong always used to have.

"I thought you came to the dance with me," he said to Shirley, ignoring me. "I paid in for you. That's rich," he said standing there feeling sorry for himself. "That's blooming rich."

Hughes came over, covered in sweat, realising immediately that something was amiss.

"What's up? Has someone dropped one?"

I didn't say anything, but if there was to be a bundle I was prepared.

"He's pinched my girl," Herbie Maxwell whined, "I paid in for her."

"You shouldn't do that," Hughes slurred, "you shouldn't pinch someone else's piece of arse," which further embarrassed and unsettled Herbie Maxwell, who acted immediately by saying to Shirley, "Come on, I'm taking you home."

I didn't say a word but I felt bloody awful inside. The four of them left together and I was left on my own, feeling a bit like Montgomery Clift, the actor, who I thought would have reacted like me, by happily munching some mints, trying to get rid of the smell of the wine, totally bemused and mesmerised by the whole experience.

I waited for the bus, wishing that I had never gone out in the first place. When I got in, Dad was listening to the news from Radio Éireann. Blast him, I thought, that bloody Irish news will be the death of me with its warnings of ground frost and *Behannie Day live* (that's God bless you in Irish). I am going to miss all the best records on Radio Luxembourg.

News, news, news, and what good does it do him? It's always full of tragedy and it's not as if you can do anything about it. I was angry with him about the radio because I couldn't take on board that I was more annoyed at the pickle I'd got myself in at the dance, while he had placidly gone through the evening without any major disturbances. So I made myself a Spam sandwich with lashings of salad cream on it and stared into the fire wondering if I would ever see her again.

Chapter 29

It was the school holidays and I was working in Scott's bakery shop for the three-week Easter period in order to get some money to travel down to London for the London Public Schools championships at the White City Stadium where I had seen Chataway beat Kuts. I must have been a natural shop assistant. That business acumen came from my father's side of the family; his brothers were all successful shopkeepers. The manager asked me if I'd like a full-time job. I told him that I'd consider it as I didn't want to offend him or dismiss instantly what he had spent his whole life achieving. But I had no intention of spending eight hours a day serving old biddies quarters of this and two ounces of that for the rest of my life.

As I stacked the shelves, I was counting off the days for the London race and the confrontation with Ground. In Lilleshall I had beaten him in the time trial and this time in London, I'd have him and the record as well. Being in this shop deprived me of the training facilities I had at school, so on the dot of half five I was out the door of the shop once the closed sign went up, with my holdall up to the Crawfords training grounds, much to the chagrin of the manager.

I followed the training schedule devised by Long, who was doing his National Service in the RAF. I would have to do National Service one day, but at least it would be better than school I thought in my simplistic way, but I later found out from Long that the bullying and intimidation that went on in the huts was a lot worse than school.

I had to keep the training up but I also needed the money to travel down to London. This wasn't forthcoming from Dad as he was always on about the mortgage in Dublin. I waited for the bus up to the Crawfords grounds, determined that no bastard was going to put me off my daily training. There were those who wanted to lead your life by their own homespun philosophies, developed to compensate for their own inadequacies and lack of courage. It took courage to train each day. The type of courage it takes to write a play, book or a poem. All of these activities ask of you to put your head on the chopping block.

The smart arses around you think that you'll only get beaten. It takes courage to put yourself up against bigger lads and better togged out ones than yourself and better-spoken blokes who sound as if they are being trained to spend the rest of their lives ordering you about. Lads with lovely new holdalls with their own initials on them that they got from their uncle and auntie. I was lucky to get a carrier bag that we brought the half-priced cakes to the cinema in. It took determination to stand up against those privileged bastards, to enter qualifying rounds and go after them. If you let yourself down, you had no place to go and no one to seek consolation from if you were defeated.

No one cared that you were not able to sleep the night before a race or that you had shit after shit before the race as you warmed up while worrying could you hold yourself and keep your bowels closed during the race. Wouldn't it be terrible that during the race, you shit yourself in front of all those people as you fought with every ounce of effort and energy for the finish? It took discipline to attempt to get the medal that few valued. All I could do to comfort myself was to believe that I went where they feared to enter. To work is to pray, so the Benedictines say, and according to them I would have banked up a few prayers for myself during this period with all my training.

As I stacked the shelves in the shop, cleaned the windows or swept the floor, my mind was never on the job in hand. All I'd be thinking of would be my running, my training and the forthcoming races. Running gave me a release from the boredom of the job and the realisation that I was on my own with nothing in common with anyone around me, as I had nothing in common with my fellow competitors. But no matter what accent they had, no matter what their Uncle Percy gave them for Christmas, when you stepped on the running track, the cards were dealt and by Harry, I was going to beat the shite out of all of them, I thought as I stacked the last tin of Heinz beans on the shelf.

They might have been more privileged than me but if there was a special reward for effort, determination, courage and the ability to stand pain, I'd win over the lot of them.

In 1955 I won the All England Schools championship in the half mile. As a reward for winning, I went for a week's special training that year in Lilleshall in Shropshire. There was this fellow there who could quote the geometry theorems in Latin. I never liked this public school blond square-headed type. He would have been a dead ringer for a recruiting poster for Adolf's army or any other army, except the good old Salvation Army.

Little Titch, he called me when we were grouped together in a training squad. He didn't call me Little Titch after the time trial when, in front of the top coaches in the country, I beat the shite out of him. "Had a bad one today," he laughed, as he came off the track looking to see where his balls were. And you'll be having further bad ones if ever I'm around, I thought to myself. He had more ability than me and he had it all going for him. When the High Church of England God made him, He made a winner and a member of the ruling classes. But when the Irish Catholic God made me, He didn't give me many special attributes, but for thinking and determination and a good appreciation for the absurd comedy all around me. These are gifts I have used all my life as I now touch wood. Not being able to read or write and certainly not conversant with any geometry and coming up to sixteen, I developed skills in other areas of life particularly when racing or time trialling, which Mr Ground had discovered much to his smiling chagrin. I was getting the message from my dad and friends that anything I won was not worthwhile, but by Christ, if someone else won it, then they were everyone's cup of tea. Day by day I was having it ingrained into me that I could never be as good as other people, while as Mr Ground got older, he exuded more confidence by the hour.

After you have won something big you find that you suddenly acquire more friends than you formerly had. People are interested in you; initially you think it's because they admire you, but eventually you find out it's because they want to advance themselves, by getting the formula that has been successful for you and which they think they can automatically use in order to bring them success.

A week or two after my victory in the All England Schools, Ken and his brother Ted, two of the Harriers, attached themselves to me, believing that some of my running magic would rub off on them and improve their performances. Ted was doing National Service. He had signed up to do three years instead of the compulsory two, because you got a couple of extra bob per week for doing the longer duration. His brother Ken, his identical twin, had failed his medical because of flat feet.

Ted had got a girl in the family way but shock of horrors, it turned out that she was a Catholic, so when the little girl was born and baptised, I was asked to be the godfather as I was the only Catholic they knew. At fifteen going on sixteen, this was pretty heavy stuff for me. One Sunday afternoon, I went to the church and then back to the house, where we had formal tea in their best cups and saucers, not a sit-down affair, but a running buffet with salmon and cucumber sandwiches, cut into triangles on white sliced loaf, biscuits and a piece of shop cake bought specially for the occasion.

We all stood around trying to balance our cups on our saucers in embarrassed silence as everyone's eyes tried to avoid the mother, who was considered the Catholic culprit in this affair. I often think of that little girl and wonder what ever happened to her as I was her godparent, a role totally unfitted to me as it stipulated that I was to be a guardian over her moral welfare and her attending church. But Ken thought that his brother was a bloody fool for getting involved with this girl. What chance did he have of ever achieving any athletics success now that he had a wife and kid to keep. I was getting a not dissimilar message from Dad and Brother Mac.

I used to train with Ken and Ted on the top field, which was used as a cricket pitch in the summer time. Round and round on the outside of the cricket crease each weekend of the winter and during the early spring evenings, we'd pound our way on the field, until we were eventually demoted to the bottom field, a much rougher area, because we had cut up the ground so much.

The English have a funny way of dealing with things that upset them, unlike the Irish, for when something is getting on their nerves, they have it out there and then and nip it in the bud as Dad used to say, which clears the air. But the English always try to avoid direct confrontation. They suffer in silence rather than bring the matter to a head or they go behind your back. Dad always warned me that you had to watch them because you were dealing with stab-me-in-the-back merchants, and he further warned that you have to keep a particular eye on them because the more an Englishman gets annoyed the more he laughs.

So no one came directly to us and said that we couldn't use the top field or asked us would we mind not using it or, as would be the case in Ireland, someone would have come up to us and said that if I see you three stooges up there using my cricket pitch, I'll cut your fecking legs off.

Instead a notice was put up in that field to say it was closed for marking out and would all the athletes, of which there were only us three, use the bottom field. But from that day to this, I swear to God the field was never marked out. Of course the groundsman might have died.

After being like a robot in the shop, dreaming of my running and my races, I'd go immediately after we closed to the Crawfords grounds, where I'd train on the bottom field with Ken and Ted, the twins.

This particular evening, I wouldn't hang around too long after training for I had decided to wash my vest and shorts to be all shipshape for the race down in London, where I was to compete at the famous White City Stadium in the London Public Schools championships.

Mr Ground, my main antagonist in the London race, had had his vests and shorts ironed or even laundered by his mother, or knowing him, by the daily help, while I boiled my vest and shorts in a saucepan after I had removed the remnants of my dad's bacon and cabbage. Dad was a notorious man for the bacon and cabbage, a habit that I have inherited. He said that our stomachs were like engines, which needed constant oiling.

I heated the iron by the fire, so after taking the shorts and vest out of the pot, I ironed them wet, which made tons of steam rise in the room just like it came out of the chimney of the Chinese laundry, which I could see out of the window at the back of the yard. No, I don't think Mr Ground ever used an iron in his life, certainly not one of these dry ones. And by the stamp of him and his attitude, I don't think that he ever intended to either.

It gave me solace to think that this same vest and shorts on this table covered with Irish newspapers, alongside an opened one-pound pot of plum jam, which cost seven pence ha'penny, could be famous, for the winner of a major championship always got their photo in the newspaper.

So it was obvious that many of the buckos that I ran with and against were heading in a much different direction from myself. Later in life, with suits, good shoes and posh accents and twice-daily clean shirts and freshly laundered kit, while mine was worn for the season, and only half-heartedly washed if there was any hint of being photographed for the newspaper. I knew that I was being prepared for a different world. My diet differed greatly from Mr Ground and his associates as well I'm sure, for my dad's basic nourishment as I've said was boiled bacon and cabbage and potatoes. A meal was not a meal to him without half a stone of potatoes on the plate, which was probably a subconscious fear inherited from the awful effects of the different potato famines. Not that you could get a good potato in Liverpool. They were always wet and not a bit floury like the ones at home. When you boiled half a stone at home in their jackets, you'd serve them up and there they'd be sitting on the plate as if trying to break out of their jackets, smiling at you.

It wasn't until I came to Liverpool and was living in full board with a rip of a landlady off London Road who started peeling potatoes, a thing that you'd never do at home, that I realised that I was in a very strange country and among a very peculiar class of people definitely when it came to handling the spud.

In the west of Ireland there were always two classes of potatoes, those for the table and those for the pigs, but I think that all this country got from Ireland were the potatoes that were only fit for the pigs.

We got lumps of brisket of beef from a butcher near Mrs Ward where I watched the Coronation. This was boiled for hours and made to last for days. Without a fridge, it never occurred to us that we were running the risks of getting food poisoning.

For ten Players, which Dad handed over to the young butcher when the manager had gone out for a pint at lunchtime, or for an early-evening drink, the young butcher would fill the bag with sausages, bacon and brisket of beef for next to nothing.

We'd boil the sausages and eat them with cabbage and spuds, but as the man says, hunger is great sauce and as a young lad you'd eat the side of a house and come back for more as long as it was filling. Across the road from the butchers was a grocers and confectionery shop where Dad would go at five to one on a Wednesday or on a Saturday. We swooped down on the manager for bargains, because he had no fridge so all of the cream cakes would be given at a knocked-down price, and then off to the pictures, a very odd-looking pair with four carrier bags of cream cakes, eating like lords in the cinema. We looked oddities in the pictures with all of our shopping but we didn't fancy the prospect of going back to a room, for that was all it was to us, to drop our bags there and have to come out again. The room was not a home for us. It was not reliable like your own home where you felt a sense of permanence. In a room you were cut off, isolated, as if you were in a cell. For one thing, unlike a home, it was an oddity to have visitors to a room, and in fact, landlords and landladies frowned upon you having guests.

Another source of food came from Ireland. A lot of food was sent illegally through the post. I heard tell of a man in London who, during the war, used to receive a couple of rashers of bacon wrapped in the *Irish Times*. He was a brave man I think, to attempt frying it in a house full of lodgers. At this time because of rationing, you could be lynched for the rind. His method of surviving was to have the room sealed off with coats and newspapers around the doors, so that the smell did not escape, causing many hungry knocks on the door.

Chapter 30

One of the most pleasurable things I'd do in preparation for a race or a time trial would be after I had done the vests and shorts, clean my spikes and coat them with dubbing, applying sparingly with a soft clean cloth and working it into the leather. This would soften and waterproof the surface, so as to get them as supple as possible so that when I put my foot into the shoe it felt as if I was putting my hand into a glove. Spikes were very expensive and not every lad could afford them. At times, there was a lot of borrowing of spikes between young lads.

My dad couldn't afford to buy me spikes but after my victory in the Liverpool Schools' Championships, Brother Mac presented me with a new pair of white spikes, which cost over five pounds.

Dad's take-home weekly pay was just a little over seven.

The next Sunday, Long would be back from his call-up duties for the weekend, so with stopwatch and whistle, which were on permanent loan from the physics lab, I would be put through my paces to find out if the winter's work had got results. The day was fast approaching when I'd have to meet Mr Ground on the same track where Chataway broke the three-mile record. I had seen this memorable race live about a year before on the telly at Crawfords with my fellow club members.

I'd have to train very conscientiously for the next week and rest up a couple of days before the time trial at Bootle Stadium on the Sunday. As soon as I stepped out on the track, the eyes would be there with their stopwatches, including Charlie Mire, the handicapper, and before the afternoon was out, Mr Ground in London would know of my form. I had no alternative but to put my head on the chopping block, for there were no other tracks in Liverpool or Lancashire worked out so early in the season.

At the end of the winter and before the summer cricket and athletics season began, the rugby posts were taken down after the 'sevens' were played and a four-forty-yard grass track was marked out as well as the cricket pitches, but it would be some weeks before that happened, so I would have to be content with the concrete Bootle Stadium as a venue to do my time trial. It is interesting how I cleaned my spikes for the time trial like a soldier would clean his gun, but it was a contradictory thing to do for I could not use the spikes in the time trial on the Sunday because at the Bootle Stadium, the track was laid out for cyclists and was banked, made of concrete where spikes could not be worn, but the cleaning of the spikes offered some kind of meditative solace for the task ahead.

No late nights this week and I'd have to psych myself up and be as pure as the driven snow, at least until after the Sunday time trial. The danger of getting yourself pumped up is that you can make a lot of tactical mistakes. The important thing is to manage one's emotions but when pumped up, your emotions take over your logic, which can lead to tactical disasters. Nerves, or in modern-day terms 'bottle', are to do with everything. You put yourself on the chopping block so you have to psych yourself up. You don't give a fuck for no one or anything.

When you are in a competition, you suspend everything, God, mankind, womankind. You go into a tunnel view of the world. You have got to focus and nothing else matters. What happened yesterday, what's going to happen tomorrow doesn't matter a hoot. All that matters is the event. You probably go to the athletics track on public transport sitting by people who know little of what you're up to. You're like a criminal among them, thinking and plotting, but having nothing to do with their insufferably boring lives. All that matters is the race.

That's one way but you won't get anywhere that way because running has got to come from within. It has to flow from inside and be an organic growth like lava flowing from a former dormant volcano, not governed by the will. As far as this approach was concerned, I still had a long way to go and a lot to learn.

The twins, Ken and Ted, took me over a couple of hundred yards of the first part of my time trial. I soon dropped both of them but I couldn't do anything against the wind and rain, which hit me as I entered into the back straight so it was impossible to know what form I was really in.

I felt reasonably OK within myself but I wasn't flowing from within, so I had to console myself that given more hospitable warmer conditions, I would run faster. I also had to accept that greater people than me had their plans skew-whiffed by the weather.

I don't think Napoleon was much of a runner, in fact I delight in my more lucid moments to think that I could have had him over the four-forty yards or the half mile. But I had to admit that the weather in Russia certainly played an important part in his career, as it had done in my time trial. I had to console myself with the adage that the best was yet to come, given that the barometers were kinder.

Chapter 31

We got on the coach outside St George's Hall at eight in the evening. Hughes and I had sandwiches for our overnight journey down to London. I had made tomato ones on white sliced bread, which the manager of the shop where I had worked for the Easter holidays let me have for half price. As his pasty hand had clinched my hand, he had said that I could always have a job with him. I hoped not otherwise one day I could be like him, an ulcerated manager looking after a shop for Scott's the bakery and working for next to nothing, while eating broken biscuits, taking home half-priced stale cakes and short-changing short-sighted old ladies, looking forward to a gold clock presentation after thirty years of being a good and faithful servant. No way, I thought as

I hung my white shop coat and apron on the peg, I hoped for the last time. I had much bigger fish to fry.

I had also made some Heinz salad spread sandwiches from a jar I had nicked on the way out of the shop when the old boy was doing up the day's receipts. Hughes' mum had made ham and egg sandwiches that we both ate with relish as we sat on the back seat of the coach, which we had requisitioned and determinedly held on to, repelling any fellow passengers who tried to invade our territory with dirty looks. We palmed the unoccupied seats beside us as if we were waiting for our friends to arrive. We intended to spread ourselves out on the seats for the duration of the night's journey. Hughes kept fantasising about going to Soho, which he hoped would show our Sylvia, who had finished with him, if he was a man of the world or not. I was dreaming of running at the great White City Stadium. It was a great adventure for these couple of Dick Whittingtons who had yet to reach the age of sixteen.

In spite of all the excitement of being let loose from Dad's ever-dominating control, I soon fell asleep. It had been a long day for me, working in the shop humping boxes and cases about and filling shelves for the manager, who tried to get a week's work out of me on my last day.

I think it was in Birmingham that I woke. The people getting on and off seemed ghostly. The driver had switched off the continuous drone of the engine, which had been the background music since we had left Liverpool. People coming and going seemed vulnerable in the silence. My ears were tuning in to the haphazard noises now that the engine was off and perhaps because I had been asleep, I seemed to hear them on a deep level of my being. We had an hour stopover in the coach station so Hughes and I went to the cafeteria, where there were vending machines and a jukebox. We were among the first recipients of the press-button services industry. We got oxtail soup, which should have been taken to the Trades Description department. On the jukebox, we played Slim Whitman's 'Rose Marie' and 'China Doll' over and over again for the whole hour.

It was pitch black and frightening outside except for the intermittent arrival of coaches from as yet unknown and faraway places with sweet-sounding names just like Slim Whitman sang of in his song, but I felt secure inside the almost deserted cafeteria with the jukebox and my best mate Hughes while most of the people in the country slept in their beds.

We arrived at Victoria Coach Station to be met by Long in his RAF uniform and highly polished black boots with a peaked cap that made his ears stick out like a donkey, but we didn't say anything as we were his guests for the weekend. We had to spend the whole of the day sightseeing as we weren't due to meet Long's RAF mates until later. We were three boys up from the provinces, gawking and laughing at everyone and everything in sight. In all honesty we were undermined by the slickness and pace of the rapid no-nonsense metropolis.

We saw Buckingham Palace and the balcony I had often seen on the Pathé newsreels where the royal party appeared and waved to the thousands of plebs, offering some sense of solace during any seemingly unsolvable crisis. The red buses were striking after the green-painted buses that I had been brought up with in both Dublin and Liverpool. Frantic black cabs busily attempted to take their passengers to meetings, measuring time and money on their clocks. The clock ran much faster than I ever could. We saw the changing of the guard in Whitehall and the Cenotaph.

There didn't seem to be much going on at number ten Downing Street and we all wondered if Winston was indoors or was he at Marlborough doing his oil paintings or building more walls as he had done in Berlin.

I had received mixed messages from my parents about the larger-than-life man. At times they'd say that there must be some good in him for he spent a few years as a child on an estate outside of Claremorris near Ballindine where my mam came from.

Sitting in splendour opposite the Albert Hall we saw the unhappy prince with his big moustache. In Trafalgar Square, we saw Nelson's Column, which put me in mind of Nelson's Pillar, which we had in the centre of Dublin. It's amazing, I thought, the cheek the British had, planting their national hero smash bang wallop in the centre of Dublin.

How would they like it if a couple of hod-carrying Paddies arrived in Trafalgar Square one morning with a bit of three be four and erected a statue of de Valera in place of the Admiral? The English take their monuments very seriously, for recently a young man was given six months for taking the head of a statue of Lady Thatcher.

Pope Pius XII, whom I'm no great admirer of, requested not to be interred close to former Popes in the Vatican because he did not consider himself worthy of such an accolade.

Hughes and Long had a great day together seeing the sights but frankly I felt like an odd man out, following them about and worrying about the heats and the job that lay ahead tomorrow, which didn't seem to affect them in the least. Anyone will tell you that sightseeing before an important race is not the ideal preparation for the forthcoming event. I felt hurt by their selfish behaviour. They were in London supposedly to support me. I had put the training in but all the hard work I had endured was now apparently secondary to their enjoyment.

We met two of Long's RAF mates in the Lyons Corner House. They were going up to Liverpool on weekend leave. One of them, a runner himself who recognised me and had seen me run in Liverpool, gave me the key of a double room that they had booked under their own names in the Union Jack Club opposite Waterloo Station. We couldn't book ourselves into the Club because we did not have the necessary services identity cards.

They both refused any money for the room, wishing me the best of luck in the race. This restored my faith in mankind. They assured us that we needn't worry about moving about in the Union Jack Club as no one bothered about identity cards. Many of the clientele would be in mufti. Their assurances did not totally blot out my anxieties.

Hughes and myself were illegally trespassing on government property and it was possible that we could be murdered in our beds and eaten by cannibals and never be seen or heard of again, except for the odd mention in the missing column of the *News of the World*.

They both left for Euston and their train journey up to Liverpool, feeling happy with themselves as I hoped to be with myself after the Sunday race when I took the coach back.

We had been in the Lyons Corner House, which was opposite the Houses of Parliament. This was where Bannister, Brasher, Chataway and the Austrian coach Franz Stampfl used to meet. It was there they planned the attempt on the first four-minute mile, which Bannister broke at Iffley Road in Oxford in May 1954. I had felt as if I was treading in famous footsteps.

At school Long had been a big fish in a small pond but now in the RAF he was just another number, which he was finding hard to come to terms with.

Hughes had asked me not to agree if Long broached the subject of changing rooms, so that he could be in with him. So I told Long that I was terrified of being on my own in a room, that I was terrified of the dark, and in a way that was true. It was in my

Uncle Tom's shop in Ballyhaunis as a very young child that I first became consciously afraid of the dark. When I woke up in this strange bedroom, which overlooked the town square, after having had a nightmare, crying that I wanted my dad, my Uncle Tom's wife became very disturbed because of how distraught I was.

I couldn't stop crying but I wasn't crying from my eyes but from the back of my throat, hiccupping and grunting like a pig. I felt that someone had cursed the pair of us because he had taken me away from my mam, brothers and sister in Ballindine to be abandoned by him in this huge bed in the darkness. He drank in the pubs of the town while my non-drinking uncle and aunt looked after me.

By the end of the day, before we had even entered the Union Jack Club, our former unbreakable triangle was disintegrating. For the whole of the weekend, Hughes and Long hardly spoke. The problem with the three of us was that we were all following different agendas.

Hughes wanted to get back at Sylvia by going to Soho. Long wanted to have the old days back and be with Hughes and I wanted to win the London Public Schools at the White City. Back in July, when I had won the All England Schools, we had presented a united front, but now there was internal squabbling within the camp, which might lead to disaster. Hughes and myself were a bit nervous as we went up the steps to the Union Jack Club but there was no need to worry because there was so much hustle and bustle going on that no one took any notice of us.

With eyes down and lungs full of the coal-saturated air that exuded from the steam trains of Waterloo Station, we quickly whisked by the reception desk along a corridor adorned with flags and rolls of honour, recalling those who had died in past conflicts for their King and Country, into a huge covered amphitheatre, which had an enormous winding staircase that led to the bedrooms. We followed the directions, which pointed to the whereabouts of the cafeteria and canteen. The message all round us seemed to be that it was more noble to die for one's country than to try to live peaceably in it. At my tender age, I felt the whole place was a shrine to sacrifice and the glorification of war and death.

In this place they seemed to be constantly recalling the gallantry of the men who had lost their lives in order to prepare the present squaddies to make similar sacrifices. It is said that Jesus gave his life for those who had been detained in limbo, a region on the border of hell where pre-Christian just men and women and infants waited to be transferred to heaven, a bit like the council might move people off a bad estate to a newly refurbished one. But I don't think that Jesus would have been all that impressed by the military yahoo on display in the corridors and the amphitheatre of the Union Jack Club.

There's always two sides to anything, so I couldn't help feeling a sense of belonging and pride as I sipped my orangeade surrounded by the actual men that I had seen portrayed in war films as heroes. As they queued up at the servery or bar, they seemed less robust than those I had seen on the screen. They were only soldiers in the Union Jack Club. Officers had their own separate club near Victoria Station.

We were all tired after a long day of sightseeing that left me feeling flat and stale to see how much some people had in London and of how little chance I had of ever getting anything. The day had begun on a high when we first met at Victoria Coach Station, but had ended in a low in the Lyons Corner House after they had had their tiff.

After a meal of sausage, egg and chips and lashings of brown sauce, we returned to our rooms. I was ready for my bed but

Hughes, whom I was sharing the room with, began playing up. He insisted that we should go to Soho there and then. I told him that I was knackered but he wouldn't have any of it, saying that he hadn't come all the way down from Liverpool to go home without visiting Soho. He had his reputation to think of and that if I didn't accompany him, he'd go on his own, which left me between the devil and the deep blue sea. I didn't fancy spending time in the room all on my own as I had been subjected to enough of that in Liverpool.

So foolishly, I gave in and we both sneaked out of the Union Jack Club, making our way across Waterloo Bridge to the Strand, past glittering theatres and hordes of people out for the night.

We had already made this journey earlier and it wasn't until we left the pigeons in Trafalgar Square, knowing that we were going into the unknown territory of Leicester Square, which had a little park in the middle and was surrounded by half a dozen cinemas all showing films that I'd never heard of, that I felt a bit nervous.

We crossed over Leicester Square, which was thronging with people of all nationalities, shapes, sizes, colours and creeds and we went up to Piccadilly Circus, where hundreds of people were sitting on the steps, the hub of the Empire, under Eros, God of Love, which was plentifully on sale to all the visitors to the West End. There were loads of women on the pavements. Tarty types, done up to the nines in high heels, furs, short knee-length dresses, openly offered men a good time. It cost between a pound and thirty bob. "This is the life," Hughes said, as if he had discovered his El Dorado.

Across from the island on which Eros stood was a large blinking neon sign saying that Guinness was good for you, which I heartily agreed with, for I myself began drinking bottled

Guinness as early as seven years of age, when I used to mix half a pint of Guinness with half a pint of milk on doctor's orders while I was recuperating from my second breakdown.

This day I had decided to have the whole bottle on its own while giving an extra portion of milk to the cat. So for a couple of hours afterwards, I found the world to be a comical place, an angle I have not moved away from since the age of seven.

Opposite the Windmill Theatre, there were salt beef sandwich bars where you could get salt beef on rye covered in fresh mustard and a gherkin. It was well beyond our means but it was lovely to witness the beef being carved as the saliva rose in our mouths.

We stood on the pavement looking in through windows at people who sat on fixed stools, which they could rotate about on, so that they could be free and mobile as they watched the man behind the counter cut slices of hot beef, which he had fixed to the carving board by enormous steel rods, so that it would not move all over the board. The joint was hurriedly replaced when the head carver tapped his knife on the board, signalling like a conductor to a lackey that a new joint of salt beef should be taken from the saucepan. Like any great artist the carver tackled the beef. He had to use skill, both in terms of thickness and the precise amount given to each sandwich, as this dictated not only how delicious it would be but also the profit that each joint of beef would yield.

What a hedonistic part of the planet we had entered, the likes of which I had never seen before in the whole of my life. This wild grotesque Rabelaisian demonstration of humanity was so different from the sheltered way that Hughes had been brought up in Huyton that he wanted to plunder the whole area and dedicate the remainder of his life in the pursuit of Mammon.

There was jazz emanating from various drinking dens but Hughes' main objective was to get to a coffee bar, which were all the rage at this time. A frothy tasteless liquid was served in see-through Pyrex cups and saucers after a tremendous rigmarole took place behind the counter. An excitable individual of Mediterranean disposition doused the place with steam from two enormous silver vats that stood on the counter, frantically turning knobs that issued forth hissing noises and steam, building up the customers' expectations of great-tasting coffee to come, but you'd get better-tasting stuff from a sluice.

But it was the hip place to be and the hip thing to drink, so we put up with all the palaver and waited to be served this tasteless frothy muck that was layered like sedimentary rock on the top of the Pyrex cup. It was tepid on the top but would burn the insides of your mouth once you got beneath the grey collected matter on top. Hughes was a great follower of the fashionable thing to do down in London, which he would boast about to Sylvia once he returned to Liverpool. This stuff cost one shilling and nine pence, an outrageous price. You could get a cup of tea or coffee in an ordinary cafe for four or five pence, but it was the place to be, surrounded by the in crowd, so we paid up, feeling very grown up sitting in the windows watching the goings-on outside in the doorways of the houses opposite. It was the first traffic-free thoroughfare I had encountered.

On the other side of the road, well-made young women stood at the doorways, enticing men to enter the houses. Hughes' eyes were popping out of his head. "I must investigate," he said as he got up, leaving his half-finished frothy coffee.

"Wait here, don't move. Watch how a man does it. You've got to sow your wild oats while you're young."

Hughes crossed the road, spoke to this girl at one of the doors and it wasn't long before he was gone, leaving me sitting in the Black Cat coffee bar wondering what was going to happen next.

No matter how I tried to rationalise the situation, I still could not help worrying. What if Hughes didn't come back? How long was I expected to wait? Of all the men I saw going into the house I never saw any of them coming back out again.

This must have meant that they were doing away with them inside by robbing them, murdering them and eating them. There was a lot of devil worship going on during and after the war. I had read of such things in the *News of the World* of this bloke who, after cutting people up, hired a plane and threw the pieces that he didn't find all that appetising into the English Channel. There might be another exit out of the house. Say if they had a back way out like they had in the Hollywood speakeasies. But all of this speculation was getting me nowhere. It all came down to a very simple thing: how long was I to give Hughes to come out and what then, if he didn't come out, was I to do? Should I break the family code and inform the police or should I go back to the Union Jack Club and tell Long? Neither alternative gave me much incentive to act. All I ended up doing was getting more annoyed with Hughes because of his wilful and irresponsible behaviour.

After about the longest twenty-five minutes I had experienced since my arrival in London, Hughes came running out of the doorway opposite. I made a quick exit from the coffee bar and set off after him, shouting, "What's up Hughes? What's the matter?"

But Hughes didn't stop until we got to Trafalgar Square, where he plunged his hand into the fountain, which people used to dive into to welcome in the New Year, as if he wanted to sterilise it. The great one-armed Admiral looked down gleefully, glad that he was out of it all.

Later he told me that he was introduced to this fairly good-looking girl by the one who had taken him in, who was sitting on a revolving stool, just like those they had in the salt beef sandwich bar in Great Windmill Street. He had to buy her a drink, which cost ten bob a glass, and one for himself, which cost another ten bob. She told him not to worry and relax. After he had bought her and himself eight drinks, which turned out to be cordial – Hughes said it tasted worse than the coffee in the Black Cat coffee bar – they could go upstairs.

He told me, "She held my hand and played about, kissing my ear, whispering sweet nothings, which tickled me, sending shocks vibrating up and down my spine, all of the time swivelling on the stool, which made me randy as hell as I shot my hand up her skirt and do you know what I found?"

"So that's why you drove your hand into the fountain and I thought that you were enthused by the historical significance of it."

"I felt like having it chopped off," he said. "I'll tell you, I'll never bless myself with it again."

"Never mind, you'll have to do worse with it," I said light-heartedly.

When we got back to the Union Jack Club, we found that Long had got in a bother with a bunch of squaddies when he had one over the eight, in the wet canteen, just for being a Brylcreem boy. It wasn't his fault because there was great rivalry between the different services.

I was worried because Hughes and myself were due to be called up soon when we were eighteen to do our National Service. Everyone said it made a man out of you. The call-up was abolished in the September we were due to go in.

Chapter 32

To get to the White City we had to go down steep escalators at Waterloo. I was used to escalators at John Lewis's store in Liverpool where I would go with Hughes to listen to the latest released records down in the basement. At the ticket kiosk we were told to follow the black Northern Line either to Tottenham Court Road or Piccadilly Circus, where we could pick up the red Central Line for the White City Stadium, which was built for the 1908 Olympic Games. It was there that the present-day length of the modern marathon of twenty-six miles three hundred and eighty-five yards was decided as the official distance so that the finish came in line with where the Royal Box was situated. The original distance for the first marathon was more like forty miles. Like a lot of young runners, I was fascinated by the Greek runner who ran with the news of the victory of the battle, dropping dead after he had delivered his message, a story to inspire most kids.

I was looking out for fellow competitors on the way to the White City track and then I saw this bloke who was probably a sprinter because he was carrying wooden starting blocks. He had this piece of three be four with two insteps of blocks of wood built on either side of it.

Behind the starting line, he'd set up his starting blocks, nailing them into the cinder track, which represented a considerable advantage over his fellow competitors who had to dig little holes with trowels into the cinders to compensate for the advantage of leverage they knew that those with starting blocks had over them.

This was the biggest athletics stadium I had been in, in the whole of my life. It was made more daunting because it was so sparsely occupied. Any time I had seen it on television or film, it was brimming to the seams with spectators.

There was no designated warming-up area, so I had to make do with trotting around under the stands. What the hell, I thought, was I to complain after all the great runners who had preceded me. I thought of Woodeson, Bannister, Chataway, Kuts, Hägg, Arne Andersson, and here I was following in their glorious steps.

I got through my heat quite easily in an almost-empty Friday-morning stadium. It would be full to capacity that evening for the greyhound racing, which began at seven. The semi-final that took place an hour and a half later was the most exquisite four-forty yards I had ever run. Running in lane three, I had total command and balance of those who had been drawn out in front of me, while I completely disregarded and annihilated the two inside of me to win, easing up coming down the finishing straight just outside of the record, which must have wiped the smile off Mr Ground's face.

In the showers afterwards I stood and basked under the hot water and wondered if these were the showers that Chataway, Bannister, Lovelock and Kuts had stood under. I was feeling certain of a victory and a new record and personal best on the morrow, given the correct weather conditions.

I had raced twice on the White City track and I had won each time, another first in anyone's book and something for Hughes to tell his grandchildren. Third time lucky tomorrow and I would retain my position as the best in the country for my age over both quarter and half mile.

I also realised that my status had radically increased and the significance of my being in London was being vindicated. The petty feuding between Hughes and Long was shown to be of no importance. Obviously I had congratulations from both of them, but now I glowed devishly inside, dismissing their congratulatory acclamations because now I was centre stage within our trinity again. With my new-found confidence, I ungraciously ditched the pair of them. What did it matter? I would have the prize, the victory and the record on the morrow.

But as my grandmother, back in the west of Ireland, who never left her village in the whole of her life, used to say, never count your chickens before they're hatched. Long had given up his weekend leave I believed to help me, but when I saw his shenanigans with Hughes, I quickly began losing respect for him. After my heats and semi-final, I felt contempt for him.

On the inner grass arena of the cinder track, eight of us spent ages bundled together like refugees, waiting for the AAA's six-mile championships to finish. This was won by Ken Norris, who booked a place for himself on the plane to compete in the Melbourne Olympic Games in November.

As I watched the runners trying to complete their twenty-four-lap ordeal, I found it hard to relax or be friends with anyone, unlike the graceful and consistent sprinter from Trinidad, McDonald Bailey, who often had similar experiences. He won fourteen AAA titles between 1946 and 1953 and was known to have fallen asleep in the centre of the arena as he waited to be called to the start. As the waiting continued, I began to get more nervous and agitated. To win races, you needed brains, balls and luck and all of these at different stages were being firmly tested out in this arena.

In my mind's eye I had picked myself as favourite so the sooner I got on the track the quicker I'd be champion and holder of the London Public Schools Challenge Cup. Officious officialdom was getting up my nose as they were holding me up from making a name for myself. The total dedication required to run in a race, to compete successfully, was beyond belief. In hindsight, it's still amazing to think that as I got on the track, everything had to be given up; the past, the future, nothing mattered. I had to focus on the present moment, the now, the race.

Formerly, my greatest fear of entering a race was the fear of coming last. If I thought that I was entering into that zone, I wouldn't put my head on the chopping block. I'd complain of cramp or injury. Some blokes didn't mind coming last as they always got a good round of sympathetic applause, but not me, I minded coming last very much.

Since I had won the All England Schools, my fear was not of coming last but of not coming first, for I had put myself up there for everyone to have a shot at.

The lane you were allocated depended on a random pick of numbered straws held by an official in the centre of the arena, literally seconds before the start. This gave you hardly any time to gauge where your main opponents were. The draw for lanes was all-important for the one-lap four-forty yards. It was a disadvantage to be on the inside lane as it could be all cut up from previous races, while if you were on the outside lane you were running blind and no one to judge your pace by. You've got less than fifty-three seconds to impress yourself on the race. If you explode out too fast in your lane and overreach yourself at the start and middle, you suffer in the latter stages of the race.

Luckily I drew lane three. I had two inside of me and would you believe it, I had Mr Ground outside of me in lane four. The gods of fate had determined my destiny and victory, all I had to do was to fulfil it. As the gun went, I flew around the top bend, cutting Ground's stagger advantage before we entered the back straight. He buckled at the knees at the audacity of my start. Down the back straight I really motored, enjoying all the power and speed that my body possessed after all the long winter's training. Around the last bend coming off the back straight, I dug in deeper and deeper, as I entered into the long continental finishing straight. Up to then, I was used to running on tracks where start and finish were in the middle of the finishing straight, but on the continent and at the White City Stadium, the start and finish were at the top of the straight so as I came round the bend into the finishing straight, I realised that I had misjudged the distance and that I had a longer straight than I normally expected to complete. My legs began to lock as I could sense them coming after me. I glanced across to my right in anguish and terror. I could see Ground majestically passing me, eating up the yards with his high lifting action, striding by me on his way up the finishing straight, leaving me floundering. I struggled to the finishing line in fourth place.

I learned a lot from the race but sadly not until fifty years later when I had time to reflect upon what went wrong. I wanted to do four things when in fact I would have been better simply concentrating upon one. I wanted to win, to break the record, to beat Ground and impress Long and Hughes. A more experienced athlete would have selected out the most important thing, which was winning, and let the other things take care of themselves.

I left the White City Stadium disappointed and shattered, constantly questioning what had gone wrong. I had trained and worked hard but what I was to discover was that I had become a victim of my own arrogance. I made the mistake of thinking as a champion when I entered the race. I was defending my last performance when in fact I should have been struggling in my humility to try to win my next race.

The next great runners to pack the White City Stadium would be the three Hungarians, Sándor Iharos, László Tábori and István Rózsavölgyi. Their 1956 Olympic hopes in Melbourne were destroyed. While they were competing abroad, the Hungarian Revolution took place. It was so firmly put down by the USSR that they were forced to flee to the land of freedom – America. They never really recovered their form, having to race twice weekly for their athletics scholarships that ensured them their university education.

It's funny to think that none of us got anything that we wanted from our visit to London. On the coach back up to Liverpool after Hughes had told me what had happened in Soho, I innocently produced a jar of cinders that I had taken from the White City where Chataway and Kuts had battled it out in their famous 1954 race.

"What do you want that for?" Hughes said dismissively. "You're soft in the head."

But I mightn't have been as soft in the head as Hughes made out because in a poll in *The Times* of 2 October 2001, the Chataway epic 5000m race with Vladimir Kuts, possibly the USSR's greatest, in 1954 in the White City when people were gripping the television urging him home, was chosen as one of the all-time sporting greats of the twentieth century. I still have the cinders in a jar. Even at that age, I could tell class from the rest.

I knew it would be torture returning to Liverpool with my tail firmly between my legs.

Chapter 33

"Fine feathers make fine birds." That's what Dad said as I put on my satin green, white and gold running shorts in our new room, which was overshadowed by the yet to be completed Liverpool Cathedral.

"The day is coming when athletes will wear all kinds of colour shorts and vests. They won't run around the track as if they are in mourning. They will introduce some entertainment and novelty to the world. Do you know that one day runners will have their names on the back of their vests and their hair dyed to match the colour of their running shoes?"

I knew that when Dad wasn't depressed, he could be outrageously flamboyant. Then he'd become a terror for colour by the shirts, ties and hats he'd wear. Now the tricolour shorts that he had had made for me as a surprise by a woman up in Brecknock Road demonstrated that he was in such an exuberant mood again.

He could read me like a book so he knew that I was reluctant to wear these shorts in school. He brushed it off as purely girlish behaviour on my part, saying that you want to take the bull by the horns and go forth boldly to meet any difficulties.

Dad was delighted about the coup he had scored with the green, white and gold satin shorts, for they fitted me perfectly. My main worry was how I could buck up enough courage to wear them and what occasion would be the most opportune occasion to do so.

"When have you got PE again?" he asked. I half whispered, "Tomorrow," thinking so that was his game, he still wanted to get back at Keegan for the way he had humiliated the both of us earlier because of the state of my kit.

I hesitated and as I said he could read my mind so he flattered me, which always made my ears stand on end, by saying you want to be different. I didn't agree or disagree with what he said, I just went along with him, he'd feel very offended after all the money he must have spent on having the shorts made. I knew that he wanted me to be different because the more he was humiliated at work, the more he used me to kick back.

The lads noisily got out of their school uniforms as I changed into my new green, white and gold shorts. Leahy said, "Look, he's wearing Neil's mum's drawers," as the lads laughed. Keegan, the head of the PE department, came out of his office, followed by Boyle his assistant, saying, "Right gentlemen, line up at the door."

I followed the rest of the lads into the queue. No one was allowed into the gym without having their kit inspected by Keegan, who in hindsight would have made a better sanitary inspector than a PE teacher.

"What's this, the pantomime season?" he said, looking at me. No one laughed at his Wigan sense of humour, for all the lads hated him much more than he hated himself, and considered Scouse witticisms much superior to the slow Wigan parochial wit.

"Mr Boyle, get Cinderella a pair of shorts."

Boyle came back from their office giving Keegan a pair of shorts, which he threw at me. Immediately I understood that he wanted me to compromise myself by backing down to him.

"There's nothing wrong with my shorts Sir."

"Nothing wrong laddie." He bit his lip. "To wear a pair of green, white and gold shorts in a PE lesson is insulting the teachers, your classmates and the school. Now grow up Doyle. If you're not in agreement with our educational policies you can always withdraw from the school."

I stood there in dumb insolence.

"Listen Doyle, you're only a boy and the Irish are safe in Ireland. We don't want to be hard on you but the only one who can help you is yourself. If you wear our vests and shorts, there'll be no more questions asked and as far as I'm concerned, the whole matter will be dropped."

"Yes Sir," I said in a low voice, not wanting to upset him. "I only mean Sir, that I am Irish and it is my duty to wear the shorts."

"Right laddie, you'd better report to the Head. I don't want any like you who can't fit in, in my class."

Normally if you were thrown out of a lesson, you were sent to the Headmaster's office but I took my time changing, knowing that it wouldn't be long before lunch break, when I'd have to change back into my kit for my lunchtime training session. After my training session, I went to History, where we had Mr Lane, the Irish teacher from Cork, who had interviewed me when I first got into the school.

"Just the man," Mr Lane said as he looked at his watch as I entered the door. "The Head wants to see you over some clerical matter."

"But what about my lesson Sir?"

"You'll soon catch up. We're only doing a bit of revision. You'll miss nothing. The sooner you go, the sooner you'll be back among us as per normal."

I couldn't understand 'Pop' Lane's attitude. If he knew, and I'm sure he did know, what had happened with Keegan, surely he would have supported me for wearing the tricolour shorts, for most Corkmen were fierce nationalists and had fought hard for the establishment of the new Free State.

I went to see Brother Mac. He was a man who'd support me as he needed me to run for the school. I naively told him what had happened with Keegan.

"As you are approaching the end of your school career and preparing to enter into the world of commerce, it's important that you start off with good recommendations from the people who have known you up to now, so if you take a bit of advice from an old-timer like myself," Brother Mac said, "and don't upset the apple cart. At your age I was the same myself. I suppose it's because we're both redheads. We're terrors for flying off the handle and making mountains out of molehills. When I look back, it's all like a puff of wind meaning nothing," he said, as he puffed on his pipe. "And time marches on," he said, looking at his watch, sounding very contented with himself.

"But Dad told me to wear the shorts Sir."

"I want you to make a good living for yourself in this country. I want you to be successful. Forget Ireland. What has she ever done for you?"

"Are you saying that I should go against Dad's wishes?"

"All I am saying is that your father has his life, as I have mine and you have yours, and sometimes for some reasons they appear to be pulling in the opposite direction."

"I am in a terrible predicament Brother Mac."

"See the Head as Mr Keegan said and it will all be sorted out in a minute. As far as I'm concerned, you're making a mountain out of a molehill."

I went to the Headmaster's office but as usual he had an engaged sign on the door. I sat and waited there until the school secretary came along to tell me that the Head would be busy for the rest of the day and that the best thing to do was to go home and that the school would contact Dad to arrange for an appointment to meet the Head when he was not so overwhelmed with work. I couldn't believe the pettiness of these people who were supposed to be there to educate us and set us an example of adult behaviour. I was glad to have the time off school. Any half-sane person would have jumped at the opportunity. But if they didn't let me back in I'd be ruled out of the English Schools' this year, for I'd find it hard to get into another school because my academic record was next to nil.

Waking up the next morning I felt terribly depressed, for instinctively I knew the plight I was in. I resolved not to let it get me down, a thing I've had to practise all my life with the consoling words that things could always be worse. If I knew any Latin I'd have it as the family motto. I lay awake wondering if a letter would arrive from the school that morning.

There were noises along the corridor and doors being banged by people hurrying out to work or more likely to sign on, who seemed intent upon waking the ones they had left behind in their beds.

Going out and being occupied was the name of the game but this morning, because of the green, white and gold shorts, I had nowhere to go.

Dad was back. I heard him at the door. He was looking for the key under the mat. Then he tried the handle and, standing like John Wayne in the doorway, he said, "You're here. Why aren't you out at school?"

Immediately I was being accused, as was always his way, until you expertly explained that you were an innocent victim. Children are not born liars as I was often accused of being. I had to become a liar in order to accommodate the shenanigans of the adults.

A big lump of a man of five foot seven, he looked tired in his dirty gaberdine coat and green cap after doing an all-night shift, working on the wall where they were trying to reclaim some land from the sea for the Ormskirk Council so that the elderly rate-payers could have a couple of extra yards of promenade to walk their dogs in front of the bowling greens.

"Are you in trouble?" he asked, closing one eye and cocking the other one as if he felt at last that he had got me cornered when he'd feel justified in giving me another dishing-out.

"I didn't hear the clock."

"Have you been cheeking them?"

"I haven't been cheeking anyone."

He didn't like me to answer him back and the friendliness left his voice instantly, that's if it had ever possessed any in the first place.

"You're just like your mother with too much to say for yourself. When will you ever learn to keep your mouth shut?"

So I decided to give him a taste of his own medicine and to attack him back and to blame him for my predicament instead of blaming myself.

"I was sent home because of the shorts," I said, trying to muster up all the power I could in my voice, stating categorically that I was in this mess because of his high-handed approach.

Just then the landlady came and stood in the doorway. At least she was comparatively sober at this time of the morning. She shouted, "Why the hell did I ever let the likes of you into my house?"

In truth, she wasn't personally attacking us for she would have said that to anyone in the house she bumped into at that hour of the morning. She had a strong Liverpool accent when drunk, but when sober she had a hint of the refined seaside resort of Southport thrown in.

Probably in her younger days, she'd been on the game, but being cleverer than the other girls, she saved her money so that she could buy this dump and fleece those who inhabited her rooms. I felt a sense of shame and personal responsibility for being sent home from school so to change the subject, I decided to pretend to lose my temper by shouting at her from the bed, "I didn't ask to come here, I was brought here."

Her voice screeched at me. It appears that she had more liquor on board than I had first estimated. "If I had anything to do with the likes of you I know what I'd do with you, you young cur, waking me up in the middle of the afternoon from my much-earned rest." I looked up into her red-painted lips and painted face and shouted, "Do you know you're better drunk than sober?" She came in through the door and tried to get at me in the bed. Dad intervened. "Now, now, Mrs Blair, if there's any dishing out to be done here I'll be the one to deal with that type of thing." He turned on me and looked at me severely. "Now give the bed a rest and get up and get washed."

Mrs Blair left the room muttering something. I quickly got dressed and went down to the communal bathroom wondering what would be my fate and what was in store for me. There were dirty basins in this cold makeshift of a washroom, not exactly the

Adelphi Hotel. A down-and-out type of man was washing out a chef's hat, which he had probably nicked from somewhere. A young man in his topcoat, his face all lathered up, was about to begin to shave while his identical twin looked on, waiting for his turn to lather his face and for his turn on the razor. I stood in line waiting for someone to finish, clutching my crumpled-up towel.

The landlady was in the passageway causing as much disruption as she could manufacture, so that she could empty the house of as many lodgers as possible and get down to the serious business of gin-drinking and cursing her lot in the world. An older lad queued in front of me, a spick-and-span type, the sort of lad I wanted to model myself on. He had dark, well-Brylcreemed hair. He rubbed his chin and smiled, saying he could do with a shave.

"Been here long mate?"

"A couple of weeks," I said, rubbing my chin too.

My face was covered with spots, probably due to bad diet. Too many fries, not that in this room we had any means of having a fry-up for all the cooking facilities we had was one solitary gas ring. If stuck you might try your luck to boil a kettle on the weak flame. Using one gas ring, it proved impossible to cook any fry-ups or stews. I had to admit by the state of my face that I had not eaten enough fresh fruit or greens. But what would you expect when we had to move as often as us two did, having to live out of suitcases.

"You Irish?"

"Yes." I nodded.

"There's lots of blokes in my billet are Irish, always on the run. More get caught each day if they don't own up to their National Service." He lowered his voice.

"They hate being in uniform. The Sergeant Major says there are two classes of Irish, those that you can do something with and those you can't do anything with."

I wondered if I was one of those type of Paddies. Most of the teachers definitely thought I was the type that no one could do anything with. The type euphemistically called their own man with their own mind and not heeding anyone.

He lowered his voice yet again. "I don't like the Scousers myself, too bloody funny for their own good. All the time creeping up the authorities' backsides. I'm from Shoreditch myself. Know where that is Padhraig?"

I could not get one bit of bread
Whereby my hunger might be fed.
So weary of my life at length
I yielded up my vital strength
Within a ditch which since that day
Is Shoreditch called as writers say?

"No," I said. I hated being called Paddy by anyone but I didn't mind this bloke calling me Padhraig. He didn't do it to belittle me but to be friendly.

"It's in London, the East End, a great place, not like this hole. I was billeted in Crosby, must be the arsehole end of the world. Here, Manchester, the whole of Merseyside and Lancashire down to Birmingham, one big bloody graveyard."

It was so different to hear the rapid fire of the Cockney speech in comparison to the slow nasal cynical whimsical accent of the Liverpudlians.

"Are you working?"

"No, I'm still at school."

"Good on you mate."

"Worse luck you mean."

"Best laugh of your life."

I wanted to sound all grown up so I said, "It's worse than nick and I'm no good at it."

"I bet you would be if you tried."

"I do try."

"Never mind eh, one day you'll get it. You don't want to take it all so seriously. Got a girlfriend?"

"No," I said solemnly.

He looked at me, which made me think that he was questioning my sexuality, so I quickly said, "I had one but she chucked me over. She wanted to get too serious, you know how they can be and I wanted to put myself about a bit before total commitment."

"I don't blame you. There's plenty of fish in the sea."

"Are you telling me?" I said as he left the sink.

"When you start mooching about with women then you'll know what real suffering is all about."

I gave myself a cat's lick, feeling elated by the grown-up conversation I had with the Cockney soldier who was truly a man of the world, a place that I was on the threshold of.

I deposited the crumpled towel behind the cistern in the lavatory, which was next door to the washroom. I dared not go back to our room as Dad would be sprawled out on the bed and if I woke him, he'd be in a hell of a temper. I decided after having my lick to go down to the Pier Head.

As I stood at the tea stall praying that someone would notice me and buy me a cup of tea and a meat pie, it suddenly dawned on me that this Pier Head was purgatory. I knew that things could not get any worse and that heaven was just around the corner. All I had to do was stick it out in this purgatory and one day I would be in heaven. When I got back to the room after roaming tea-less around Liverpool all day, Dad was up and shaved and dressed up to the nines.

I looked at him, wondering what he was up to, but he quickly read my mind, which he was always adept at.

"So, I'm straightening out a few things. I'm doing something I should have done years ago," he said as he wiped his shoes with the crumpled towel. "In this life, you've got to take the bull by the horns son, never forget that. From where we stand we've got no other choice, otherwise we're trampled underfoot. They might think they can treat us like shite because they have degrees and letters after their names, but I'll show them," he said, going out slamming the door.

It must have been nearly two hours before Dad returned. Naturally I was anxious to know how he had got on.

"Oh I got on all right."

"But what happened?" I was dying to know. As Dad changed into his work clothes to get ready for the night shift on the wall, he told me that he was shown into a room by the maid to see Brother Mac. He immediately asked him the time.

"You mean on the smuggled watch you gave him?"

"Exactly, I wasn't going to beat about the bush and told him that if he didn't lay off, I'd go to the papers accusing them of receiving smuggled watches."

"But Brother Mac didn't know that the watch was smuggled when you gave it to him."

"That's his lookout."

"But Dad, you smuggled the watches in the first place."

"It doesn't matter a damn who smuggled them. The fact of the matter is that they received them."

"But someone in the school or associated with them paid the hundred pounds fine to stop you from going to prison."

"That was then, this is now. And in the eyes of the law, they are as guilty as if they received stolen goods."

I didn't dare say anything. Dad was in one of his moods when everyone else was in the wrong and he was in the right.

"Then I told him that I'd been up all night," Dad continued, "and that I'd be up again tonight while you buckos are snugly in your beds. If you lot lived in the real world you wouldn't be living like a lot of old women, gossiping about the type of shorts my son wears. My son has put this school on the map. Now if you think that was easy for him, tell me why all the rest of them aren't doing the same. He does it because he's different but then when he comes back down to earth after getting you more headlines and a load of medals, you expect him to be the same and be treated like everyone else in the school. Well it can't be done. It won't work and it never will. You can't have your cake and eat it Brother Mac."

"Does that mean that I go on wearing the shorts?"

"Well I don't think they will want to see me again."

Chapter 34

The cover teacher who took us probably didn't have a clue about Mathematics. We hadn't had a Maths teacher for months so to give himself an easy lesson and to gain our attention, he explained, after a short prayer, that all of us were war babies. Our poor academic achievements were not due to bad teaching or to our lack of determination to work hard, but to the fact that we had all been subjected to air raids, evacuations, families being split up, stress, infidelity, deaths, bad rationing, anxiety etc etc etc. For that reason, a group of underachieving lads existed within the school, the 'war babies' and that was our label.

In Dublin when we had to see the school doctor, he only looked at your head for lice from a distance, but the English were meticulous masters of inspections, including medical ones.

I stood there, vulnerable and miserable before them, my hands covering my private parts, as they looked me up and down. The doctor then came from behind the table and asked me to open my mouth and say "Ah". I ah, ah, ahed like a whistle on a fast train passing through a station. He then looked into my left ear and tutted, then the other one, when he tutted so much that I thought that his tutter had gone out of control.

He put his cold stethoscope, which he wore around his neck like a scarf, to my chest and back and asked me to cough, which I timidly did. Then he put his hands under my balls and asked me to cough louder he said, louder, as he apparently tried to pull them off. Then he sat me on a chair and told me to cross my knees, which he tapped. My right leg went up immediately, nearly hitting him in the face, but when I reversed the position of the knees, the left one hardly moved at all. Again he knocked it with his little wooden hammer but, not getting any reaction from the left knee, he kept banging it like a carpenter would when driving a nail home. I was beginning to feel very tense, as I am naturally a hypersensitive character, so he gave it up as a bad job and asked me if I was feeling all right.

I replied that I was free of shrapnel, a remark that came totally out of the blue.

"I'm not asking you what you are free of, I'm only looking at what you've got," he said. Oh, to be a man like this, to know everything and have everything in its place must be great. To have a good suit, polished shoes, clean shirt and tie, and a change of underpants whenever you fancied it, and nice fingernails.

But how was I to get where he was? Not that I wanted to be a doctor, but he made me feel that I wasn't right the way I was at present. It seemed that I was going in the opposite direction to him by concentrating on my running so much. Maybe I had made a rod for my own back by going down the wrong road and there was no turning back. At sixteen, instead of keeping my options open, I had closed them down by specialising too early. By dedicating myself to running, I had cut myself off from many other avenues.

But running was the only thing that I was any good at, as many people gleefully remarked. They were probably jealous of my cavalier attitude in doing my own thing.

I could never make a career as a runner. The world was so cut and dried and all about earning a living. It was all well laid out before I had arrived and someone like me was not going to change it one iota.

"Get dressed," he said.

The nurse escorted me back along the corridor to the hall.

I've had more discussions with my dad about making money than Edward VII had glasses of champagne. On the way to the pictures, which we still went to nightly, he'd have some new hare-brained scheme. During the interval in the cinema he wouldn't talk about the film we'd seen but he'd be expostulating on some new operation he had in mind.

On the way home, which invariably involved a detour by the fish and chip shop, he'd be on about making money. His aim was to start a new business up by finding a gap in the market. He would have to borrow from some kind of a half eejit in order to start up the new venture, as the banks, or more precisely the bank managers, didn't want to know you in those days, as indeed they don't today if you don't have the collateral.

There were nights when we had seen all the films on in Liverpool, so there was nothing left for us to do, as we couldn't be expected to sit in the room all evening, looking at each other and the four walls, so we'd walk up and down the main streets of the city, wandering through Hope Street, Duke Street, London Road down Dale Street, past Victoria's statue to the Pier Head, while all the time the main topic of conversation was how to make money.

Dad despised the man who took a job to work for someone else, which he considered made him a weakling, an inferior and non-profit-making slave.

"You're giving your manhood away when you take a jobeen," he'd say.

This day Dad came in as I was sitting by the table looking out of the window, staring at the summer heat that was stinking out the old Victorian building. A couple of flowers were growing on the side of the wall, which had to be admired because they must have been tough hard little bastards to survive in the stench from the laundry at the back in the filthy and polluted Liverpool air. Apart from the doors of the houses, there wasn't a bit of green around the neighbourhood; in fact you had to take a bus ride to Parliament Street and if you were lucky you might see a residue of grass there between the dog shit.

"I'm going to Hector Grey's in Dublin to buy some watches."

Hector Grey's was a big wholesale shop in Dublin who sold all kinds of watches and jewellery.

"I met this fellow in a pub and he says that there is great money in watches because of the Customs and Excise Tax. You can buy them over in Dublin for next to nothing and once you get them here, you can sell them at double the price. You're lucky son. Mark my words, you've got a clever old dad here."

"Yes," I sighed.

"I can see us living in the lap of luxury. And this will come off; I've got a feeling about it in my bones."

"Are you calling in to see Mam?" I asked.

"No, I won't have time. This is just a business trip, in and out, haven't got time for visiting."

No, you'd have some explaining to do, I thought, if she was to ask you why you were making such a brief visit, which said a lot about the integrity of the whole scheme and the childlike way he behaved in his relationship.

"How are you going to get the watches over?" I asked.

"There's a fellow on the boat, I've not met him yet."

Not Kilroy I thought.

"But I've been given his name and I'm told he'd take Dev himself over if the price was right."

As ten o'clock struck on the Royal Liver Building, the gang-plank was dumped on the shore and Dad waved goodbye from the little third-class deck as the B&I boat went out into the Mersey, heading for the Irish Sea. There wasn't much for me to do so I went home to listen to Radio Luxembourg, where my favourite singer at the time, Mario Lanza, had his own programme on at ten forty-five. I thought his voice the most saintly thing I've ever heard and he could move me to tears. While I listened to his Ave Maria I would stand in front of the mirror and mime to his voice as the tears rolled down my face, making me wish that I had a voice like his.

Next morning after breakfast, I polished my shoes, put my best shirt and tie on and, with the ten shillings Dad had given me, I got the number nine to Dale Street. The News Theatre opened at ten so I went in, and by the evening I had been to four separate picture houses and by the time I got home, I had a headache and my eyes were sore. But I had a big helping of fish and chips, so I sat happily listening to Luxembourg and reading the sports page of the *Evening Echo*, which resulted in a late night for me.

The next morning Dad shook me from a heavy sleep.

"I'm back," he said, "take a look at these."

He pulled up his sleeves and there were ten watches on each arm.

"How did you do it?" I asked.

"I came through the Customs. I've also got two down here," he said, pulling up the leg of his trousers.

"But say if they had caught you?" I asked.

"Oh if I was a blackbird, I'd whistle and sing," Dad said, dismissing any such possibility as ridiculous.

"Did the Customs examine your case?"

"No, I looked as innocent as a saint!"

"It's very dangerous," I warned him, "you could have been caught and locked up in prison. What would have happened to me then?"

"Yes I suppose there is that in it," he said, half reflecting, "I suppose I took a bit of a chance but you see the fellow I was to meet was on the other boat and it meant that I'd have to stay in Dublin another day to meet him. I didn't want that, so I had to take the chance."

"Oh Dad," I said, "say if you had been sent to prison to Walton."

"Why, wouldn't you have come along to visit me?" He laughed.

"Dad, don't do it again. It's too dangerous."

"I won't."

"Promise me you won't," but I could see that he wasn't listening to me.

"I want to promise," he said, "but I had no other choice. Look on the bright side. Do you know what I'm going to make on these? There's twenty-two watches and I've got this buyer already. I'll make ten pounds on each watch clear. That's two hundred and twenty pounds."

I said "Great," but the sum didn't mean anything to me as it was beyond my experience.

"Now if I do that each week for a month, mind you only once a week, that would be over eight hundred pounds, multiply that into eight months, that's six thousand and four hundred pounds. And turn that into five years and that's thirty-two thousand pounds. That's nearly as much as you'd get for winning the Irish sweepstake."

"It's a lot of money Dad."

"I'll tell you son, you're on to it now. You'll never have to soil your hands for the rest of your days. You'll have money to burn.

"Sounds great Dad," I said, "shall I put the kettle on?"

The fellow came along to the house as I hid in the recess. He was a well-spoken chap who had a number of markets in Manchester. He bought the twenty-two watches and Dad made two hundred and twenty pounds' profit. He stuck the money in his waistcoat with a great safety pin across the top pocket.

When the chap had left, the arrangement was that he would call again next week for more watches. Dad undid the safety pin on his waistcoat, kissed the bundle as if it were a holy relic and then gave it to me to kiss.

"Now then," he said, "this time next week with the help of God, this little bundle will have grown into over four hundred pounds. That's a clever old fellow," Dad said, winking, never slow to give himself a compliment.

For the next couple of weeks, Dad flitted in and out of Dublin visiting Hector Grey's just off Lower Abbey Street along-side the Ha'penny Bridge and passed on the purchases to this bloke on the B&I boat, a steward who took over the consignment of watches, all cloak and dagger stuff.

They'd travel back together on the same boat so that Dad

could keep an eye on him and then follow him to a pub in the docks where money and watches would be exchanged. On the Wednesday night the bloke from Manchester was due to come along to pick up the watches, so Dad packed me off to the pictures at the Rialto so I wouldn't have to hide in the recess.

When I got back home with two portions of fish and chips, one for myself and one for Dad, he wasn't in the room so I put his in the oven to keep warm and turned on the radio, but I began to worry when Luxembourg closed down at midnight and Dad still hadn't appeared. At one, I was really in a state and wondered if I should get in touch with the police to see if he had been in an accident as he was never in this late.

It was ironical in a way that our roles were reversed, for now instead of him worrying about me being out late, I was in the position that he was normally in, which was not an altogether comfortable one. At three I decided to wait till morning as I had been brought up in a culture that it was the last resort to contact the law, for all they'd do is ask me sticky questions.

In the morning I decided before I'd take any action that I'd wait until after I'd been to school. I went to school as I had to get my training in and I could get something to eat there. I accepted that if he'd gone, he'd gone, but I still had to survive.

When I got home I saw a light coming from under the door, which assured me that he was in.

"Where in the name of God have you been?" I said. "I've been worried to death about you."

"I've been arrested. I've been down in Dale Street Police Station all night with them trying to find out who took the watches over for me."

I let him keep on talking as I could see that he was really wound up like the spring on a clock so I said, "I'll put the kettle on."

"Tell us who took the watches over for you. Tell us and we won't press any charges against you. You should have seen it son, it was just like being in the pictures. They had the table, the chairs, the spot lamp on my face. There were three of them, probably the three greatest bastards that God ever created."

"The kettle won't be long."

"Tell us and you can go free. Well I wouldn't son. That's one thing you should never do is tell on one of your own. I'd do many things I'll tell yeh, many things that people could throw up to me later, but I'd never tell on one of me own especially to those bastards."

"But how did they know about the watches? Who told about them?"

"That fellow who pretended that he was from Manchester."

"No, you mean the one that came here. It's better than the pictures."

"Well I told him. I said if I had to do what you do for a living I'd cut me fecking throat. It would be a more decent thing to do for your wife and kids."

They fined Dad a hundred pounds. Confiscated the watches, all for trying to take tax out of Her poor Majesty's purse.

"A hundred pounds, where am I to find a hundred pounds? What kind of a God is there up there at all for me to suffer this awful curse? I'd be better off to slit my throat. What's the use in believing in anything? I'd be as well thought of if I was like those whore-minded bastards I see every day, the type of filth you read about in the *News of the World*."

"I'll just wet the tea!"

"Do you know it's the ones who don't believe in anything, they're the ones who manage in this world?"

"Drink your tea Dad," I said, knowing well that what was

done was done and could never be undone and I was never consulted about it in the first place, but now I would have to suffer the consequences as he ranted and raved.

"They talk about carrying crosses but no one talks about the cross I have to bear. I've lost the watches, they cost me all the money I had and now they want a hundred pounds. I haven't got a job. That's some life isn't it?"

You make your own cross, I thought, as most of us seem to do.

"Nearly fifty years on this earth fighting and struggling and what have I got, ten bob in my pocket and a mortgage around my neck which is choking the life out of me."

I accepted that Dad had a run of bad luck and whatever luck is, it seems you need it to succeed, but it never seemed to come his way.

"God Almighty, what did I do to deserve this? Of course if I had a proper partner, if only I had the good sense to marry someone who would have backed me."

I felt embarrassed because I felt that it wasn't right to attack someone if they weren't here to defend themselves.

He sighed and then he revved himself up again as if he was some kind of engine starting out on a long journey of anger and regrets. "And that curse of God payment is due on Tuesday and I haven't got it. Three non-payments and they'll take the place off me."

"Do you want a drop of hot?" I asked, hoping to take his mind off the continuous persecutory pain he was suffering.

"A hundred pounds, where am I going to get that kind of money? Money, money, that's their fecking God. It's money from first you breathe. You walk it, talk it, sleep it, fart it, for without money in this life or for what I can see any other life, you're shagged, finished, caput."

"Should I make you a sandwich or something?"

"If I haven't got that hundred pounds within a month, they'll take me to Walton and they'll lock me up for six months and then they'll have no one to pay the mortgage in Dublin while I'm sewing mail bags."

It was pitiful to listen to Dad raking up the past with all this negative stuff but when he was in one of these spins it was best I found to let him get it, albeit momentarily, out of his system. He got some relief for a brief interlude, which were becoming less frequent as time went on.

"She's turning the kids against me, poisoning their minds telling lies about me."

This frantic despair that was threatening him is still painful to recall.

"But for you son I could happily die now. I could happily sit here and die, just happily drop dead now, and there wouldn't be anyone in the world to shed a tear. Not one, not the devil of one."

"I'd shed a tear," I said, "and your sister the nun would get the old hankie out I'm sure."

"Ah what's the good of tears, I'll have to get that hundred pounds from some place."

Thank God he was coming round from feeling sorry for himself, because he started jig-acting about, demonstrating his instantaneous mood swings.

"Do you know," he said in an English accent, "what that old bastard with the white hat said, 'You have been found guilty of smuggling, which is a very serious offence'."

I could have said that the Catholic Church don't think it's an offence at all, or the Church of England. What commandment says thou shalt not smuggle?

"Could you tell me?" he said, cocking his eye, as Dad went off on one of his monologues.

"'I fine you a hundred pounds,'" the old git says. "'Will you indeed you old bastard,' I says to myself looking at him. Why not fine me another one and six and you could get yourself a haircut you big parasite."

I went out to get the *Evening Echo* while Dad put something together for tea. But Dad had beaten me again for he had got on the front page of the *Evening Echo* while I had only ever made the back sports page. Now it will be all over the school that my dad is a smuggler. Of course I'll deny it. There's lots of Doyles and loads of them in the phone book.

A letter came from Dublin next morning from Mam, whose slanted writing I always recognised. I put the letter on the cluttered mantelpiece and said a little prayer hoping that it wouldn't upset him too much.

"Oh," he said, when he came in from Mass. "More good news from Dublin. I wonder what's wrong this week?" he asked, taking hold of the letter and swivelling it in his hand, trying to decide without having to actually open it. "The lavatory last week, the sink blocked the week before and slates off the roof before that. Perhaps," he said with a sense of irony, holding the envelope up to the sunlight, "they've sent some money."

I had heard it all before so I made ready to go to school to get away from all of it and to do my training.

"Well, well, well," Dad said, halting me in my tracks, as he tore open the envelope, producing a cutting from the *Irish Evening Press*.

IRISH MAN FINED FOR SMUGGLING IN LIVERPOOL

"Christ, that's done it now, there won't be a cat or canary that won't know about the smuggling." Dad paused for a moment and moved from despair to anger as quickly as the clouds would cross the sun, apparently putting it out on a summer's day.

"Ah feck them anyway. Why do I have to feel that I owe them anything. They're over there and I'm over here, the craw thumping bastards."

"I'll be off then."

"What's the hurry?" Dad said, "Put the kettle on."

"I've got to go Dad. I've got an important training session today."

I had to break the umbilical cord yet again or I could end up in the foetus position on the floor listening to him go on all day.

I went to school and as usual went out training during the lunch hour, but this time I was on the new four-forty-yard grass track that Brother Mac had just marked out for the beginning of the athletics season. This day it was decided that I'd do a time trial over the full lap to see if the training I had put in since my dismal London appearance had improved my all-round fitness. I had organised four time-keepers at the hundred and ten yards splits to call out my times as I went on to complete the lap.

I started off with a great rush and burst of energy, throwing all caution to the wind as I got around the first bend and down the back straight, where I was really striding out more like a two-twenty-yards runner than a four-forty-yards one.

At that moment, Brother Mac was looking out of his ground-floor classroom window, probably wondering how fast his new-laid-out track would turn out to be, when he saw me hitting for the final bend at a thunderous pace. He ran from the building in his black soutane to the finish to see what time I had done.

I had run a phenomenal sub-fifty-second four-forty yards, which would have walked the race I had competed in down in London and was seconds faster than any other lad of my age in the country.

"Well done Doyle," Brother Mac said proudly. "Well done boy, you're going to make a name for us this season."

As he said this, I broke down crying uncontrollably.

"What is it boy?" he asked as he handed me my tracksuit.

"It's nothing Sir," I said.

"Is that your father in the paper, boy?"

"Yes Sir," I said.

"I'm in my classroom. Just pop in after you've shacked," a term used by athletes in those days that meant warming down.

In the classroom I told Brother Mac how I was worried about Dad. They were going to put him into prison and how I'd be sent to an approved school if he couldn't pay the fine.

"Now don't you worry there boy. You go off to your lessons and concentrate upon your work and running and I'll see to the rest."

"Yes Sir," I said. And I went off feeling a load lifted off my round shoulders.

Next morning a letter came from the law courts in Dale Street acknowledging the receipt of a hundred-pound payment of the fine. Dad felt intrigued about who had paid it. He felt undermined that someone had done such a thing and he considered that they had a hold over him. One thing Dad hated was to be beholden to anyone.

He went through his brothers and sisters in Ireland but quickly decided that they were all a pack of mean bastards; he didn't want to have to alter his opinion of them because they'd rather see him fry in hell than help him out. I decided to put him out of his misery by telling him that I thought it was Brother Mac, telling him about our meeting after the time trial.

"Did he now? I'm not surprised, for when Brother Mac first met me he knew I was the genuine article," he said by way of giving himself a compliment.

Next day I met Brother Mac in the corridor and thanked him for paying the fine but he adamantly denied it, saying, "Where do you think a poor Christian Brother would get a hundred pounds? It was an anonymous donor who has followed your running career up to now who paid the fine." So I felt obliged to keep running for the season trying to win as many trophies for the school as possible by way of restitution.

After school Hughes came round to the class to collect me.

"Got the time?" he asked.

"You don't want to believe everything you read in the news-papers," I quipped.

Chapter 35

We had not been home for Christmas for years. But now the case for compensation for Dad's broken leg was pending. It had happened at work, since when he had been placed on light duties, helping Jimmy the Spanish cook out in the kitchen, so things between Mam and Dad had improved considerably. She had written to ask him to forgive and forget, and to come home for the holiday and the festival when we could all be together once again as one big happy family.

On 23 December, my last December in Liverpool, they had a party out on the 'wall' at Crosby, where Dad played the accordion for them and Taffie and Alex waltzed together. Singing and crying, everybody was mad drunk. I sang 'Galway Boy' and

'Kevin Barry', the forbidden song, and 'The Wild Colonial Boy', accompanied by Dad on the accordion. Dad had drunk a lot of whiskey and the tears came slowly down his face as I sang to the hushed audience.

I will ask my God to let me make my Heaven
In that dear little land across the Irish Sea

"Cor you Paddies know how to turn it on," Jimmy the Spanish cook said in the Cockney colloquialisms he had picked up here and there.

"Good old Ted's son," someone shouted and then they went into an old-time waltz. With the men dancing with the men. Happy men with other happy men for this was the last day of work before Christmas.

The men danced a reel. Then they sang 'Auld Lang Syne'. I went in through the kitchen and opened the back door of Jimmy's and Dad's workplace and I listened to the sea in the darkness, bashing against the reclaimed land that the men had been salvaging day and night, from the sea for the council. Promenaders would walk their dogs there in the future, long after most of us were dead, gone and forgotten.

The tears came into my eyes because I was happy for the happy men.

I was happy for Dad, for myself and for the fact that we were going to Dublin for Christmas, for the first time for six years.

And each time I think of that area, which has stood still in my repertoire, the kitchen, the sea, the men and the dancing. I always feel happy. Because I know that there's nothing in the world to fear, when people can create such wells of happiness with simplicity, and hope and be immersed in humble humanity.

We had six Christmases in Liverpool. We had one with Mum and Winnie when Dad threw the bones of the duck carcass we had secretly smuggled into our room onto the top of the wardrobe, sending me into hysterics at the thought of what they'd say when they found them, long after our welcome had run out.

We had one where we had a leg of lamb, which in a way I felt was sacrilegious as all of the previous Christmases we always had a fowl. One Christmas Day, Dad brought some men back from the pub whom he'd just met during the morning session, in a fit of sentimentality, brought on by the 'Free Drink'. I thought they must be like the Three Wise Men, until one of them began to pick his teeth, which he did with a matchstick. And continually spat whatever he found out of his mouth with great gusto upon the floor, while we waited for whatever we were going to eat, which turned my stomach and put me off any thoughts of food for the day.

We had a Christmas when we had a duck, which Dad said if you put it into hell it still wouldn't cook. We had a Christmas when we had a knocked-off turkey, which was so big that we had to saw the bastard in half to get it in the oven.

We had Christmases that were so lonely that they are best forgotten. They were like days that you just sit down and wait for death.

But now all of that was behind us. Because by my watch, the party would be wound up by six, and we'd be down the Pier Head at nine, then we were going home to where we belonged and where we came from. To the land of poetry, drama, tragedy and song. We were going home to the twenty-six counties, home to the 'Soldier's Song', home to the tricolour, home to a nation once again, home to the Dublin Mountains and the Wicklow Hills where the River Liffey rises, which eventually takes the

Guinness Barges with their consignment of porter to the North Wall for export to England. Guinness was later made at Park Royal in London, which never tasted the same or had the same colour as that produced at home.

We were going home to O'Connell Street where Nelson's Pillar dominates, showing what the British think of us, erecting their one-armed conquering hero within our midst, in opposition to Daniel O'Connell, who worked to introduce Catholic Emancipation. We were going home to Middle Abbey Street, where I collected the morning papers from the *Independent* office for our shop, which gave me a penchant for early mornings that I've held throughout my life. We were going home to Morgan Place and to Morgan United, the home of the soccer team formed by Joey Rice. It never won a game in the whole of its ignominious existence. We were going home to Stephen's Green, which was held in the Troubles, disrupting the genteel and well shod from exercising their dogs and relationships in the normally sedate Capability Brown surroundings. We were going home to Dame Street and Grafton Street and to Trinity College and to the land of privilege and to the grand shops that made you wish and hope, no matter what your left-wing-leaning propensity, that one day you might have enough to shop in them. We were going home to Usher's Quay and the Auction Rooms, where many an eye was wiped by the staged bidding. Home to Moore Street where the ould ones put the rotten fruit in the bottom of the bags, topped up by a few edible ones. Home to Parnell Monument, the edifice erected to the man who nearly got a united Ireland, but who was hounded out of office by the establishment, because of his love for a woman. A similar fate befell Oscar Wilde, not with a divorcee, but with Alfred Lord Douglas. We were going home to Tara Street baths where I learned to swim. Home to the

Iveagh Baths where they had the Free Monday wash house for the Liberty Dwellers who lived outside of the city walls and thus avoided paying taxes. Home to the Hollis Street Hospital where I was born. Home to Westland Row where my Auntie Maggie took me to be baptised. Home to the Fifteen Acres where I first began to run. Home to the Phoenix Park where I tried to play hurley and football, which I failed at abysmally. Home to Adam and Eve's where I first served Mass in the Franciscan Friary. Home to the Brazen Head, the oldest pub in Dublin. Home to Dolly Flossits, one of the most popular brothels in North Dublin, opposite which we had the Little Horseshoe Shop, our second premises in Dublin. Home to Slattery's Pub, outside of which I used to wait for Dad to finish his pint and patiently stand observing the world. It had private snugs, where the ould ones and the clergy could drink in peace with the painted women. Home to Mrs O'Riordan, who at just over four foot could out-drink any man, woman or child in Dublin, if it was going free. Home to Mrs Kennedy, who had a lovely daughter, who half of Dublin had screwed, with the other half living in envy. Home to the GPO in O'Connell Street, where the statue of Brian Boru stands. Home to Cafolla's, the Italian ice cream makers of Knickerbocker Glorys, which cost three and ninepence, whose ancestors brought and worked the Italian marble in the ornate churches. Home to the GAA in Parnell Square, who organised the hurley and football of a Sunday at Croke Park. Home to soccer matches at Dollymount Park, religiously attended by Joey Rice, founder of Morgan United, who never won a game but who was partial to witnessing the good and great, whose moves he would assiduously recount to the little kids who joined him. He had thoughts of being famous on the soccer pitch, which soon evaporated. His admission to the grounds was normally paid for by his elderly widowed mother, who doted upon her son. Home to Lansdowne Road where rugby was played by the well shod, and socially advantaged, Anglo-Irish stock.

Home to St Anthony's in Fairview, where my mam and dad were married after running away from Mayo, which must have been terribly romantic, and exciting and ahead of its time, when love was young and thankfully foolish and they were much happier, believing that their love could surmount any difficulties.

Home to the Savoy opposite the Carlton Cinema, a notorious cottage and meeting venue whose tales I was told about later in London, by ex-participants who in spite of leasing their bodies out could not afford to live in Dublin, and who were forced to emigrate to the London scene.

Home to the Theatre Royal where the comedian and film star Noel Purcell parked his car illegally. He was reputed to be one of the meanest men in show business, in a profession noted for parsimonious individuals. Home to the Gaiety Theatre, where Jimmy O'Dea and Maureen Potter appeared as the pantomime dame and principal boy. Home to a city of entertainment and swank and to Arnott's, where Dad said that once you shopped there you'd never want to shop anywhere else. Home to Clerys where the young priests were fitted out in suits for the Missions to convert the black babies. Home to Glasnevin where James Joyce buried poor Paddy Dignam in *Ulysses*. Home to Deans Grange, a much posher graveyard, where our dad was to end up in a simple unmarked grave. Home to Grangegorman, the lunatic asylum where Mam said we all came from when we got out of hand and annoyed her, which was many the time.

But now we were going home. We were going home. For good or for bad, with warts and all. We were going home. We were going home. We were going home.

305